THE TOMB OF SAINT PETER

SUPPLEMENTS

TO

NOVUM TESTAMENTUM

VOLUME VIII

LEIDEN
E. J. BRILL
1964

THE TOMB
OF SAINT PETER

A REPRESENTATIVE AND ANNOTATED
BIBLIOGRAPHY OF THE EXCAVATIONS

BY

ANGELUS A. DE MARCO, O.F.M.

LEIDEN
E. J. BRILL
1964

PRINTED IN THE NETHERLANDS

CONTENTS

PREFACE

The excavations beneath the Vatican basilica of St. Peter between 1940-49 and the reaction of the scientific world to the results of the archeological findings have given a new impetus to the much-studied question of the Roman tradition that Peter is buried in Rome on the Vatican hill. At the present time the entire matter is still controversial. Opinions range from almost a complete acceptance to a total rejection of the archeological findings and their interpretation. The mass of literature, pro and con, has increased to such a degree that it is practically impossible to obtain a thorough grasp of all the diversified points of view.

For this reason it appears to be necessary to have a complete annotated bibliography of the entire problem which involves not only the tomb of St. Peter venerated at the Vatican, but also the Memoria Apostolorum at San Sebastiano on the via Appia which tradition associates with Peter's grave.

Intimately connected with the problem is, of course, the question of Peter's Roman sojourn and martyrdom in the Eternal City as well as his position as head of the College of the Apostles and the Universal Church.

Far from taking a position of his own in this vexed problem, the compiler of the present annotated bibliography endeavors merely to present an aid for anyone who wishes to study the issues that have become involved. While he is aware that one or the other title on the subject may have escaped his attention, his hope is that this bibliography will serve as a contribution to the cause of securing the greatest possible truth to this vital discussion.

It would have been impossible to present a work of this kind without the assistance of the Library of Congress, Dunbarton Oaks Harvard University Research Library and the Library of Catholic University of America, all in Washington, D.C.; also, the Widener Library of Harvard University, Cambridge, Massachusetts, the Vatican Library and the Library of the Pontifical Institute of Christian Archeology, Rome, Italy. To their staffs the compiler owes a debt of gratitude.

At the same time, he must thank the editors of Novum Testamentum and Messrs E. J. Brill, Leiden, Holland, for publishing this work.

Finally, he acknowledges a special indebtedness to Dr. B. A. van Proosdij, assistant manager of Messrs E. J. Brill, for his interest and suggestions.

Catholic University of America   ANGELUS A. DE MARCO, o.f.m.

Washington, D.C.

LIST OF ABBREVIATIONS

AAS   Acta Apostolicae Sedis. Vatican City, Rome, 1909 ff.
AB   Analecta Bollandiana. Brussels, 1882 ff.
AJA   American Journal of Archeology. Princeton, 1885 ff.
BAC   Bollettino degli Amici delle Catacombe. Rome, 1931 ff.
Bess   Bessarione. Rome, 1896 ff.
BibZ   Biblische Zeitschrift. Freiburg i.B., 1903-1939; Paderborn, 1957.
BLE   Bulletin de littérature ecclésiastique. Paris, 1899 ff.
BM   Benediktinische Monatsschrift. Beuron, 1919 ff.
CC   Civiltà Cattolica. Rome, 1850 ff.
DACL   Dictionnaire d'Archéologie Chrétienne et de Liturgie, ed. F. Cabrol and H. Leclercq. Paris, 1907-1953.
EC   Enciclopedia Cattolica, ed. P. Paschini and others. Rome, 1949-1954.
EL   Ephemerides Liturgicae. Rome, 1887 ff.
HJ   The Hibbert Journal. London, 1902 ff.
HJG   Historisches Jahrbuch der Görresgesellschaft. Cologne, 1880 ff.; Munich, 1950 ff.
HZ   Historische Zeitschrift. Munich, 1859 ff.
IKZ   Internationale kirchliche Zeitschrift. Bern, 1911 ff.
JAC   Jahrbuch für Antike und Christentum. Münster i. W., 1958 ff.
JBL   Journal of Biblical Literature. New Haven and Boston, 1881 ff.
JBR   Journal of Bible and Religion. Wolcott, N. Y.; Brattleboro, Vt., 1933 ff.
JL   Jahrbuch für Liturgiewissenschaft. Münster, 1921-1941.
JRS   Journal of Roman Studies. London, 1911 ff.
JThSt   Journal of Theological Studies. London, 1900-1905; Oxford, 1906-1949; N.S.: Oxford, 1950 ff.
MAH   Mélanges d'Archéologie et d'Histoire. Paris and Rome, 1881 ff.
Mnem   Mnemosyne. Bibliotheca philologica Batavorum. Leiden.
NC   La Nouvelle Clio. Brussels, 1947 ff.
NRTh   Nouvelle Revue Théologique. Tournai, 1879 ff.
NTSt   New Testament Studies. Cambridge, England, 1954 ff.
OCP   Orientalia Christiana Periodica. Rome, 1935 ff.
RAC   Rivista di Archeologia Cristiana. Rome, 1924 ff.
RGG³   Religion in Geschichte und Gegenwart. 3rd ed. by K. Galling. Tübingen, 1957 ff.
RH   Revue Historique. Paris, 1876 ff.
RHE   Revue d'Histoire Ecclésiastique. Louvain, 1900.
RHL   Revue d'Histoire et de Littérature Religieuses. Paris, 1896-1907.
RHPR   Revue d'Histoire et de Philosophie Religieuses. Strasbourg, 1921 ff.
RHR   Revue de l'Histoire des Religions. Paris, 1880 ff.
RivB   Rivista Biblica. Rome, 1953 ff.
RQ   Römische Quartalschrift. Freiburg i.B., 1891 ff.
RQH   Revue des Questions Historiques. Paris, 1866 ff.
RSR   Recherches de Science Religieuse. Paris, 1910 ff.
RSRUS   Revue des Sciences Religieuses. Paris, 1921 ff.
SAB   Sitzungsberichte der Preussischen Akademie der Wissenschaften. Phil.-hist. Klasse. Berlin, 1882 ff.

ST   Studi e Testi. Pubblicazioni della Biblioteca Vaticana. Rome, 1900 ff.
TB   Theologische Blätter. Leipzig, 1922-Mai, 1942.
ThLZ   Theologische Literaturzeitung. Leipzig, 1878 ff.
TR   Theologische Rundschau. Tübingen, 1897 ff.
TZ   Theologische Zeitschrift. Basel, 1945 ff.
ZKG   Zeitschrift für Kirchengeschichte. (Gotha). Stuttgart, 1876 ff.
ZkTh   Zeitschrift für katholische Theologie. Innsbruck, 1877 ff.
ZNW   Zeitschrift für die neutestamentliche Wissenschaft und die Kunde der älteren Kirche. Giessen, 1900 ff.
ZST   Zeitschrift für systematische Theologie. Gütersloh, 1923 ff.
ZTK   Zeitschrift für Theologie und Kirche. Tübingen, 1891 ff.

PART ONE

PETER'S ROMAN SOJOURN AND POSITION

1 ALAND, K., "Wann starb Petrus?" — NTSt, 1 (1955/56), 267-275.

>At the time when Paul writes I Corinthians, Peter is making missionary journeys. This is the only information that can be gleaned from Paul's letters concerning this of Peter's life. Since Paul's letters do not report Peter's death, Heussi concludes that he died long before Paul —as early as the year 55. When Paul wrote Galatians, Peter was no longer alive.
>
>In this study our author challenges the validity of such an hypothesis. He also defends the Roman tradition of Peter's death basing himself on John 13, 36 and chapter 21.

2 ALAND, K., "Petrus in Rom" — HZ, 183 (1957), 497-516.

>This is an answer to Heussi's later writings refuting his contention that St. Peter never came to Rome and could not be buried there. Our author strenuously defends the Roman tradition.

3 ALAND, K., "Petrus in Rom. Eine notwendige Bemerkung" —Deutsches Pfarrerblatt, 58 (1958), 79-81.

4 ALAND, K., "Eine abschliessende Bemerkung zur Frage "Petrus in Rom" — HZ, 191 (1960), 585-587.

>This is a reply to K. Heussi's essay dealing with the presumed evidence of Peter's sojourn in Rome (HZ, 186 (1958), 249-260), (see no. 155).
>
>In this study our author takes a final strong stand against Heussi's invective style and constant variable mode of arguing. (Aland refers to his study "der Tod des Petrus in Rom. Bemerkungen zu seiner Bestreitung durch Karl Heussi," in Kirchengeschichtliche Entwürfe, Gütersloh, 1960, pp. 35-104). Aland charges Heussi with arbi-

trary interpolations of the sources, of assigning later dates
to the origin of early Christian writings without sufficient
justification, and of giving wilful interpretations (all
according to a previously assumed intention), namely, to
reach certain conclusions. Our author points out that Heussi's main failure lies in the manner of his general approach.
He begins from presuppositions which are unhistorical.
He demands demonstrating proofs and statements of the
Church in the first and second centuries as would be
expected if one were dealing in the realm of modern history.
If he does not find what he seeks, he assumes that his
denial of it has been proved. Actually, the sources of Peter
and his death are relatively sufficient and quite satisfying
when compared with those of other persons and events in
the early Church—including St. Paul and others.

5 ALAND, K., "Der Tod des Petrus in Rom"— *Kirchengeschicht-
liche Entwürfe*, (Gütersloh: Gerd Mohn, 1960), 35-104.

Observations on criticism by K. Heussi.

6 ALLNATT, C. F. B., *Cathedra Petri*, (London: Burns & Oates,
1879), 112 pp.

The object of this work is to present a brief summary or
abstract of the Patristic evidence regarding the Titles and
Prerogatives ascribed to St. Peter and to his See and
Successors in the first ages of the Church. His leadership
in the primitive Church and his Apostolic commission are
unquestionably evidenced in such testimony. The question
of his stay in Rome is taken up in the appendix (pp.
113 ff.). That St. Peter was the first Bishop of Rome is
shown by the various testimonies contained in this work.
Since the fact was disputed, the author appends a letter
to a Protestant friend, containing notes on the Reverend
R. Maguire's work entitled: "St. Peter non-Roman."

7 ALTANER, B., "Der I. Klemensbrief u. der Römische Primat" — TR, 35 (1936), 41-45.

This is a critique of R. van Cauwelaert's: *L'intervention
de l'Eglise de Rome à Corinthe vers l'an 96*, (see no. 239)
which deals with the well-known Epistle of St. Clement:

unequivocal proof of the primacy of the Roman Church. The relationship between the Church at Rome and Peter must obviously presuppose Peter's early coming to that city.

8 ALTANER, B., "War Petrus in Rom?" — TR, 36 (1937), 178-187.

Though one would have good reason to think that the old question of Peter's Roman sojourn and martyrdom had been terminated, this has not been the case. Despite the positive attitude in recent times of many Protestant theologians to favor the traditional view (e.g. Harnack, Lietzmann), some have again voiced themselves against it.

In the first part of this study the author reports his views regarding the very recent work by K. Heussi: *War Petrus in Rom?* (see no. 142). According to Heussi, individual testimony in this matter has been evaluated in too sentimental a fashion. For this reason the whole problem remains in the realm of mere possibilities. However, he feels that he has succeeded in finding (for the first time) a fixed point according to which all uncertain points of the tradition are to be judged. Altaner does not question this methodical principal. The heated point of the discussion for Heussi is *I Clement* 5, 1-6, 2. He claims that Clement knows nothing about Peter's sojourn. The reference of the two Apostles suffering at the same place does not refer to Rome. It indicates only that they had found a place together in heaven. Altaner says that Heussi draws these conclusions from an *argumentum silentii*. How is this possible? Further, Heussi's rejection of the idea of a martyr-death is hard to reconcile with all the sources. Though he does not endeavor to answer all of Heussi's charges, Altaner feels that Heussi's conclusions are the consequence of an unjustified skepticism regarding the ancient Christian sources in general. He tries to destroy all the evidence of the indications in Christian literature of the second century.

In the second part of this critique, Altaner speaks of H. Lietzmann's work: *Petrus und Paulus in Rom*, 1915 (see no. 177). The recent negative publications of H. Dannenbauer, J. Haller, and K. Heussi, which attacked

Lietzmann's positive position, are answered in: *Petrus, römischer Märtyrer* (see no. 178). Against Dannenbauer, in particular, Lietzmann defends the testimony of Clement and Ignatius of Antioch.

In the third part, Altaner reports on Heussi's reply to Lietzmann: *War Petrus wirklich römischer Märtyrer* (see no. 143) in which Heussi reiterates his interpretation of *I Clement* 5, 2. Altaner feels that he reveals a rare gift in being able to allege (without any proof) that early Christendom did not have the slightest sense of historical tradition, and that on this account, there was no historical knowledge independent of literary sources.

9 ALTANER, B., "Omnis ecclesia Petri propinqua" — TR, 38 (1939), 130-138.

This is a critique of the works of two Protestant scholars: H. Stoeckius, *Ecclesia Petri propria,* (Archiv für kath. Kirchenrecht, 117 (1937), 24-126) (see no. 235), and W. Köhler, *Omnis ecclesia Petri propinqua,* (Heidelberg, 1937/38) (see no. 171).

Altaner points out that the traditional interpretation of Tertullian's *De pud.* 21, 9, (both by Catholics and Protestants) was that Tertullian is objecting to the edict of penance allegedly issued by Pope Callistus, and the arrogant justification of the Pope who seems to refer to himself, and so to "every Church that is near Peter," the text of Mt. 16, 18. While this was the traditional interpretation of earlier Catholic research, it is now almost quite generally rejected. It was G. Esser who first gave an entirely different interpretation to the text. According to him, it was not Callistus, but the bishop of Carthage who is Tertullian's opponent. It was pope Zephyrinus who issued an edict of penance. This interpretation was readily accepted by Catholic scholars. Protestants, however, did further research into the concept of the primacy of the Roman bishop. Altaner feels that Stoeckius bases his view on unfounded textual emendations. He changes "id est ad *omnem* ecclesiam Petri *propinquam*" into "id est ad *tuam* ecclesiam Petri *propriam*" basing this on the meaning of the term "proprius" in Roman civil law. And "non quae solverint vel alligaverint" to "solverit vel alligaverit." Altaner observes that the interpretation of Mt. 16, 18, according to Tertullian, refers to nothing else but the episcopal power of binding and loosing, not to a particular and different authorization of Peter that was to be transferred only to the Roman bishop. Altaner views W. Kohler's hypothesis (see no. 171) as unacceptable. Granted the kind of pagan mentality even at that time in Rome and in Africa, it is hard to understand how a man like Pope Victorinus, who was aware of his hierarchical stature, would have relied on the ideas indicated. The lists of monarchical bishops of the Roman Church presented by Hegesippus and Irenaeus point to the fact that the mere historical presence of Peter in Rome and his episcopacy there, as well as his tomb, were the only reasons for relying on Mt. 16, 18.

10 ALTANER, B., "Neues zum Verständnis vom 1. Clem. 5, 1-6, 2" — HJG, 62-69 (1949), 25-30.

In studying the question of the Roman residence and martyrdom of Peter, the author deals with 1 *Clement, chapter* 5, in which he gives a detailed analysis of the text which forms a solid basis for the Roman tradition. Among other things, he shows that chapter 9 of the Epistle of Polycarp used 1 Clement chapter 5, almost word for word, and he seeks to show that Polycarp understood the passage to mean that Paul, Ignatius, Zosimus and "other Apostles" suffered martyrdom in Rome.

11 ANONYMOUS *Resoconto autentico della disputa fra sacerdoti cattolici e ministri Evangelici intorno alla venuta di San Pietro in Roma*, (Roma, 1872: tipografia Lombarda), 102 pp.

The Catholic-Protestant arguments on the important question of Peter's sojourn in Rome. This is a compilation of these discussions which took place in Rome between Catholic scholars and Protestant (Methodists) on February 9th and 10th, 1872.

12 ANONYMOUS "Sulle Memorie e i Monumenti dei SS. Apostoli Pietro e Paolo a Roma" — CC, 86, 2(1935), 247-257; 587-594. 86, 3(1935), 166-173; 582-589.

In this essay the author is concerned with the monumental testimony that strengthens the arguments favoring the Roman sojourn, martyrdom and burial of Peter
(and Paul). He divides his study into the following main
headings:
1. The first testimony of the Apostle's grave and its
   importance.
2. The monuments that developed over the Apostolic
   grave.
3. The Constantinian sarcophagus and altar of Peter.
4. Observations regarding the Vatican cemetery.
5. The vicissitudes of Peter's grave from Constantine to
modern times.
6. The grave and basilica of Paul on the via Ostia.

The cumulative evidence points to the fact that Peter's
tomb in the Vatican is genuine and that all the traditions
connected with it point to his prolonged residence, death
and burial in the Eternal City.

13 BACCHUS, F., "The Twenty-Five Years of Peter" — *Dublin
Review*, 120 (1897), 386-396.

The purpose of this essay is to examine the hypothesis
of Lipsius which accounts for the traditional twenty-five
years of Peter's Roman episcopate. The author also
shows how this hypothesis is indirectly supported by the
researches of Lightfoot and Hort into the origin of the
episcopal lists of Eusebius.

14 BALBONI, D., "Natale Petri de cathedra" — EL, 68 (1954),
97-126.

While basically concerned with the origin of the feast
of the 'Cathedra' and its meaning, this scholarly study
contains information of related value for the study of the
question of Peter's martyrdom and the date of the event.

15 BARDY, G., "Pélerinages à Rome vers la fin du IVe siècle" —
AB, 67 (1949), 224-253.

This study deals with the numerous testimonies of the
Fathers of the Church, scil., Jerome, Ambrose, Chrysostom,
etc., with regard to the pilgrimages made to the martyrs'

tombs at Rome. The most popular places of pilgrimages were the Apostles Peter's and Paul's tombs. Incontestable evidence of the Roman tradition that Peter and Paul were martyred and buried in the Eternal City.

16 BARNES, A. S., *St. Peter in Rome and His Tomb on the Vatican Hill*, (London: S. Sonnenschein & Co., 1900), 391 pp., 37 illus.

In this voluminous work the author marshals cumulative evidence to refute the objection that Peter never came to Rome and could not have been martyred and buried there. His evidence is gathered from Scripture, the ancient writers, archeological monuments, and the traditional portraits of Peter and Paul. His conclusion is: such well substantiated testimony leaves no room for serious doubt regarding the Roman tradition of Peter's sojourn and death. The fifteen interesting chapters contained in this book are as follows:

1. St. Peter at Rome.
2. The first coming to Rome.—A.D. 42-49.
3. Absence of St. Peter from Rome.—A.D. 49-63.
4. Return of St. Peter to Rome and martyrdom of St. Peter and St. Paul.—A.D. 63-67.
5. The wanderings of St. Peter's body.
6. The first tomb on the via Appia and on the Vatican.
7. The building of the basilica.
8. Vicissitudes of a thousand years.—A.D. 325-1400.
9. Buildings and Monuments with which the Tomb of Peter may be compared.
10. Old St. Peter's.
11. Old St. Peter's.
12. Changes in the fifteenth, sixteenth, and seventeenth centuries.
13. The discoveries in 1626.
14. Present appearance of the tomb.
15. Can the tomb still be reached?

17 BARNES, A. S., "The Apostles at Rome" — *The Early Church in the light of the Monuments*, (London, New York, Bombay, Calcutta: Longmans, Green and Co., 1913), 1-18.

Though the New Testament does not present clear and

doubtless proof of St. Peter's apostolate and death in
Rome, yet when we look outside Scripture, there is manifold evidence to prove the Roman tradition. The author
asserts that the presence of Peter (and Paul) in Rome is a
fact established beyond doubt and based on monumental
evidence. The object of this essay is to present the traditions in connection with the Roman monuments. The
author points out the following:

1. The places of martyrdom.
2. The tombs on the Vatican and via Ostia.
3. The Platonia ad catacumbas.
4. The chair of St. Peter.
5. The Mamertine Prison or Tullianum.
6. Other and doubtful traditions.
7. The wooden altar of St. Peter.
8. St. Peter's chains.

All these memorials are associated with Peter at Rome.
Recent excavations and research have strengthened this
evidence.

18. BARNES, A. S., *The Martyrdom of St. Peter and St. Paul*,
    (London: Oxford University Press, 1933), 184 pp.

In this work the author finds evidence to help solve the
difficulties associated with Peter's and Paul's residence
and martyrdom in Rome.

According to him, during the Neronian persecutions,
Peter and Paul resided in a villa near the third mile on the
via Appia in Rome. (Presently covered over by the basilica
of San Sebastiano). Both were martyred on June 29, (67)
and were provisionally buried in a little garden close to
their residence. Nineteen months later (69) (*Acta Petri*)
on January 22 and 25 respectively, they were transferred
to their permanent graves on the Vatican and via Ostia.
Anacletus subsequently erected a *Memoria* over the
original site of burial, the *platonia*. The author supports
his hypothesis on the basis of the discovery of some
fragments of the inscription *hic habitasse* found in the
debris of San Sebastiano. These help to reconstruct the
famous epigram. The largest contains ASE—which would
seem to explain *habitasse* and *habitare*. Further evidence

is furnished by a reexamination of the consular reference: *Tusco et Basso* (= 258), as seen in the *Depositio Martyrum*. He feels that this date in only an interpolation of the copyist, since many other interpolations are to be seen in the same source.

19 BARRETT, C. K., "Paul and "Pillar" Apostles" — *Studia Paulina in honorem J. de Zwaan, Haarlem*, 1953, 1-19.

This study is concerned with the question of Peter's presence in Rome and the interpretation of Gal. 2,6 (δοκοῦντες, ἦσαν and διαφέρει). Since ἦσαν is used in the past tense and refers to δοῦντες, Heussi concludes that Peter is dead since he includes him among the δοκοῦντες and therefore he could never have come to Rome. Our author writes: "in any case the tense of ἦσαν is to be noted and contrasted with that of διαφέρει. Even though he was privileged to have intercourse with the Lord during his earthly ministry, this does not necessarily prove that God showed any particular favor toward him, nor that his fellow-Christians were subservient to him."

20 BATIFFOL, P., "Papa, sedes apostolica, apostolatus" — RAC, 2 (1925), 99-116.

A history of the formulas which have been used through the centuries to designate the Papacy—papal authority. Such evidence is connected by tradition with the position of Peter in the Roman Church which includes his residence in the Eternal City.

21 BATIFFOL, P., "Natale Petri de Cathedra" — JThSt, 26 (1925), 399-404.

This is concerned with the earliest mention of the feast of the Cathedra of Peter found in the Depositio Martyrum of the Roman Chronograph of 354. The author traces the origin of the feast and the event or fact in the life of Peter to which it is related. The tradition in its connection has a reference to Peter's coming to Rome and his position in the Church.

22 BAUER, A., "Die Legende von dem Martyrium des Petrus und Paulus in Rom" — *Wiener Studien*, 38 (1916), 270-307.

H. Lietzmann's conclusion which established the tradition that Peter and Paul were actually buried in Rome
and their graves are in the two places which today are
venerated as their graves (Peter at the Vatican, Paul on
the via Ostian), is opposed by the author in this study.

23 BAUS, K., "Aufenthalt und Tod des Apostels Petrus in Rom"
— *Von der Urgemeinde zur frühchristlichen Grosskirche*, I
(Freiburg, Basel, Wien: Herder, 1962), 134-136.

In this brief account the author sums up the literary
testimony that speaks of Peter's sojourn and death in
Rome.

24 BERNARDI, J., "Le mot τρόπαιον appliqué aux martyrs."

See no. 490.

25 BERRA, L., "Vaticano: II, La tomba di S. Pietro alla luce
degli ultimi scavi."

See no. 492.

26 BESSON, M., *Saint Pierre et les origines de la primauté romaine:
Tu es Petrus*, (Paris, 1934: Bloud & Gay).

A general work on Peter from the Catholic viewpoint
with regard to his position in the Church and the Roman
primacy. One section deals with the question: Saint Pierre
a-t-il été à Rome? In this respect the author gives an
excellent expose of the question with illustrations from
archeological monuments.

27 BETZ, O., "Felsenmann und Felsengemeinde" — ZNW, 48
(1957), 49-77.

This scholarly study is a parallel on Mt. 16, 17-19 in the
psalms of Qumran. According to the hymns of praise of
(Hodajoth) of the Qumran sect, God establishes the
community of the final period upon a Rock. In this
framework the author sees a new view regarding the interpretation of Matthew. The study is divided into the following sections:
1. The community in the Qumran writings.
2. The Qumran psalms (IGH 5, 20 ff.).

3. The concepts for the community: εκκλησία and
מול

4. The rock-foundation and the temple.
5. IQH 6, 26 ff. as a free interpretation of Is. 28, 16 ff.
6. Kaphis.
7. The individual and the community.
8. The doors of death and Belial's might.
9. Peter the mouth of God and of the devil.
10. The key of the kingdom of heaven.
11. Human knowledge and divine revelation.
12. Final observations.

The author claims that the question of the authenticity of Mt. cannot be decided by a comparison with Qumran parallels though they do speak for a Palestinian origin of the word. According to this manner of speaking, Christ could be referring to a single individual as well as to the community—Peter—the Church.

28 BOEHMINGHAUS, E., "Vom Grabe des heiligen Petrus, Funde und Feinde" — *Stimmen der Zeit*, 95 (1918), 251-267.

See no. 268.

29 BULTMANN, R., "Die Frage nach der Echtheit von Mt. 16, 17-19" — TB, 20 (1941), 265-279.

This study deals with the interpretation of Mt. 16, 17-19 which defines the primacy of Peter among the Apostles (according to Catholic interpretation). The author attempts to challenge the genuineness of Mt. 16, 17 ff. He claims again (as formerly) that the text is spurious. He tries to refute F. Kattenbusch and K. L. Schmidt; he points to the absence of the word 'church' in the teaching of Christ and above all tries to show that Jesus spoke only of a kingdom to come in the future, not of a Church that is now being realized.

30 BURGER, J. D., *La tombe de saint Pierre est-elle identifiée?*

See no. 495.

31 CAMPICHE, M., "S. Pierre et son martyre" — *Revue de l'Université d'Ottawa*, 22 (1952), 249-273.

The author evaluates the importance and distinction between the theological and historical questions in the matter. "Fundamentally, if we could prove that Peter never set foot in Rome, nor died there, Pope Pius XII would still be for us the successor of Peter as pastor of the entire flock ... It would be totally useless to deny Peter's coming to Rome if the purpose is to destroy the Catholic Church" (p. 251).

32 CAPPOCI, V., "Gli scavi del Vaticano, Alla ricerca del sepolcro di S. Pietro e alcune note di diritto funerario romano."

See no. 501.

33 CECCHELLI, C., *La tomba di N. S. Gesù Cristo e le "Memorie" Apostoliche.*

See no. 525.

34 CECCHELLI, C., "Un vecchio errore" — *Osservatore Romano,* Nov. 18, 1951, p. 3.

Despite Lietzmann's *Petrus in Rom* published after the excavations beneath San Sebastiano ad catacumbas, some still hold a negative view regarding the Roman tradition of Peter's sojourn and death. This is a critique of writers as M. Goguel, K. Heussi, etc. While the Papacy and the foundation of the Roman Church are based upon faith, the historical fact of Peter's coming to Rome and his death there can also be substantiated. There may be discussions with regard to such matters as the date and character of the translation of Peter's remains ad catacumbas, the origin of the liturgical feast, etc. These minutiae in the documentary interpretation in one way or another cannot infringe on the primary fact of Peter's coming to Rome, which fact is based on the solid arguments of incontestable documentation. Nor is it possible to overlook the positive value of the present-day Vatican excavations.

35 CLAVIER, H., "Πέτρος καὶ Πέτρα" — *Neutestamentliche Studien f. R. Bultmann, 2 Aufl.,* 1957, 94-109.

This scholarly study deals with the Reformer's interpretation of the text Mt. 16, 17-19, and a examination of the meanings of the name itself.

36 CONGAR, Y., "Cephas-Céphalè-Caput" — *Revue du Moyen Age Latin*, 8 (1952), 5-42.

The important question of the name of Peter—which is linked with his role among the Twelve—is examined in this scholarly study.

37 CORTE, N., *Saint Pierre est-il au Vatican?* Bibliothèque Ecclesia, 29 (Paris: A. Fayard, 1956), 154 pp., with illus.
Also in Italian: *San Pietro e'sepolto in Vaticano?* Tempi e figure, 19 (Roma: ed. Paoline, 1957), 157 pp. with illus.
In German: *Ist der heilige Petrus im Vatikan?* Bibliothek Ekklesia, Band 1 (Aschaffenburg: Paul Pattloch, 1957).

The author, who uses the pseudo-name Leon Cristiani, deals with the same subject in these monographs. Here we find a compilation of the literary testimony confirming Peter's sojourn and death in Rome. The testimony of later scholars is also quoted, and the results of the recent Vatican excavations are examined in an endeavor to answer some of the doubts raised by scholars. The author also indicates that the facts of history are not totally unrelated to the foundation and validity of the Roman Papacy. This useful study contains the following chapters:
1. The importance of the question.
2. Tu es Petrus.
3. Jerusalem, Antioch, and Rome.
4. Literary proof of Peter's coming to Rome.
5. Gaius' trophy and the excavations of the catacombs (San Sebastiano).
6. The excavations under St. Peter's 1939-1949.
7. The discussions of the scholars.
8. St. Peter at the Vatican.

38 CORTI, G., "Pietro fondamento e pastore perenne della Chiesa" — *La Scuola Cattolica*, 84 (1956), 321-335; 401-462. 85 (1957), 25-58.

The endeavor on the part of some Protestants to justify their anti-Papal position was answered by the well-known

Protestant theologian O. Cullmann (see no. 42). By his contribution he has done much to promote the ecumenical movement and deserves the attention of his coreligionists on this essential problem. The author takes up an examination of the Papacy under the following aspects:
1. The replies of Catholic exegetes.
2. The juridic-institutionalistic concepts of the Primacy.
3. The mystic-personalistic concept.

In the second study the author adds the literary testimony of Leo the Great and of his times.

39 CRISTIANI, L., "Saint Pierre inhumé au Vatican."

See no. 546.

40 CULLMANN, O., "Les causes de la mort de Pierre et de Paul d'après le témoignage de Clément Romain" — RHPR, 10 (1930), 294-300.

This is a masterful essay on *I Clement* 5 in which the author concludes that we derive by inference from this text concerning the circumstances of the two martyrdoms of Peter and Paul, that Rome was the place of their martyrdom.

41 CULLMANN, O., "Πέτρα-Πέτρος-Κηφᾶς" — *Theologisches Wörterbuch zum Neuen Testament*, vol. VI, 94-112.

The author examines the name Peter. He concludes that Jesus did give this name to Peter and that, according to tradition handed down only by Matthew, Jesus explained this name on a special occasion by His intention of founding His Church on the Apostle whom He designated as the Rock.

42 CULLMANN, O., *Saint Pierre, Disciple, Apôtre, Martyr*. Bibliothèque Théologique (Neuchâtel-Paris: Delachaux Niestlé, S.A., 1952), 232 pp. Also in English: Peter; Disciple-Apostle-Martyr. (Trans. by F. V. Filson, Philadelphia: Westminster Press, 1953), 229 pp. In German: *Petrus, Jünger-Apostle-Märtyrer*. Das historische und das theologische Petrusproblem, (Zürich: Zwingli-Verlag, 1952), 282 pp. A new edition published in Zürich-Stuttgart, 1960.

The noted Swiss Protestant theologian reexamines the
problem relative to St. Peter from the literary and liturgical sources and the results of the Vatican excavations.
This is surely a detailed scrutiny of the evidence—exegetical and theological—in favor of the Petrine tradition
with all the arguments that have been advanced against
it. The recent Vatican excavations and the explicit Papal
pronouncement that Peter's burial place had been found
had received widespread discussion among the experts.
While in no way dependent on these results, the historical
tradition of Peter's Roman sojourn and martyrdom and
the Roman primacy did enter into the discussions. It is
in this framework that the author—according to a rigorous
method—examines all the evidence for this tradition. His
negative and positive conclusions are as follows: Peter
probably went to Rome late in his life and, after a short
ministry, suffered martyrdom. Neither liturgical nor
archeological data proves this, but I Clement (95 A.D.)
and Ignatius, *Ep. ad Romanos*, 4, 3 makes it highly probable. The place of martyrdom was without doubt remembered, but the place of burial was not known.

Before the end of the 2nd century a memorial was built
at the site of his martyrdom. This was Gaius' trophy-
probably the columnar evidence discovered in the Vatican
excavation. A square cavity lies below this monument. It
could have been a cenotaph commemorating the martyrdom—not claiming to be the actual burial place.

No actual grave is found under this monument. The
oldest graves here are not earlier than 70 A.D. and therefore are not from Nero's time. The bones found near the
supposed burial-place show nothing that proves they are
Peter's.

The Papal pronouncement that Peter's bones were
found cannot be accepted with certainty.

Since no interest in relics or burialplaces in Rome can
be shown before the end of the 2nd century, the probable
conclusion is that the burial place is and will remain
unknown. The monument site, however, even if not the
place of burial, became increasingly important to the
Christians. This is seen in Constantine's church which he

built overcoming gigantic and hazardous difficulties. He must have had strong reasons to undertake such a project. The excavations do not support the statement of the *Liber Pontificalis* which claims that Constantine covered the grave of Peter with large bronze slabs and built a Confessio over it.

43 CULLMANN, O., "Πέταος"— *Kittel*; *Theologisches Wörterbuch*, vol. 6 (1955), 99-112.

This is one of the later surveys on the interpretation of Mt. 16, 17-19. In dealing with the text of Gal. 2, 7 ff. our author points out that here Paul writes Πέτρος, perhaps because he quotes an official document.

Among the many critiques of O. Cullmann's Peter-book we enumerate the following:
In general it can be said that the reviewers discuss the exegetical aspects in the framework of its theological ramifications. Practically all are unanimous in their praise of Cullmann for a better formulation of an old problem in which certain elements are utilised that are so often neglected by others. However, according to some, there is a need for a reexamination of various questions which he deals with, in the light of recent positive results, and to which Cullmann attributes only hypothetical value. Others are inclined to a strong skepticism, particularly regarding Peter's position in the Roman Church and his sojourn and martyrdom in the Eternal City.

44 AFANASSIEFF, N., *La Pensée Orthodoxe*, n.X, 7-32 (in Russian) — *Theologia* (July-September, 1955), 465-475.

45 ALLEN, E. T., JThSt, 5 (1954), 59-62.

46 BEAUPÈRE, R., *Istina*, 2 (1955), 347-372.

47 BENOIT, P., *Revue Biblique*, 60 (1953), 565-579.

48 BOISMARD, M. E., *Divus Thomas*, 21 (1953), 233-237 — *Lumière et Vie*, 1953, n. 11, 194-198.

49 BONNARD, P., *La Tribune de Genève, January* 15, 1953 (taken from *Bulletin luthérien d'information et de documentation*,

n. 1-2, January 30, 1953). — *Revue de Théologie et de Philosophie, n.s.* 3(1953), 31-34.

50 BOTTE, B., *Irénikon*, 26 (1953), 140-145.

51 BOUTTIER, M., *Foi et Vie*, 51 (1953), 497-517.

52 BOUYER, L., *Bible et Vie chrétienne*, 1 (1953), 119-121.

53 BRAUN, F. M., *Revue Thomiste*, 53 (1953), 389-403.

54 BRUCE, F. F., *The Evangelical Quarterly*, 26 (1954), 45-46.

55 BURROWS, M., JBL, 73 (1954), 48-50.

56 CAMBIER, J., *Ephemerides Theologicae Lovanienses*, 29 (1953), 646-653.

57 CERFAUX, L., RHE, 48 (1953), 809-813. — RSR, 41 (1953), 188-202.

58 CONGAR, Y., *La Vie Intellectuelle*, 25[1] (1952), 17-43.

59 CREVOLA, C., *Gregorianum*, 34 (1953), 543-546.

60 DANIÉLOU, J., *Etudes*, 86 (1953), 206-219. — *Credo*, (Uppsala), 34 (1953), 55-64.

61 DANKBAAR, W. F., *Nederlandsch Theologisch Tijdschrift*, 7 (1952), 307-308.

62 DEJAIFVE, G., NRTh, 75 (1953), 365-379.

63 DUMAS, A., *Christianisme social*, 61 (1953), 543-546. — *Esprit*, April, 1954, 637-638.

64 FENTON, J. C., *The American Ecclesiastical Review*, 130 (1954), 209-212.

65 FRISQUE, J., *Église Vivante*, 5 (1953), 269-270.

66 FRUSCIONE, S., CC, 104, 3 (1953), 275-289; 595-611.

67 FULLER, R. H., *Theology*, 57 (1954), 28-30.

68 GAECHTER, P., ZkTh, 75 (1953), 331-337.

69 GELIN, A., *L'Ami du Clergé*, 63 (1953), 583-584.

70 GIRARDET, G. M., *Protestantesimo*, 8 (1953), 40-50.

71 GOGUEL, M., *Verbum Caro*, 6 (1952), 181-182. — RHPR, 35 (1955), 196-209.

72 GREEN-ARMYTAGE, A. H. N., *The Downside Review*, 72 (1954), 201-204.

73 GREENSLADE, S. L., *The Scottish Journal of Theology*, 6 (1953), 203-207.

74 GROSCHE, R., *Catholica*, 10 (1954-1955), 143-147.

75 GUTZWILLER, R., *Orientierung*, 16 (1952), 201-203; 215-217.

76 HAMER, J., *La Revue Nouvelle*, 19 (1954), 92-97.

77 HILLERDAL, G., *Svensk Teologisk Kvartalskrift*, 29 (1953), 139-140.

78 JOUBERT, L., *L'amitié*, May, 1953, 7-12.

79 JOURNET, C., *Primauté de Pierre dans la perspective protestante e dans la perspective catholique*, Alsatia (Coll. Sagesse et Cultures), Paris, 1953.

80 KARRER, O., *Um die Einheit der Christen. Die Petrusfrage. Ein Gespräch mit E. Brunner, O. Cullmann, H. von Campenhausen* (Frankfurt-am-Main: J. Knecht, 1953).

81 LAMPE, G. W. H., *The Church Quarterly Review*, 155 (1954), 176 ff.

82 LEMEER, B. M., *Angelicum*, 31 (1954), 161-179.

83 LEENHARDT, F. J., *The Ecumenical Review*, 6 (1953-1954), 95-97.

84 LE GUILLOU, M. J., *Vers l'Unité Chrétienne*, n. 52, 1953, 4-9.

85 MANTHEY, G., RAC, 28 (1953), 205 ff.

86 MAURER, C., *Kirchenblatt für die reformierte Schweiz*, 109 (1953), fasc. 2.

87 McCAUGNEY, J. M., *Reformed Theological Review*, 13 (1954), 21-22.

88 MEHL, R., *Le Monde*, April 2, 1953.

89 MEINERTZ, M., *Zeitschrift für Missionswissenschaft und Religionswissenschaft*, 37 (1953), 235-239.

90 MEJIA, J., *Criterio*, 28 (1953), 605-606.

91 MITCHELL, G., *Irish Theological Quarterly*, 21 (1954), 210-212.

92 MOREL, B., *Réforme*, February 28, 1953.

93 MURPHY, F. X., *The Irish Ecclesiastical Record*, 81 (1954) 436-443.

94 NEIL, W., *The Scottish Journal of Theology*, 7 (1954), 207-210.

95 NELSON, J. R., *The Student World*, 47 (1954), 216-218.

96 OVERNEY, M., *Nova et Vetera*, 28 (1953), 206-229.

97 POTTERIE, I. DE LA *Streven*, 6 (1953), 405-407.

98 SCHMEMANN, A., *St. Vladimir's Seminary Quarterly*, 2 (1953-1954), 31-32.

99 SCHMITT, J., RSRUS, 28 (1954), 58-71.

100 SCHOEPS, H. J., *Zeitschrift für Religions und Geistesgeschichte*, 5 (1953), 80-81.

101 SEGERS, H., *Revue du Clergé africain*, 9 (1954), 11-25.

102 SIMMEL, O., *Stimmen der Zeit*, 151 (1952-1953), 459-462.

103 SPICO, C., *Revue des Sciences philosophiques et théologiques*, 37 (1953), 180-183.

104 VÖGTLE, A., *Münchener theologische Zeitschrift*, 5 (1954), 1-47.

105 CULLMANN, O., "L'apôtre Pierre instrument du diable et instrument de Dieu: La place de Mt. 16, 16-19 dans la tradition primitive" — *New Testament Essays in memory of T.W. Manson*, (Manchester, 1959), 94-105.

This study deals with the interpretation of Mt. 16, 16 ff.

106 CURETON, W., *Ancient Syriac Documents*, (London, 1864), 61-62.

We have here testimony of an apocryphal source—the Syriac martyrdom of Sharbil— alluding to the bodies of

the two Apostles at Rome. The event is placed in the time of
Pope Fabian (236-51). The excessive number of foreigners
in Rome caused the Praetor to expel them; they demanded
and received permission to take with them the bodies of
their dead and began to remove the bodies of the two
Apostles. The Romans objected, but finally consented.
An earthquake interrupted their sacriligious attempt and
they abandoned it. There is no reference to the hiding
place ad catacumbas.

107 DANIEL-ROPS, H., "St. Peter and the Church at Rome" —
The Church of Apostles and Martyrs, Trans. by A. Butler,
(London: J. M. Dent & Sons Ltd., 1960), 92 ff.

The man who contributed most to this eminent foundation was none other than the very person to whom Jesus
had entrusted the task of directing His Church—Peter—
the ancient "rock" of Christianity. It is absolutely certain
that he came to Rome. It is certain that he remained there
for a very long period (about twenty-five years), broken
by various brief absences—notably by his journeys to
Jerusalem. There is no doubt whatsoever of his martyrdom
in the Eternal City. According to the author, all the literary documents of the period agree on these points. This
is further substantiated by liturgical and archeological
evidence. Pages 94, note 3, 100-102, provide interesting
information regarding the excavations at the Vatican, and
conclusions to be drawn.

108 DANNENBAUER, H., "Die römische Petruslegende" — HZ,
146 (1932), 239-262.

Lietzmann's thesis that the two Apostles were actually
buried in the two places in Rome which today are venerated as their graves—Peter on the Vatican and Paul on
the Ostia—is challenged by the author. However, his
arguments do not seem too convincing. He actually
formulates the result of his investigation in these words:
"Every little village in Palestine can claim with greater
justification, than can the imperial capital, to be the
place of Peter's death." In his commentary on *I Clement*
he asserts that the author is completely ignorant of Peter's

fate. He explains this by the fact that the Neronian persecution completely destroyed the Roman Church and broke the chain of all living Christian tradition.

109 DANNENBAUER, H., "Nochmals die römische Petruslegende" — HZ, 159 (1939), 81-88.

> Arguments are again marshalled against the Roman tradition in much the same vein as above.

110 DAVIS, G. M. Jr., "Was Peter buried in Rome?" — JBR, 20 (1952), 167-171.

> This study demonstrates the point-by-point correspondence of the study in *Acts 12* to the passion story, using elements from John, Matthew, Mark as well as Luke. According to the author he feels that F. Robinson's suggestion "that the twelfth chapter of Acts, when interpreted, states that Peter died in Jerusalem in the spring of the year 44," is a new exegesis which seems to him to be an interesting and very real possibility. "What then is it that the Pope is digging up presently under the Vatican? All the claims of these bones discovered could possibly be true." "Meanwhile, *Acts 12* may be telling all of us who have ears to hear that he to whom the resurrection faith first came never left home."

111 DE VOOGHT, P., "L'argument patristique dans l'interprétation de Matth. 16, 18 de Jean Huss" — RSR, 45 (1957), 558-566.

> On several occasions Huss endeavored to demonstrate —according to Wyclif—that *petra* in Mt, 16, 18 does not refer to Peter, but Christ. The latter thus promised to build His Church not upon Peter (*Petros*) but upon Himself (*petra*). In arguing his case Huss has recourse to two of the Fathers of the Church: St. Augustine, whose authority he invokes; St. Ambrose, whose authority he rejects. In this study the author examines the Patristic arguments established in this manner.

112 DIBELIUS, M., *Rom und die Christen im ersten Jahrhundert,* Sitzungsberichte, Heidelberg Academy, 1942. (Botschaft und Geschichte II, 1956), 177-228.

In these pages the author concerns himself chiefly with the most important indirect witness for Peter's martyrdom—*I Clement, 5*. He sides with Lietzmann but endeavors to explain the brevity of the notice chiefly by the literary character of the author. Clement is strongly influenced by Hellenism and is concerned to apply to the Bible and to the history of the beginnings of the Church the literary artistry and concepts of the Cynic-Stoic philosophy. In this framework the relative silence about Peter (which was proposed as an argument against his martyrdom in Rome) becomes understandable if we realize that Clement does not go into the question of the martyrdom for political reasons and those stated above.

113 DIEKMANN, H., "Das Zeugnis des Polykrates für die Apostelgräber in Rom" — ZkTh, 45 (1921), 627-634.

In endeavoring to explain the tradition of the Apostles' graves and the reference to the 'trophies' made by Gaius, the author examines the testimony of Bishop Polycrates of Ephesus who in the Easter Controversy (under Pope Victor, 189-198) appeals to the graves as witnesses of tradition. The author deals with an analysis made of the text (found in *Eusebius*) by two scholars: H. Kock and C. Schmidt. From these he draws his conclusions phrased as the following questions:

1. Could Victor be referring to the Roman graves of the Apostles? His answer is in the affirmative.
2. Whether or not there is a reference in Polycrates' letter, and soon after him, in Gaius' testimony? His answer is that there is a greater probability but not a certainty.

114 DI GIOVANNI, V., *San Pietro in Roma*, (Palermo: Bacione del Povero, 1895), 34 pp.

This little brochure is invaluable for the monumental evidence proving Peter's sojourn and martyrdom in Rome.

115 DINKLER, E., *Die ersten Petrusdarstellungen. Ein archäologischer Beitrag zur Geschichte des Petrusprimates.*
Marburger Jahrbuch für Kunstwissenschaft XI, (Einzelausgabe Marburg-Lahn 1939), 80 pp. and 7 plates.

This scholarly study examines the position occupied by Peter in the Church. According to the detailed account the author thinks that *Mt. 16, 17* is not Christ's authentic words, and there is no proof that Christ Himself gave Peter the name Kephas-Petros. This was merely an honorary name which the community gave Peter after Easter because (he became for them the Kephas-Petros) he was the first to profess the resurrection of Christ.

116 DINKLER, E., "Petrus Apostel" — RGG³, 5 (1961), 247-249.

A useful treatment intended to furnish the reader with general information.

117 DINKLER, E., "Die Petrus-Rom-Frage" — TR, 25 (1959), 189-230; *ibid.*, 289-335; 27 (1961), 33-64.

The results of the excavations under St. Peter's between 1940-1949 have caused increased attention on the "Peter-Roman-Tradition." The question is asked: how old and reliable is this tradition and can it be proven that Peter died a martyr in Rome and that he was buried on the Vatican Hill? The Pope announced in 1950 that a grave had been found in which Peter had been buried. What really have the excavations proven? The purpose of these scholarly studies (3 of them) is to answer these questions. In a rigorous manner and illustrated with extensive bibliography the author gives an analysis of the discussions of the literary sources. This is an excellent survey of much of the literature by both competent and non-competent writers who have attempted to answer these questions according to the literary evidence. In his second study, the author given an analysis of the discussions on the excavational findings by the various experts.

In the third, he gives a recapitulation of the observations regarding Peter's martyrdom in Rome and his burial there. Basing himself on the various opinions in all phases of the above discussions he concludes as follows: "The archeological excavations prove without doubt a fruitful field for both the Old Testament and the history of the ancient Church from the year 220. However, as regards the history of the first two Christian centuries, thus far they have proved little of any value. In any case, the archeologist must be earnestly warned against any hasty methods which would endeavor to prove theological truths from archeological evidence. Just as the empty tomb of Christ does not prove His resurrection, neither does the "tomba scomparsa" of Peter prove the Roman primacy. In fine, however, it must also be noted that the archeological findings in no respect are intended to call into question the historicity of Peter's martyrdom in Rome."

118 DRAGUET, R., "Heussi et Lietzmann: Petrus in Rom" — RHE, 34 (1938), 88-91.

The author deals with the whole controversy between Heussi and Lietzmann regarding the Roman tradition of Peter's martyrdom and burial.

119 ERBES, C., "Das Alter der Gräber und Kirchen des Paulus und Petrus in Rom" — ZKG, 7 (1885), 1-49.

This is a historical-archeological examination of the antiquity of the graves and Churches of Peter and Paul in Rome. The evidence associated with these monuments has an essential bearing on the much-discussed tradition of Peter's (and Paul's) sojourn and death in Rome. The author endeavors to establish that no cemetery existed at the Vatican before the fourth century. In regard to Gaius' testimony, the word "trophy" means here simply the places where the Apostles were executed. It does not refer to *tombs*. However, it could be said that Erbes is rather reserved in his judgement concerning Peter's Roman sojourn.

120 ERBES, C., "Die Todestage der Apostel Paulus und Petrus und ihre römischen Denkmäler" — *Texte u. Unt.* N.F. IV/I, (Leipzig: J. C. Hinrichs, 1899), 1-138.

This is a critical examination of the sources pertaining to the date and death of the Apostles Peter and Paul in which the author takes a negative view of the traditional Roman interpretation. He feels the topographical and historical data (re: Vatican cemetery) are in need of correction.

121 ERBES, C., "Petrus nicht in Rom, sondern in Jerusalem gestorben" — ZKG, 22 (1901), 1-161.

> The author rejects the tradition that Peter died in Rome. He bases his argument on interpretations of the *Apocryphal Acts of Peter*, the *Syriac Martyrology* of 412, and *Mt. 23, 24*, though at the same time he endeavors to show how general, from the middle of the second century, was the belief that Peter had come to Rome.

122 ESSER, G., "Tertullian de pudicitia 21 und der Primat des römischen Bischofs" — *Katholik*, 92, 2 (1902), 193 ff.

123 FERRUA, A., "Sulle orme di S. Pietro" — CC, 94, 3 (1943), 36-45.

> This study is concerned with the monumental evidence that gives testimony of Peter's prime position in the Church of Rome. The traditions in connection with some of the Roman monuments also point to his presence and death in the Eternal city.

124 FLAMION, J., "Saint Pierre à Rome" — RHE, 14 (1913), 249-271; 473-488.

> This is a critique of C. Guignebert, *La primauté de Pierre et la venue de Pierre à Rome* (see no. 137). The question of Peter's coming to Rome has once again been brought to the fore by the voluminous work of Guignebert. In his analysis of the work Flamion endeavors to investigate Guignebert's method, to examine its value from a strictly historical viewpoint and to determine what method should have been employed in the solution of this problem. It is with the second part of the work that Flamion mainly concerns himself, scil., the fact itself of the founding of the Roman Church by Peter and his coming to Rome and sojourn in that city. The ancient tradition, as found in Sacred Scripture, the works of the Fathers and other writers, is studied by Flamion. He does not accept Guignebert's hypothesis nor his criticism of the Roman tradition.

He feels that Guignebert's examination of the evidence
does not adhere to the elementary principles of historical
criticism.

125 FOAKES-JACKSON, F. J., *Peter, Prince of the Apostles*: *A
Study in the history and tradition of Christianity*, (New York:
George H. Doran, 1927), 320 pp.

In this large work the author endeavors to give the
ordinary reader:
1. An interest in the first days of Christianity by an
attempt to portray the Apostle who took the lead at
its inception and acted as a pioneer in its diffusion.
And also to arouse scholars:
2. To study the problem it suggests, namely, how far
tradition is to be respected where direct historical
material is scanty. Chapter XII (pp. 151 ff) is directly
concerned with "did Peter visit Rome according to
literary evidence?" The author concludes that though
the archeological testimony is weak, still the probability of his visit to Rome is strong.

126 FORGET, J., "Le témoignage de St. Irénée en faveur de la
primauté Romaine" — *Ephemerides Theologicae Lovanienses*,
5 (1928), 437-461.

There is no passage in the Fathers nor among the ancient
Ecclesiastical writers that is so often studied and so minu-
tely discussed as the famous text of Irenaeus concerning
the Roman Church and its position among the other
Churches. (Scil., *"ad hanc enim Ecclesiam propter poten-
tiorem principalitatem necesse est omnem convenire Ecclesiam,
hoc est eos qui sunt undique fideles, in qua semper ab his
qui sunt undique conservata est ea quae est ab apostolis
traditio."*)
In this study the author endeavors to give a minute
interpretation and analysis of the text. He concludes that
the ancient interpretation of Irenaeus' testimony—that
one which was up to the end of the last century unani-
mously accepted by Catholic Theologians—remains the
most natural, not only as regards the first part, but also
the second. Assuredly, Irenaeus makes no distinction

between the primacy of honor and primacy of jurisdiction. And one could not (without an anachronism) attribute to him concepts and theological precisions which were derived from later centuries of deeper studies and after long controversies. However, he clearly established the foundation on which the logic of posterior ages could support the doctrine and the supreme power of the Bishop of Rome and of his dogmatic infallibility.

127 FOUARD, C., *St. Peter and the First Years of Christianity,* (Trans. by G. F. X. Griffith, New York: Longmans, Green and Co., 1903), 415 pp.

This is a general work on Peter the Apostle. Chapter XVIII (pp. 335 ff) takes up his ministry in Rome. An appendix (pp. 398-410) deals with the important question of Peter's stay in Rome. Herein all the literary and (some) liturgical evidence is marshalled by the author to establish the fact of the foundation of the Roman Church by the Chief of the Apostles. According to the author, there is no tradition that contradicts it—no Christian community has ever claimed him as its first pastor.

128 FRIDRICHSEN, A., "Propter Invidiam. Note sur Clém. V." — *Eranos,* 44 (1946), 161-174.

This study deals with *I Clement, ch. 5.* Following Cullmann's conclusions (with the addition of some supplementary points), the author agrees with him that we derive by inference from this text concerning the circumstances of the two martyrdoms of Peter and Paul, and that Rome was the place of their martyrdom.

129 FUCHS, E., ZTK, 48 (1951).

The author sees no identity between Symeon (Acts (Acts 15, 14) and Peter (II Peter, 1, 1).

130 GAECHTER, P., *Petrus und seine Zeit,* (Innsbruck-Wien-München: Tyrolia Verlag, 1958), 450 pp.

This informative study deals with the Apostle Peter in the framework of the following chapters:
1. The triple command: "feed my lambs."

2. The election of Matthias (Acts 1, 15-26).
3. The hatred of the house of Annas.
4. The seven (Acts 6, 1-6).
5. Jerusalem and Antioch.
6. Peter in Antioch (Gal. 2, 11-14).
7. James of Jerusalem.
8. The alm-bearers from Corinth. (in I Cor. 9, 1 ff).
9. The extent of Paul's apostolate.

131 GALTIER, P., "Le véritable édit de Calliste" — RHE, 23 (1927), 465-488.

In this scholarly study the author distinguishes between the true edict of Callistus and the *edictum peremptorium* (not to be identified) which provoked the well-known text of Tertullian: *De pudicitia*, (21). It represents a powerful polemic against the penitential discipline of the Catholic Church of North Africa. According to the most probable opinion it was directed against the Roman Bishop Callistus, and specifically against the *edictum peremptorium*. The author endeavors to examine the quoted words in which are found: *id est ad omnem ecclesiam Petri propinquam*, i.e., "that is, to every Church akin to Peter." These make sense only if they refer not solely to the Bishop of Rome, but to that of *every* church related to Peter by faith or origin.

132 GALTIER, P., "Ecclesia Petri propinqua" — RHE, 24 (1928), 41-51.

This concerns the famous expression that has been conjectured as referring to the privileged position of the Roman Church, formed and continuing to exist near the Apostle's tomb.

133 GIET, S., "Le témoignage de Clément de Rome sur la venue à Rome de St. Pierre" — RSRUS, 29 (1955), 333-345.

One of the principal sources on the question of Peter's coming to Rome is *I Clement* (c. 5), in which he exhorts his correspondents to banish all spirit of contention. In the second part Clement speaks of the order established in the Church by Christ and makes a brief reference to the

Apostles Peter and Paul. O. Cullmann in his famous work
(see no. 42) gives a detailed study of the Epistle and
concludes from its indications that the martyrdom of
Peter took place at Rome. While the author accepts
Cullmann's conclusions, he feels that the interpretations
on which he bases his reason appear hardly probable. On
this account Giet appeals to a new examination of the
text.

134 GILG, A., "Die Petrusfrage im Lichte der neueren Forschung"
— TZ, 11 (1955), 185 ff.

135 GRABOWSKI, S. J., "St. Augustine and the primacy of the
Roman Bishops" — *Traditio*, 4 (1946), 89-113.

St. Augustine has long become the common and universal boast of Christianity. The Catholic Church sees
in him one of the foremost witnesses of her tradition of
teaching.

But the early Protestant reformers, too, have turned
to him as their forerunner, alleging their own doctrine to
be his. He must belong either to the *Catholics*, which he
so indefatigably defended, or be an Anglican, or a Protestant of some sort. One of the principal testing stones of
his allegiance to one church or another is the relation of
St. Augustine to the Roman Bishops. It is evident that
his position as an advocate and promotor of the Roman
Bishops cannot a priori be admitted by Protestants or
Anglicans without compromising their religion. The
impression left us by some Protestant scholars in Augustine's notion of the Church—excludes the power of
jurisdiction of any bishop over others. They thereby
exclude the monarchic form of government in the consti-
tution of the Church. And since only Roman Bishops can
come into consideration here, it is precisely to them that
they deny a primacy of jurisdiction in interpreting the
works and times of St. Augustine. It is, therefore, the
intention of the author in this study to give a brief presentation of St. Augustine's doctrine on the Roman See.

136 GRISAR, H., "The Tomb of St. Peter in Topography and
History" — *History of Rome and the Popes in the Middle Ages*,

I (Trans. by L. Cappadelta, London: Kegan Paul, Trench,
Trübner & Co., 1911), 277-305.

In the first part of this study the author discusses the
earliest history of Peter's tomb in full historical and
topographical detail. It contains many of the points
discussed in the most recent Vatican excavations. The
author then takes up the question of Peter's coming to
Rome and his martyrdom in the Eternal City, and he
discusses the modern opposition to the tradition. That the
Roman tradition is incontrovertible is seen in the cumulative evidence afforded by the manifold literary and
archeological testimonies. The matter is discussed in the
framework of these aspects:

  1. The graveyard of the neighborhood.
  2. The Christian cemetery of the Vatican.
  3. The earliest memorial church of St. Peter.
  4. The earliest mention of St. Peter's tomb at Rome.
  5. Monumental evidence of St. Peter's sojourn.
  6. The tomb on the via Appia.
  7. The mythical claims of Montorio.
  8. Modern opposition to the tradition of Peter's sojourn.
  9. Constantine's sanction of the tradition.
  10. Importance of St. Peter's tomb for the whole Christian
      world.

137 GUIGNEBERT, C., *Le primauté de Pierre et la venue de
Pierre à Rome*, (Paris: Libraire critique, Emile Nourry, 1909).

This voluminous work is concerned with Peter's coming
to Rome and the relationship between the Church of
Rome and the origin of Peter's primacy. It consists of two
main sections. In the first, the author endeavors to re-
examine the interpretation of Biblical texts which are
used by Theologians to establish the primacy conferred
upon Peter by Jesus. In the second, which constitutes the
greater part of the work, he attemps to take up the historical arguments regarding the founding of the Roman
Church by Peter and his coming to Rome and sojourn
there. The author holds the opinion that the foundation
of the Roman Church cannot be attributed to Peter (and

Paul) nor to either of them. "It is a spontaneous creation of the Gospel" (according to Sabatier). It is the work of a few followers of Paul whose names remain unknown. He then examines the three traditions concerned with Peter's coming to Rome and concludes that it cannot be historically proven. But while he denies the fact of the tradition, he endeavors to give some explanation of the origin of the tradition. (P. Monceaux refutes Guignebert's objections in RHL, 1 (1910), 216-240).

138 GUIGNEBERT, C., "La Sépulture de Pierre" — RH, 168 (1931), 225-253.

One of the dissenting voices against the Roman tradition of Peter's sojourn and burial.

The author examines the literary and liturgical sources (Martyrology and Calendar) which refer to "ad catacumbas" and also the Damasian inscription and the graffiti. The "trophies" of which Gaius speaks could not mean "relics" or "tombs." From his investigation he concludes that evidence of the Roman tradition regarding Peter's burial does not confirm this theory. The implication is that all is purely legendary and a hagiographic invention.

139 HAENCHEN, E., "Petrus-Probleme" — NTSt, 7 (1961), 187-198.

This author endeavors to answer some of the opinions expressed in O. Cullmann's work: *Petrus-Jünger-Apostel-Märtyrer*, (Zurich/Stuttgart: Zwingli Verlag, 1960), (see no. 42). Basing himself on the interpretation of the Scriptural evidence he concludes: "tradition says that Peter went to Rome and died there. However, the Acts tell us nothing of his end. We do not know why he went to Rome."

140 HALLER, J., *Das Papsttum*. Vol. I (Stuttgart & Berlin: J. G. Gotta'sche Buchhandlung, 1934), 8-20; 443-451.

Here we have a polemic denying the tradition of Peter's sojourn, death and burial in Rome. The author asserts: "who knows how many have protested in silence (against the acceptance by modern scholars of the Roman tradition) without raising their voice!

I know concerning the most learned and acute church historian of the last fifty years, Karl Holl, that he did not share the *prevailing view*."

Speaking of *Mt.* 16, 17-19 our author contends that it could only have originated after the year 70, when events proved that the temple rock had no permanence.

141 HERMANN, L., "La mort de Saint Paul et de Saint Pierre (en 58)" — *Revue de l'Université de Bruxelles*, 41 (1936), 189-199.

142 HEUSSI, K., *War Petrus in Rom?* (Gotha: L. Klotz, 1936), 80 pp.

> The chief arguments of the opponents of the tradition that Peter was actually buried in Rome and his grave today is venerated at the Vatican are gathered up in this brochure and directed against H. Lietzmann.
>
> In his main chapter the author endeavors to show that *I Clement* (para. 3 & 4) reports only vague and empty generalities about Peter, and that μαρτυρήσας (having borne witness) does not refer to the martyr-death. He finally concludes (as a reliable result) that "Peter never set foot in the city on the Tiber." (See B. Altaner: War Petrus in Rom? no. 8).

143 HEUSSI, K., *War Petrus wirklich römischer Märtyrer?* (Leipzig: L. Klotz, 1937), 24 pp.

> This is a separate printing of the study that appeared in *Christliche Welt* 51, 1937, n. 4. It is a reply to H. Lietzmann, wherein Heussi repeats his negative interpretation regarding *I Clement* 5, 2 ff. He asserts that the word-usage of μαρτυρήσας in the meaning to "die a martyr's death" can be proven only from the time after 150. He defends his thesis that the tradition of Peter's martyrdom at Rome, therefore, is purely legendary.

144 HEUSSI, K., *Neues zur Petrusfrage*, (Jena, 1939).

> The author takes up a new thesis in a second reply to

H. Lietzmann. He deals with *I Clement* (which is, according to some, a decisive literary witness to the martyr-death of Peter at Rome) and endeavors to supplement his original view with the hypothesis that the passage concerning Peter (in para. 3 & 4) can be a later *insertion*.

145 HEUSSI, K., "Das Grab des Petrus" — *Deutsches Pfarrerblatt*, (Essen) 49 (1949), 82 ff.

In this article the author rejects the thesis that Peter was buried under the dome of the Basilica at the Vatican since the reasons which speak a priori against the possibility that Christians buried Peter in the neighborhood of Nero's garden are almost overwhelming.

146 HEUSSI, K., "Papst Anekletus I und die Memoria Petri auf dem Vatikan" — *Deutsches Pfarrerblatt*, 49 (1949), 301 ff.

The report of the *Liber Pontificalis* according to which Pope Anacletus had already erected a Memoria for Peter in the first century is proven false. The author emphasizes the fact that this statement cannot be trusted.

147 HEUSSI, K., "Die Nachfolge des Petrus" — *Deutsches Pfarrerblatt*, 49 (1949), 420 ff.

The author continues to defend his position that Peter was never in Rome and therefore did not die there as a martyr and was not buried there.

148 HEUSSI, K., "Der Stand der Frage nach dem römischen Aufenthalt des Petrus" — *Deutsches Pfarrerblatt*, 49 (1949), 501 ff.

Here again the author attempts to deny the historicity of Peter's martyrdom in Rome. He raises the question whether Peter died as a martyr at all. Speaking of the testimony of *John 21, 18 ff.* he endeavors to minimize it by claiming that this tradition (which he concedes the author must have found already in existence) deals with the transfer of Paul's martyrdom to his rival Peter.

149 HEUSSI, K., "Gal. 2 und der Lebensausgang der jerusalemischen Urapostel" — ThLZ, 77, 2 (1952), 67-72.

In a previous work "War Petrus in Rom?" (pub. 1936) the author attempted to disprove the age-old tradition of the Church regarding Peter's Roman sojourn and martyrdom. Despite the criticisms which this thesis provoked among Protestants as well as Catholics, the author again redevelops his theory partly with a new argument to disclaim the Roman tradition, the interpretation of Gal. 2.

150 HEUSSI, K., "Die Entstehung der römischen Petrustradition" — *Wissenschaftliche Zeitschrift der Friedrich-Schiller-Universität*, Jena, 4 (1952-1953), 63-78.

The author continues his debate. Now faced with the results of the Vatican excavations he claims that the Pontifical Archeologists are speaking in a vicious circle. Obviously not being fully acquainted with the Official Report on the matter his attempt to explain away an authoritative tradition is a glaring contradiction.

151 Heussi, K., (Concerned with Cullmann's Petrusbuch), *Deutsche Literaturzeitung*, 74 (1953), 273 ff.

This is against O. Cullmann's thesis which accepts the authenticity of *Mt. 16, 17-19* as the word of Christ and which also indicates Peter's leading role during Christ's lifetime. The author also rejects Cullmann's arguments defending Peter's martyrdom in Rome.

152 HEUSSI, K., *Die römische Petrustradition in kritischer Sicht*, (Tübingen: J. C. B. Mohr-Paul Siebeck, 1955), 78 pp.

This is a critique of those texts which are recognised as *the classic texts* favoring the presence of Peter at Rome. The author attributes to them a mere psychological character and without any foundation-basis for substantiating Peter's Roman sojourn and martyrdom.

153 HEUSSI, K., "Petrus und die beiden Jakobus in Gal. 1-2" — *Wiss. Zeitschrift d. Univ. Jena*, 6 (1956/7).

154 HEUSSI, K., "Ist die römische Petrustradition bereits im Lukasevangelium und schon kurz nach dem Jahre 70 bezeugt?" — *Deutsches Pfarrerblatt*, 57 (1957), 565-567.

155 HEUSSI, K., "Die vermeintlichen Beweise für das Kommen des Petrus nach Rom" — HZ, 186 (1958), 249-260.

> This is a reply to K. Aland's study: *Petrus in Rom* (HZ, 183 (1957), 497-516), (see no. 2), wherein Heussi challenges Aland's conclusions.

156 HOLZMEISTER, U., *Vita Sancti Petri Apostoli*, (Paris: P. Lethielleux, 1937), 80 pp.

> The first part of this monograph is concerned with the life of St. Peter. (The author also includes an explanation of the Epistles of St. Peter and St. Jude). The numerous exceptions which provide legends and traditions regarding the life and death of the first Bishop of Rome are combined here with the fundamentals of Sacred Scripture. At all times the author is careful to separate historical truth from that which is doubtful and merely legendary. The aspects treated are as follows:
> 1. The life of St. Peter before his call by Christ.
> 2. Peter the disciple of Christ.
> 3. Peter's apostolate after Christ's Ascension and the office of Primate exercised in the Orient.
> 4. The apostolic and primatial office exercised at Rome.
> 5. A chronology of Peter's Roman ministry.
> 6. Other pertinent matters regarding Peter.
>
> Peter's coming to Rome, his precise relationship with the Church at Rome so far as the origin of Papal authority is concerned and his subsequent martyrdom there are historically certain.

157 JACQUIN, A. M., "Saint Pierre à Rome" — *Histoire de L'Église*, I (Paris: Desclée, 1928), 61-67.

> In this brief study the author endeavors to discuss the question of Peter's Roman sojourn and martyrdom from the historical point of view. The objection to the tradition by Erbes, Guignebert and others, has been refuted by two of the most competent modern critics, Harnack (see no. 248) and Lietzmann (see no. 177). The author makes his own personal contribution to the subject by pointing out that the tradition was constant and universal from the end

of the second century. In support of his view he cites the testimony of the various Churches:

1. Alexandria, Clement.
2. Africa, Tertullian.
3. Gaul and Asia, St. Irenaeus.
4. Greece, Eusebius.
5. Rome, liturgical and archeological evidence.

In the second part of this study the author takes up the chronological question of Peter's coming to Rome and the duration of his ministry. To this end he examines the testimony of Eusebius, the Liberian catalogue and of other witnesses.

158 JOSI, E., "Pietro" — EC, II-IV, VI & IX, 9 (1952), 1401-1410; 1414-1420; 1423-1427.

Basing himself on the literary evidence the author demonstrates with scientific conviction—the Roman sojourn and martyrdom of Peter. The grave of Peter is discussed in the light of the earliest and most recent excavational findings. He then takes up the matter of the veneration of Peter with its concomitant problem of the via Appia and the various theories associated with it. In the last section of this study the author examines the legendary accounts of Peter and those things associated with him.

159 JOSI, E., "Il martirio di S. Pietro" — Roma Nobilis, L'idea, la missione, le memorie, il destino di Roma, (Ed. I. Cecchetti, Rome: Edas, 1953), 274-277.

In this brief study there is found a remarkable synthesis of the literary sources pertaining to Peter's martyrdom at Rome. The author also takes up the question of the exact date of his martyrdom mentioning the various opinions of scholars. He concludes, that while it may not be possible to indicate the year with absolute certainty, one thing is positive even today—during all these centuries no other Church has ever claimed the privilege of possessing the place of martyrdom or the tomb of Peter except Rome.

160 JOURNET, C., The Primacy of Peter from the Protestant and from the Catholic point of view, (Trans. by J. Chapin, Westminster, Md.: Newman, 1954).

This is a presentation of the Protestant-Catholic views on the important question of the Primacy of Peter in which the author includes an interesting chapter on the work of the famous Protestant theologian, O. Cullmann. The chapters are as follows:

1. Popes-Primacy.
2. Apostolic Succession.
3. Catholic Church-Relations-Protestant Church.
4. Protestant Church-Relations-Catholic Church.
5. O. Cullmann.

161 KATZENMAYER, H., "Das Todesjahr des Petrus" — IKZ, 29 (1939), 85-93.

162 KATZENMAYER, H., "Zur Frage ob Petrus in Rom war. I Klemensbrief, Kap. 5 bis 6" — IKZ, (Bonn) 39 (1949), 243-249.

This scholar seeks in his own peculiar way to establish that both the Roman sojourn (which he assumes) and the death of Peter occurred long before the Neronian persecution, in the year 55.

163 KATZENMAYER, H., "Ignatius ad Romanos, 4, 3" — IKZ, 43 (1953), 67-73.

In this, as in his other studies, the author endeavors to prove that Peter died in 55. He also seeks to prove that a primacy of Rome or of its Bishop is lacking until the end of the 3rd century.

164 KATZENMAYER, H., "Petrus in Rom?" — IKZ, 46 (1956), 28-40.

165 KIRSCH, J. P., "Arthur Stapylton Barnes: St. Peter in Rome" — RHE, 2 (1901), 103-108.

This is a review of this famous work. The reviewer states that the author arrives at the same conclusions as other Catholic authors on the subject. He is to be commended for the monumental work in which he uses all sources— literary and archeological—to examine the question of Peter's tomb. The first four chapters present a very complete study on all the questions which are connected with Peter's coming to Rome—In endeavoring to fix

certain details, i.e., Peter's stay in Rome, Kirsch feels
that he uses legends a little too heavily. In the second part
he takes up the question of the translation of Peter's body
(and Paul's). He comes up with a new theory that it was
Pope Marcellus rather than Cornelius (as the Liber
Pontificalis states), who was responsible for translating
the bodies from the via Appia to their original tombs on
the Vatican and via Ostia. In this section he speaks in
detail on the following matters:
a) The tomb on the via Appia.
b) The original tomb.
c) The Confessio.

While Kirsch highly commends the author for this
monumental study, he does not, however, agree with
him in all his observations.

166 KLAUSER, T., See no. 674.

167 KLEIN, G., "Galater 2, 6-9 und die Geschichte der Jerusa-
lemer Urgemeinde" — ZthK, 57 (1960), 275-295.

The author deals with the complex problem of the
parallelism between Peter and Paul as found in Galatians
concerning which he offers some new possibilities of
solution.

168 KLIJN, A. F. J., "Die Wörter "Stein" und "Felsen" in der
syrischen Übersetzung des NT" — ZNW, 59 (1959), 99-105.

169 KNELLER, C., "C. Erbes, die Todestage der Ap. Paulus und
Petrus" — ZkTh, 26 (1902), 351-361.

This is a critique of C. Erbes, *Die Todestage der Apostel
Paulus und Petrus und ihre römischen Denkmäler* (see no.
120), and *Petrus nicht in Rom, sondern in Jerusalem
gestorben* (see no. 121). The reviewer rejects various
points marshaled by Erbes who denies Peter's sojourn
and martyrdom in Rome. Kneller feels that Erbes gives
a wrong interpretation to some of the true historical
witnesses while, at the same time, he accepts the testimony
of less reliable sources upon which he bases his arguments.

170 KOCH, H., "Petrus und Paulus im zweiten Osterfestreit?" —
ZNW, 19 (1919/1920), 174-179.

This is a critical analysis of the text of Bishop Polycrates of Ephesus recorded in Eusebius where there is a reference to the graves of Peter and Paul in Rome.

171 KÖHLER, W., "Omnis ecclesia Petri propinqua" — *Sitzungs-berichte, Heidelberg Academy*, 1937/8, vol. 3 (Heidelberg: C. Winter's Universitätsbuchhandlung, 1938), 38 pp., 2 plates.

In dealing with the literary sources of Peter's grave there is the well-known text of Tertullian (*De pudicitia, 21, 9*) which was directed against an unnamed Pope (Callistus?) and specifically against the edict regarding penance for sins of unchastity. Tertullian turns against what seems to him, the arrogant presumption of the Pope who refers to himself, and so to "every church that is near Peter," the saying of Jesus to Peter concerning binding and loosing (Mt. 16, 18), when in fact this saying was directed to Peter alone.

In this study the author asserts that the Roman Church is called "Petri propinqua" because she preserves the tomb of Peter. According to this interpretation, the power to loose and bind which had been given Peter actually streams forth in a physical manner and passes over to the Bishop of the Church in whose district the grave is located. Connected with this is the idea of a *derivatio potestatis* originating not in a Christian but in an old pagan religious mentality, in the imagination of a mystico-magical power emanating from the tomb of the hero. The δύναμις τοῦ δεῖν καὶ λύειν may be regarded as one aspect of the vivifying "flowing power of the hero." Whoever is in possession of the tomb is also in possession of the hero's power. "Propinqua" has to be understood in an analogon to the hero and ancestor-cult in the pagan family-community. As Romulus was the founder of Rome, so is Peter the founder-hero of the Roman Church. This sort of mentality did not yet invoke Mt. 16, 18 in its belief, but this would necessarily be the next step. (See B. Altaner, no. 9).

172 KRÜGER, G., "Petrus in Rom" — ZNW, 31 (1932), 301-306.

In this study the author champions the traditional thesis chiefly on the basis of *I Clement*.

173 LAKE, K., "Simon, Cephas, Peter" — *Harvard Theological Review*, 14 (1921), 95-97.

> In this study the author questions the common identification of Simon, Cephas and Peter. He points out that Paul's reference to Cephas and to Peter are extremely curious on the usual view, and he cites the interpretation of Clement of Alexandria's understanding (as quoted by Eusebius) that Cephas was a member not of the *Twelve*, but of the *Seventy*.

174 LANCIANI, R., *Pagan and Christian Rome*, (Boston and New York: Houghton, Mifflin and Co., 1892), 361 pp.

> A famous book by a famous scholar whose testimony is frequently quoted to substantiate the Roman sojourn and martyrdom of Peter. Writing from the strictly archeological point of view, he endeavors to avoid the questions which pertain to the religious controversy. He states: "for the archeologist the presence and execution of Saints Peter and Paul in Rome are facts established beyond a shadow of doubt by purely monumental evidence" (p. 123). "There is no event of the imperial age and of imperial Rome, which is attested by so many noble structures, all of which point to the same conclusion—the presence and execution of the Apostles in the capitol of the Empire" (p. 125). This informative work contains the following chapters:
>
> 1. The transferal of Rome from a Pagan city to a Christian city.
> 2. Pagan shrines and temples.
> 3. Christian Churches.
> 4. Imperial tombs.
> 5. Papal tombs.
> 6. Pagan cemeteries.
> 7. Christian cemeteries.

175 LEBRETON, J., & ZEILLER, J., "St. Peter and the beginnings of the Roman Church" — *The History of the Primitive Church*, (Trans. by E. C. Messenger, New York: Macmillan Co., 1944), 284-298.

> In this chapter the author examines the early Scriptural

and Patristic sources and the archeological data which provide information on the apostolic life of St. Peter and his final arrival in Rome. While the actions and doings of Peter at Rome remain unknown to us, two things are certain: he went to the Eternal City, and after governing the Roman Church, he was martyred there under Nero. The time of his arrival is conjectural, but the fact of his coming is established. All written tradition, dating to the Apostolic period (or its immediate neighborhood) testifies to this historic reality, and archeology confirms it, scil., excavations at San Sebastiano ad catacumbas, the Damasian inscription, the graffiti, the "Domus Petri." With regard to the duration of Peter's stay in Rome, the testimony of Lactantius (*De mortibus persecutorum, II*) echoes a tradition more in harmony with the truth: the twenty-five years of Peter's activity does not refer to the time of his Roman stay but only marks its end.

176 LECLERCQ, H., "Saint Pierre" — DACL, 14 (1939), 822-922. See no. 686.

177 LIETZMANN, H., *Petrus und Paulus in Rom. Liturgische und archäologische Studien*, (Bonn: A. Marcus and E. Weber, 1915), 189 pp., 6 plans. *Petrus und Paulus in Rom*, (2nd. ed.) (Berlin-Leipzig: Verlag W. de Gruyter, 1927), 316 pp., 13 plates.

The old question of the Apostles' presence and death in Rome. Once denied but quite out of date even in Protestant circles. In this epoch-making study the famous Protestant scholar aims to discover and evaluate additional testimony if such is possible. To this end he broadens the circle of sources by including the liturgical and archeological findings beneath San Sebastiano. He first examines the texts of the ancient Roman liturgies. He concludes that on June 29, 258, the bodies of Peter and Paul were transferred ad catacumbas; that this day was observed annually thereafter, but it did not become a great popular success until after the relics were retransferred to their respective Constantinian basilicas. From the excavational evidence at San Sebastiano he concludes that the forecourt of the triclia was constructed in 258 when the Apostles' bodies were transferred (for reasons of safety) ad catacumbas.

The author then briefly examines some literary tradition prior to the Apostles' transferal in 258 . In the next section he takes up the results of the excavational findings in 1615 and 1626 under St. Peter's. It seemed obvious that Peter was buried in a pagan cemetery in use from the first half of the second century to the end of the third. The erection of the Constantinian basilica indicates that the precise position of Peter's grave was known to the architect. The author then gives some brief consideration to St. Paul and the excavations on the via Ostia.

In final answer to the question: are the graves genuine? his answer is YES. Beneath the Hall of the three Emperors there actually rests the remains of Paul, and under the mighty dome of Bramante, those of Peter. (These conclusions were soon to be contradicted by A. Bauer, see no. 22). In the second edition (1927), Lietzmann includes a critical reexamination of the objections leveled by the Viennese Theologian, and reiterates his previous conviction. "To sum up, all the early sources about the year 100, become clear and easily understandable, agree with their historic context, and with each other, if we accept what they clearly suggest to us, namely, that Peter sojourned in Rome and died a martyr there. And any other hypothesis on Peter's death heaps difficulty upon difficulty, and cannot be supported by a single document. I cannot understand how, in the face of this state of things, there can be any hesitation in accepting the conclusion" (p. 238, 2nd ed).

178 LIETZMANN, H., "Petrus römischer Märtyrer" — SAB, 29 (1936), 392-410.

This is an answer to the criticism raised by K. Heussi's *War Petrus in Rom?* wherein our author is challenged for the conclusions he had reached in his former work: *Petrus und Paulus in Rom*, (2nd ed 1927) which defended the Roman tradition of Peter and Paul's martyrdom and burial.

In this reply the author refutes the arguments against this tradition. In proof of this he develops the details of Peter's tomb (can any other country claim his burial-place) and the Memoria. With regard to the Memoria Apostolorum on the via Appia, he believes that there was a translation in 258. While there are difficulties in this explanation, yet it seems to correspond best with all the archeological and literary evidence.

179 LIETZMANN, H., "Petrus römischer Märtyrer" — *Kleine Schriften*, I (Berlin, 1958), 100-123.

The material found in his original book is found printed here.

180 LOVE, J., *Saint Peter*, (New York, London, Toronto: Oxford University Press, 1956), 80 pp.

181 LOWRIE, W., SS. *Peter and Paul in Rome*, (New York, London, Toronto: Oxford University Press, 1940), 164 pp.

This little book written in 1940 is rather succinct. Though the author claims that he is giving us an objective and factual account of the burial place of Peter and Paul ad catacumbas, it is far from the case. He states that the facts which this tradition alleges are controversial if not disputable.

182 LUDWIG, J., "Die Primatworte Mt. 16, 18-19 in der altkirchlichen Exegese" — *Neutestamentliche Abhandlungen*, *XIX/4*, (Münster Westf., 1952).

183 MARCORA, C., "San Pietro" — *Storia dei Papi*, I (Milano: Edizioni Librarie Italiane, 1961), 51-58.

The coming of Peter to Rome and his laying of the foundation of the Roman Church are firmly established. This is based on Eusebius (*Chronic. ad annum* 43) and St. Jerome, who assign his coming to Rome in the first years of the reign of the Emperor Claudius (about 42 A.D.). Tradition assigns a twenty-five year duration to Peter's Roman episcopacy, though it is admitted by all that this was not a continuous residency. It was during the persecutions (67—though the year is not certain) that

Peter and Paul were martyred. Peter was crucified on the
Vatican hill; Paul was decapitated on the via Ostia. There
is no serious historical doubt as to Peter's coming to Rome.
The testimony of Clement of Rome, Ignatius of Antioch,
and others substantiate the tradition. Furthermore, the
tradition of Peter's tomb beneath the Papal altar of the
Vatican basilica has been confirmed by the most recent
archeological excavations (1940-49). The author then
speaks briefly of the excavational results and also refers
to a temporary translation of the body of Peter (and Paul)
to San Sebastiano on the via Appia in 258, and their
return to their original graves in 260. In speaking of Peter's
tomb, the author cautions that one is not to imagine that
a grave containing his body has been discovered. On the
contrary, it is merely sufficient to know that the place of
his burial has been identified.

184 MARUCCHI, O., "La crocifissione di S. Pietro nel Vaticano"
— *Nuovo Bullettino d'Archeologia Christiana*, 11 (1905), 135-179.

The controversy with regard to the exact place where
Peter was crucified in Rome (under Nero) has agitated
much discussion among scholars. Up until (and including)
the fourteenth century, the Vatican hill was always
designated as the place. It was only after this time that a
reference was made to the Janiculum. This erroneous
theory was held even in more recent times. However,
it is definitively confuted by the author after Msgr. G. B.
Lugari's publication on the same subject (Le lieu du
crucifiement de saint Pierre, Tours, 1898. V., *Nuovo Bull.*
1899, 113 ff.). According to the author the place of Peter's
crucifixion is to be sought at the Vatican, and not on the
Janiculum.

185 MARUCCHI, O., "Un insigne sarcofago cristiano Lateranense
relativo al primato di St. Pietro ed al Gruppo dell'antico
Laterano" — RAC, 2 (1925), 84-98.

Among the ancient sarcophagi to be seen in the Lateran
Museum and of great importance is that one designated
as no. 174 which comes from one of the many mausoleums
that surrounded the ancient Vatican basilica. Though it

was published and illustrated many times (from Bossius on), the author endeavors to give an interpretation of the scenes on the sarcophagus which give testimony to Peter's position and authority in the Roman Church. In this respect the sarcophagus is regarded as the most important among all the others found in the Lateran Museum.

186 MARUCCHI, O., *The Evidence of the Catacombs*, (New York, Cincinnati, Chicago: Benziger Bros., 1929), 113 pp.

In this little volume the author presents a synthesis of the archeological arguments that can be drawn from the study of ancient Christian monuments in defense of the doctrines and organization of the Catholic Church. It is mainly a critique of T. Roller's writings on the catacombs (see no. 221). Chapter V (pp. 76-87) is pertinent here. It deals with the Apostolic foundation and the supremacy of the Roman See, the coming of Peter to Rome and his martyrdom there. According to the author we must conclude quite definitely that the tradition of Peter's sojourn and death in Rome is firmly established by literary and archeological testimony. The silence of the New Testament could be explained by the chronological order of occurrences, but it is not necessary since most critics admit that Peter wrote his first Epistle from Rome, designating this city by the symbolical name of "Babylon." An argument of greater weight is the fact that no Christian Church in all these centuries has ever claimed Peter as its founder except the Church of Rome, nor has any Church claimed his body. The tomb of Peter in the Vatican is genuine beyond doubt. The traditions in connection with the Roman monuments all point to a prolonged stay of Peter in Rome. In Chapter VIII (pp. 109 ff) the author discusses the discovery of a monument of the Apostles (Peter and Paul) on the via Appia which gives additional evidence for Peter's stay in Rome. These finds prove that Peter and Paul were buried here for a short time. The tradition is attested by literary and liturgical sources.

187 MARUCCHI, O., "Il cimitero del Vaticano" — *Le Catacombe Romane*, posthumous ed. by E. Josi (Rome: La Liberaria dello Stato, 1932), 34-54.

In this section the author discusses the origin of the Christian cemetery at the Vatican which commences with the true story of Peter's burial here. Peter's coming to Rome is an undeniable fact presently admitted not only by learned Catholic scholars, but also Protestants, as Harnack. Literary testimony confirms the irrefutable authenticity of Peter's grave at the Vatican. The precise location of Peter's crucifixion at Rome, under Nero, had at one time been a subject of controversy. The Apostle was buried in an area along side the via Cornelia which divided the circus of Nero from the place where the basilica is located. The space to the right of the so-called via was certainly destined for burials. The place of Peter's crucifixion is to be sought at the Vatican and not on the Janiculum. The author then takes up the reasons for his conviction.

188 MARUCCHI, O., *Pietro e Paolo a Roma*, 4th ed. (Revised by C. Cecchelli, Torino: Casa Editrice Marietti, 1934).

This revised work of the famous archeologist is a historical and archeological survey pertaining to the Apostles Peter and Paul. It supplies information on the following matters:

1. The first relation of the Apostles Peter and Paul with the Roman world. Paul's journey to Rome.
2. Peter's sojourn and death in Rome.
3. The place of the martyrdom.
4. The graves at the Vatican and the via Ostia with some information regarding the ancient basilicas of both Apostles.
5. The temporary Apostolic grave on the via Appia.
6. The Cathedra of Peter.
7. Some Roman Churches of Apostolic origin and their relation with the catacombs.
8. The other 'memorie' indicated in documents of a later period.
9. The ancient images of the Apostles.
10. The primacy of the Roman Church confirmed by monuments.

189 MARTIN, P., "Saint Pierre, sa venue et son martyre à Rome"
— RQH, 13 (1873), 5-107.

This study deals with the controversy on the Peter-
Roman question. St. Peter's coming to Rome and his
martyrdom there has a bearing on the Papacy. It is
amazing that one would doubt this fact. One does not
destroy the Roman tradition without undermining the
basis on which it is founded and the innumerable proofs
in its behalf. The cumulative uninterrupted evidence that
dates back almost to the time of Peter himself: literary,
epigraphic, iconographic, etc., all unite to defend the
Catholic thesis and come to the aid of the historian to
acknowledge the primacy of the Bishop of Rome in as
much as he is the successor of Peter.

In this unusual study the author quotes the writings
of the Orientals from all periods of history. How could
this witness of tradition—the voice of immemorial history
—have penetrated the East? Thus it is seen that the
tradition has been constant not only in the Latin Church,
but in the Eastern Church as well.

190 MARTIN, P., "Saint Pierre, sa venue et son martyre à Rome"
— RQH, 15 (1874), 5-92.

In this study the author takes up a continuation of the
controversial question between Protestants and the
Catholic Church. He gives a history of the development
of the Protestant rejection of the Roman tradition.
Scientific treatises and discussions denying the historical
fact were not wanting. But to what avail? One does not
build an edifice as the Catholic Church on a false hypothesis. One does not construct the origin of the Papacy
on error. Antiquity affirms with the most authentic evidence that Peter came to Rome and died there.
Such witness of antiquity is unquestionable proof of truth.

191 MARTIN, P., "De quelques travaux récents sur la venue et le
martyre de Saint Pierre à Rome" — RQH, 18 (1875), 202-210.

In this study the author passes in brief review over the
Protestant endeavor to take away the primacy of the

Roman See by repeating the error that Peter never came to Rome and therefore his martyrdom there is unfounded.

How do Catholics answer the Protestants? This is a question of science and good sense and not only written testimony. One does not explain a system such as Catholicism by an apocryphal legend. As for the scientific arguments:

1. All the ancients who have spoken of Peter's death state expressly (or imply) that it was in Rome.
2. Although they may differ on the manner of death, they agree on the place.
3. The tradition is thus one, constant, universal, and explicit, found not only in the Latin Church, but in the Greek, Armenian, Syrian, Nestorian, Coptic, Arabic, and Ethiopic Churches as well.

192 McGIFFERT, A. C., "Peter's sojourn in Rome" — *American Journal of Theology*, 1 (1897), 145-149.

While the fact of Peter's presence is established, the date of the Apostles' arrival in Rome and the length of his stay demands a renewed investigation. The author's conclusions are as follows:

If Festus became procurator in the year 55, Paul must have arrived in Rome in the Spring of 56, and his death, which ended two years imprisonment, must have occurred in 58. It is quite possible, then, to suppose that Peter came to Rome very soon after and spent six full years in that city. (A stay of that length is more than sufficient to satisfy all the conditions the author refers to, so he thinks). That Peter suffered martyrdom is too well attested to admit of a doubt. Though it cannot be proved with certainty that he met his death in the great persecution of 64, it is altogether probable that he did. All the literary evidence confirms this assumption.

193 McNABB, V., *The New Testament Witness to Saint Peter*, (New York, Cincinnati, Chicago: Benziger Bros., 1928), 13 passim.

The purpose of this little volume is to justify the divine-given prerogative of St. Peter according to the witness of St. Mark, St. Matthew, St. Luke, St. Paul and St. John.

The theological and exegetical question of the Primacy of
Peter, the relationship between the Church at Rome and
St. Peter is obviously connected with his stay in the
Eternal City. The tradition connecting Peter with Rome
and his martyrdom there remained unbroken and un-
disturbed until the thirteenth century. The Reformers,
following the Waldenses, raised the doubt again. Rejecting
the personal Primacy of Peter they even went so far as
to deny that he ever came to Rome and died there. Pere
Lagrange makes some pertinent remarks in the preface of
this work: "But the progress of historical criticism forces
independent thinkers to admit that Peter came to Rome
and had there his tomb . . . That presence and tomb were
surely of some influence in the new Christian cult of Rome.
And now M. von Harnack proposes to attribute the privilege of the See of Peter to the sole influence of the tomb."
(*Ecclesia Petri propinqua*).

194 MEINERTZ, M., "Peter" — *Lexikon für Theologie und Kirche*,
8 (1936), 131-135.

195 MERRILL, E. T., "St. Peter and the Church in Rome" —
Essays in early Christian History, (London: Macmillan & Co.,
1924), 267-333.

> According to the author, the choice of a historical
> foundation stone for the Roman Church was not made all
> at once. It was the outcome of a gradual process. The
> origin of the belief that connected Peter with Rome bears
> every earmark of a myth. It lacks any support in historical
> evidence. The only reason it is not rejected universally
> by all competent scholars is that is has come to be a
> doctrine so tremendously imposing by the age-long repe-
> tition of millions. The Church of Rome regards herself
> founded on it. Yet, the historical base is not rock but
> incoherent sand. (See S. Jones remarks no. 346).

196 METZNER, E., *Die Petrustradition und ihre neusten Gegner*,
(Warthe: Schwerin, 1937).

197 MOHLBERG, C., "War und wann starb Petrus in Rom (Eine
Abwehr)" — *Neue Züricher Nachrichten*, 31 (1935), no. 71.

This is a defense of the Roman tradition.

198 MOLLAND, E., "Besprechung von K. Heussi: War Petrus in Rom? 1936; H. Lietzmann: Petrus, römischer Märtyrer, 1936; K. Heussi: War Petrus wirklich römischer Märtyrer?" — TL, 62 (1937), 493-444.

The author bases his work on an analysis of Heussi's: *War Petrus in Rom.* and *War Petrus wirklich römischer Märtyrer?* and also Lietzmann's: *Petrus römischer Märtyrer.* He rejects Heussi's attempt to deny that Peter resided and died in Rome. With Lietzmann, Cullmann, and most modern historians, he holds that we derive from literary testimony (*I Clement, Chapter 5*, which he analyzes) the circumstances of Peter's martyrdom and burial in Rome. "If this discerning hypothesis (which I believe) is correct, then we cannot only say with Lietzmann and the majority of present-day church historians that the martyrdom of Peter in Rome is a fact, but that we can even go a step further and grasp a glimpse of the dismal background of his martyrdom." Among the other dissenting voices mentioned are C. Guignebert, A. Bauer, E. T. Merrill, H. Donnebauer, J. Haller.

199 MOLLAND, E., "Le développement de l'idée de succession apostolique" — RHPR, (1954), 1-29.

200 MONCEAUX, P., "L'apostolat de Saint Pierre à Rome" — RHL, 1 (1910), 216-240.

This is a refutation of C. Guignebert's attack against the Roman tradition which appeared in 1909: "La primauté de Pierre et la venue de Pierre à Rome." The author studys the liturgical sources containing statements concerning the date and place of martyrdom of the Apostles. From the *Depositio Martyrum* for June 29th we read "Peter in the catacombs, Paul on the via Ostia in the consulship of Tuscus and Bassus." So the date of the Apostles' martyrdom is fixed by naming the consulate of Tuscus and Bassus which falls in the year 258. Bassus is identified with the consul of the same name under Nero. The author expands the text as follows: Passi sub Nerone, Basso (et Crasso consulibus; translati in Catacumbas Basso) et Tusco consulibus, that is "suffered under Nero in the consulship of Bassus (and Crassus; transferred to the catacombs in the consulship of Bassus) and Tuscus."

201 MOULE, C. F. D., "Some Reflections on the 'Stone' Testimonia in Relation to the Name Peter" — NTSt, 2 (1955/56), 56-58.

In this brief study the author proposes the idea that there is a possibility of a wider and more flexible additional range of association between 'Petrus' and 'Rock' or 'Stone,' besides the straight identification. Is it not possible that the name 'Rock' or 'Stone' evoked, for early Christians, a range of associated ideas wider than merely the foundation-theme of Mt. 16?

202 MUNCK, J., *Petrus und Paulus in der Offenbarung des Johannes*, (Copenhagen, 1950).

In this investigation made by the famous Danish scholar, there is an interesting attempt to find in *Revelation* 11, *3-13* the earliest testimony to the martyr-death of the two Apostles at Rome. The Apostles Peter and Paul are meant here by the "two witnesses," who, after they had given their witness, are attacked, overcome, and killed by the "beast from the abyss." In the same passage it says that the corpses of the two witnesses continue to lie upon the street of the "great city" where earlier their Lord had been crucified. For 'three and a half days' men of all peoples saw them lying there and refused to permit their burial, etc. These witnesses, who were previously always interpreted to be Moses and Elias, could in fact be Peter and Paul.

203 MURPHY, F. X., "Round the Tomb of St. Peter: The Vatican Excavations" — *The Tablet*, 193 (April 2, 1949), 215-216.

See no. 725.

204 NESBITT, C., "What did become of Peter?" — JBR, 27 (1959), 10-16.

The author is concerned with the problem of what became of Peter in the New Testament materials, after the author of the Acts dropped him suddenly in the

midst of his story. The writer believes the trail is fairly
clear through subsequent scriptural writings that Peter
left Jerusalem for missionary work among Jewish-Christ-
ians in Judea and Samaria. Then he returned to Jerusalem
for the Council and then went to Syrian Antioch. From
there he probably went into the provinces of Asia Minor
and Galatia. He crossed the Aegean to go westward to
Rome if that was his ultimate destination (Corinth would
have been a natural stop-off). It may well be that Peter
may have had the same plans of travelling westward to
Rome (as the Acts show that Paul had in later years).
And he may also have reached his goal, as Paul, and may
have achieved martyrdom at Rome which Christian
tradition accorded him.

205 NUNN, H. P. V., "St. Peter's Presence in Rome" — *Evangelical Quarterly*, 22 (1950), 126-144.

206 O'CONNOR, D. W., Jr., "Peter in Rome: An investigation into
the literary, liturgical and archeological evidence for the
residence, martyrdom, and burial of Peter of Rome" —
Columbia University Dissertation Abstracts, 21 (1960), 691.

In this doctoral dissertation the author takes up a
study of the Roman residence, martyrdom, and burial of
St. Peter in the light of the latest critical literature and
archeological discoveries. The discussion is divided into
the following three main headings:
1. A brief historical survey of the problem and the literary
   evidence for the residence of Peter in Rome.
2. The literary and liturgical evidence for the tradition
   of the martyrdom of Peter in Rome.
3. The literary, liturgical, and archeological evidence for
   the tradition of the burial in Rome.
   The author's conclusions are as follows: It appears most
plausible to believe that:
1. Peter did reside in Rome at some time during his
   lifetime, most probably at the end of his life.
2. He did not found the Church at Rome.
3. He did not serve as its first Bishop for a quarter of a
   century as is claimed by the Liber Pontificalis.

4. He probably was martyred by crucifixion as a member of the Christian religion.

5. He was remembered in the traditions of the Church and in the erection of a simple monument near the place where he died.

6. His body most probably was not recovered from the burial by the Christian group which later (when relics became of great importance for apologetic reasons) came to believe with complete honesty, that that which originally had marked the general area of his death also indicated the precise placement of his grave.

207 O'HARE, C. M., "St. Peter in Rome" — *The Irish Ecclesiastical Record*, 37 (1931), 337-354.

In this study the author endeavors to refute the arguments of two Cambridge scholars, Rev. E. Milner-White and Rev. W. L. Knox, who claimed that it is "a quite serious doubt whether St. Peter ever went to Rome at all." According to O'Hare, the fact that St. Peter's connection with Rome was never questioned for some twelve centuries, causes some suspicion. For this reason he discusses the question from the historical point of view and then takes up the evidence of the catacombs.

St. Peter's First Epistle was addressed from Babylon and it is a tradition that *Babylon* is Rome. All the ancient writers understand Babylon in this sense. Contrary opinions are insignificant exceptions. Other historical proofs are the Fathers: Ignatius of Antioch, I Corinthians of Clement, Eusebius, Irenaeus, Tertullian. Of these he quotes extracts which leave no room for doubt as to St. Peter's presence in Rome. By the middle of the third century it was the common opinion that the Bishop of Rome was Peter's successor, and it is extremely unlikely that this could have arisen from a baseless legend.

The author then takes up the evidence of the catacombs with regard to Peter's Roman sojourn and death. Basing himself on O. Marucchi (*The Evidence of the Catacombs*, see no. 186) he states that the traditions in connection with the Roman monuments all point to the unquestionable fact that Peter lived and died in the Eternal City. After

an enumeration of the archeological evidence, he concludes
that there are absolutely no grounds for calling this
historical fact into question.

208 PENNA, A., *San Pietro* (Brescia: Topografia ed. "Morcelliana,"
1954), 336 pp., 25 plates.

This is a useful work with many general details of the
life of Peter according to the following divisions:
1. The Disciple.
2. The Apostle.
3. The Master.
Pages 215 ff. deal specifically with the question of
Peter's coming to Rome which was denied for the first
time (in writing) by Marsilius of Padua in the fourteenth
century. The author has recourse to the literary sources
that speak of Peter's sojourn and also brings out the
principle objection of those who deny the tradition, viz.,
the silence of Acts and the Pauline Epistles. He then
takes up the question of Peter's martyrdom and grave
(pp. 217 ff) basing himself on the liturgical and literary
data, including the most recent archeological evidence
(the Vatican excavations of 1940-49). In this last instance
he gives a cursory survey of the archeological finds. He
concludes that while there has been diverse reaction to the
discoveries beneath the Confessio of St. Peter's, competent
authority has recognized and conceded the fact that
Peter came to Rome, was martyred there, and was buried
on the Vatican hill.

209 PERLER, O., "Ignatius von Ant. u. die röm. Christen-
gemeinde" — *Divus Thomas*, 22 (1944), 413-451.

210 PERLER, O., "Zeugnisse für Aufenthalt und Tod des P. in
Rom" — *Lexikon für Theologie und Kirche*, 8 (1963), 340-341.

In this brief study the author sums up the non-Biblical
testimony that speaks of Peter's sojourn and death in
Rome.

211 PETERSON, E., "Policrate di Efeso" — EC, 9 (1952), 1672-
1673.

Mention is made of Pope Victor's (189-199) letter to Polycrates in which he speaks of the Roman tradition regarding the tombs of the Apostles at Rome. (Cf. *Eusebius, H. E. V. 24, 2-8* to which Polycrates replied).

212 PETERSON, E., "Das Martyrium des h. Petrus nach der Petrus-Apokalypse" — *Miscellanea G. Belvederi*, (Collezione "Amici delle catacombe," 23) (1954/55), 181-185.

In discussing the Peter-question the author evaluates the two Egyptian texts (indirect witnesses to Peter's martyrdom in Rome), viz., the apocryphal writing "The Ascension of Isaiah," and the "Apocalypse of Peter." There is a question of dating the texts to which the passages belong and which determine their value as witnesses. They presuppose a knowledge of the Peter-tradition and may be dated to the end of the first or beginning of the second century.

213 RHEINFELDER, H., "Philolgische Erwägungen zu Mt. 16, 18" — BibZ, 24 (1938), 139-163.

This study examines the question regarding the understanding of the surname Christ promised Peter. The author's scope is similar to O. Cullmann's interpretation of the text found in the Evangelist wherein Christ utters those well-known words. The author thinks that Christ called Peter a rock only metaphorically, and that only later on did this become a surname which was preserved in the often-used connection "simon-peter" which finally led to the understanding that this surname was his real name.

214 RIDDLE, D., "The Cephas-Peter Problem, and a possible solution" — JBL, 59 (1940), 169-180.

This study was prompted by Prof. Lake's essay (Harvard Theological Review, 14 (1921), 95-97, see no. 173) who questioned the common identification of Simon, Cephas, and Peter—he pointed out that Paul's reference to Cephas and to Peter are extremely curious on the usual view, and cited the interpretation of Clement of Alexandria's understanding (as quoted by Eusebius) that Cephas was a

member not of the *Twelve* but of the *Seventy*. The purpose
of this study is not to secure a definitive answer to the
question whether Cephas and Peter are names for the
same person, or the names of two persons. The purpose
is to examine the incidence of the occurrence of the names
in the hope of discovering how the common identification
was made. The problem is an aspect of the process of the
growth of gospel tradition, so that the possible solution
throws some light on the development of the gospel
materials.

215 RIESS, F., "Der hl. Petrus in Rom" — *Stimmen aus Maria-
Laach*, 2 (1872), 461-487.

This is a historical-critical essay with particular reference to the disputation held in Rome between Catholic
priests and Protestant ministers on the Peter-question
(see no. 11), and also with regard to R. A. Lipsius' *Chronologie der römischen Bischöfe bis zur Mitte des 4. Jahr-
hunderts*, Rome, 1872. It is divided into the following
sections:
1. The various testimonies.
2. The silence of the Scriptures.
3. The scientific critique and the origin of the Peter-
   question.
The cumulative evidence, afforded by the statements
of early writers, the witnesses of tradition—and archeological testimony, points to the incontestable conclusion
that relates the foundation of the Church at Rome to
Peter, his coming there, and his martyrdom and burial
in the Eternal City.

216 RIMOLDI, A., "L'Apostolo S. Pietro nella letteratura apocrifa
dei primi sei secoli" — *La Scuola Cattolica*, 83 (1955), 196-224.

In this engaging study the author examines the legends
of Peter of the first six centuries (which form apocryphal
literature) to show in what measure this type of literature
had influenced the cult and devotion of the early Church
to the prince of the Apostles. It includes the following:
1. The Petrine apocryphal writings
2. The Petrine apocryphal Acts.

3. Pseudo-Clementine writings.
4. Apocryphal writings of Petrine interest.

217 RIMOLDI, A., "L'Apostolo San Pietro" — *Analecta Gregoriana*, 95 (1958), 346 pp.

We have here a scholarly and illuminating study of Peter. The author describes the following chapters with lucidity and impartiality:
1. St. Peter in the Fathers of the first three centuries.
2. St. Peter in the Latin Fathers from the fourth to the middle of the fifth centuries.
3. St. Peter in the Greek Fathers from the fourth to the middle of the fifth centuries.
4. St. Peter in the archeological sources; the cult of Peter at Rome from the third to the middle of the fifth centuries. The Petrine titles with regard to the Primacy. In this section he treats of:
   a. The archeological sources of iconographic character from the third to the middle of the fifth centuries. (St. Peter on sarcophagi, decorated glass, frescoes, mosaics and the minor arts; The Apostle Paul and the other Apostles in early Christian art from the third to the fifth centuries.
   b. The cult of Peter at Rome from the third to the middle of the fifth centuries; The cult of Peter at the Vatican; Peter and Paul on the via Appia; St. Peter in Chains.
   c. The Petrine titles regarding the Primacy; Peter the first of the Apostles; the Primacy of Peter; Peter the prince of the Apostles; Peter the currier of the Apostles; The keeper of the heavenly keys; The parallelism between Moses and Peter.

218 ROBINSON, D. R., "Where and When did Peter die?" — JBL, 64 (1945), 255-267.

Quoting *Acts 12, 17*, the author says that Peter died in Jerusalem in prison at this time (44). He thinks the phrase "went to another place" really meant Peter went to his glory. (The author does not say whether Peter was executed in prison by Herod because he was one of the Church leaders, or whether he died a natural death). He

notes that *Acts 12* makes "very good sense" as "a somewhat garbled allegory of Peter's death" (as it stands, it is
incredible), and points to the similarity between Peter's
"angel" and the resurrected Jesus. He suggests that
Peter's martyrdom, when the supposed early evidence is
analyzed, may well be a "piece of devout fiction," and
indicates further how "extremely flimsy" the tradition
that Peter was in Rome actually is.

219 ROBINSON, J. A. T., *Epochs in the life of Peter*. (New York,
1933).

220 ROCKWELL, W. W., "The Latest Discussions of Peter and
Paul at Rome" — *American Journal of Theology*, 22 (1918),
113-124.

> In this study the author endeavors to answer the ques-
> tion: was Peter really in Rome? Since H. Lietzmann had
> already discovered and evaluated the additional testimony
> (liturgical and archeological), the author gives an expo-
> sition of Lietzmann's findings which give positive value
> to the Roman tradition that venerates Peter's tomb on
> the Vatican and Paul's on the via Ostia.

221 ROLLER, T., *Les catacombes de Rome, Histoire de l'art et des
croyances religieuses pendant les premiers siècles du christianisme*,
(Paris, 1881).

> Though never intended as an apology of Catholic dogma,
> J. B. De Rossi's *Roma Sotterranea*, by its very nature, did
> become an archeological apology.
> This work is the Protestant theory of the catacombs.
> It is a confutation (of De Rossi's work) which many times
> enters into the field of dogmatic controversy. Among the
> many points examined by the author is the Primacy of the
> Roman See. He finds no allusion to the supremacy of
> St. Peter and of the Roman See in the monuments of the
> Roman catacombs. Peter's coming to Rome is mere
> legend, and the tomb of the Apostle on the Vatican is a
> myth.

222 SALTET, L., "St. Irenée et St. Cyprien sur la primauté
romaine" — BLE, 21 (1920), 179-206.

223 SANDERS, J. N., "L'Hellénisme de St. Clément de Rome et
le Paulinisme", *Universitas Catholica Lovaniensis*, *1943*,
(Studia Hellenistica, 2), 182 pp.

Speaking of the martyr-death of Peter there is testimony
of this fact about the time of the writing of 1 Clement.
This monograph is a comprehensive study with the idea
that Clement is strongly influenced by Hellenism and is
concerned to apply to the Bible and to history of the
beginnings of the Church the literary artistry and concepts
of the Cynic-Stoic philosophy. This work was written
independently of a work of the same nature by M. Dibelius.

224 SCHMALTZ, W. M., "Did Peter die in Jerusalem"? — JBL,
71 (1952), 211-216.

The author expands Robinson's thesis that Peter died
in prison in Jerusalem a short while before the demise of
Herod Agrippa I in 44 A.D.

225 SCHMÜTZ, S., "Petrus war dennoch in Rome" — BM, 22
(1946), 128-141.

For the first ten centuries in the history of Christianity
there never was any doubt regarding Peter's sojourn and
martyrdom in Rome. It was finally attacked by a number
of scholars and even used by politicians to further their
cause. This study is a critique of the critics. The author
takes up the earliest literary testimony from all areas
which testify to the tradition—Rome, France, Africa,
Greece, Asia Minor, Palestine, Egypt. But where could such
a conviction of Christians of the East and West come from
in such early times? What other place or city could claim
any title to this tradition? If one considers the consequence
of the tradition—the claim of Papal power— why was there
no protest against the assertion of a Roman sojourn for
more than a millenium of years?

226 SCHULER, M., "Klemens von Rom und Petrus in Rom" —
Trierer Theologische Studien, 1 (1941), 94 ff.

The famous text of *1 Clement*—a literary source proving
the Roman tradition—is the subject of this study.

227 SCHULZE-KADELBACH, G., "Die Stellung des Petrus in der
Urgemeinde" — TLZ, 81 (1956), 1-14.

228 SEPPELT, F. X., "Das Petrusgrab" — *Hochland*, 42 (1950),
456-466.

The first part of this study is a critique of the critics
with regard to the Roman sojourn and death of Peter.
Noteworthy among them was F. Bauer, who succeeded in
establishing a negative attitude conditioned by deno-
minational prejudice and bias. After H. Lietzmann, there
was a readiness to recognize the Roman tradition more or
less as a historical fact. (However, H. Dannenbauer in his
Die römische Petruslegende (see no. 108); and J. Haller in
Nachweisungen und Erläuterungen of the 1 vol. of his
Papsttum (see no. 140), seriously challenged H. Lietzmann,
but without scientific conviction).

None were successful. According to Bihlmeyer and
Altaner (among others), the general attack against the
Roman tradition was a failure.

In the second part of this study the author takes up the
question of San Sebastiano and examines the literary
testimony with regard to the translation-theory. The
excavations seem to have supplied incontestible proof
for the theory, though Catholic scholars as Delehaye and
Kirsch have objected to this hypothesis. In the last part
of this study the results of the Vatican excavations and
the tomb of Peter are discussed with some final observations about the tradition that speaks of the separation
of the heads of St. Peter and Paul.

229 SEPPELT, F. X., "Petrus in Rom" — *Geschichte der Päpste*,
I (München: Kösel, 1954), 12 ff.

According to the author, the laying of the foundation
of the Roman Church, the Primacy of the Roman See,
Peter's coming to Rome, his death and burial in the Eternal City, are all substantiated by literary and archeological
testimony.

230 SHOTWELL, J. T., & LOOMIS, L. R., *The See of St. Peter*,
(New York: Columbia University Press, 1927), 737 pp.

This is a documentary study containing extracts of the essential texts (from accredited sources) that relate to the growth of the tradition of Peter's presence at Rome, his foundation of the Roman episcopacy, and martyrdom there. The contents of Book I which holds our Interest here are as follows:

Part I — New Testament texts.

1. Jesus and Peter.
2. Peter and the other Apostles.
3. Peter in Rome and the founding of the Roman Church.

Part II — The tradition accepted as historical.

1. Peter the Preacher in Rome.
2. Peter the Roman martyr.
3. Peter the founder of the Roman Episcopate.

Part III — The Apocryphal tradition.

1. Beginnings of the Simon Magus legend.
2. The legend of Peter and Simon.
3. References to the Petrine legend in third century literature.
4. Development of the Petrine legend during the third century.
5. Development of the legend during the fourth and fifth centuries.
6. References to the legend by the Fathers of the fourth and fifth centuries.
7. Later elaboration of the legend.
8. Relics in evidence of the legend.

231 SIEFFERT, F., "Petrus, der Apostel" — *Realenzyklopädie für Theologie und Kirche*, 15 (1904), 186-212.

The author considers the possibility of giving a psychological basis for the unique position of Peter and for the giving him of his name.

232 SIGRIST, F. A., *Petrus der erste Papst*, (Switzerland: Verlag Weggis, 1930), 151 pp.

This comprehensive survey of Peter, the first Pope, includes the author's analysis of the question of Peter's

sojourn and death in Rome which takes him through the
following considerations:

1. Peter in Rome and the Bible.
2. Peter in Babylon?
3. The stories of Peter in Rome.
4. Written (documentary) evidence of Peter's sojourn
   in Rome.
5. Clement of Rome.
6. Ignatius of Antioch.
7. Irenaeus of Lyons.
8. Tertullian.
9. Clement of Alexandria.
10. Gaius in Rome and other literary testimony.
11. Peter's grave in Rome.
12. The fate of Peter's relics.
13. The feast of the Cathedra.

233 SMITH, M., "The report about Peter in I Clement, 5, 4" —
NTSt, 7 (1960), 86-88.

> The author discusses the most important passage of
> Peter's martyrdom. No one until the end of the second
> century is equally explicit as to Peter's fate. The fact that
> all Clement chose to say about Peter came from *Acts*
> creates an argument from silence, admittedly slight, but
> perhaps sufficient to change *I Clement, v. 4,* from evidence
> in favor of Peter's martyrdom at Rome to evidence
> against it.

234 SPENCE-JONES, H. D. M., "The Foundation of the Church
in Rome. The Influence of St. Peter" — *The Early Christians
in Rome,* (New York: John Lane, 1911), 7-20.

> In these pages the author endeavors to answer the
> question: was Peter in any way connected with the begin-
> ning of the foundation of the Christian community in
> Rome? Can he be considered the founder of that Church?
> On what grounds is this tradition based? To answer these
> questions he gives quotations from the Patristic writers of
> the first three centuries that bear on the foundation of the
> Church in Rome, including the oldest catalogue of the
> Bishops of Rome. According to the author, these and

other literary notices more or less definitely ascribe the foundation of the Roman Church to Peter and Paul. But how could Peter be the founder of the Church at Rome if he never appeared in Rome before A.D. 64 ? The traditional notices of the early presence of Peter in Rome are many and various. Taken by themselves they are, no doubt, not convincing (some are even legendary). But taken together, they constitute an argument of no little weight. All serious historians now agree that Peter taught in Rome, wrote his Epistle from Rome and suffered martyrdom there. Everything points to this conclusion. The cumulative evidence of the early writers, the testimony of the cata-combs, the witness of tradition and the voice of what may be termed "immemorial history."

235 STOECKIUS, H., "Ecclesia Petri propria" — *Archiv für katholisches Kirchenrecht*, 117 (1937), 24-126.

The relationship between the Church at Rome and St. Peter has an obvious bearing on Peter's coming to Rome.

This is an examination of the Primacy-question according to Tertullian from the point of view of Church history and Canon law. The text in question is *De pudicitia*, 21, in which Tertullian criticises an unnamed Bishop (Callistus ?) and specifically the edict which declared (contrary to the practice of the early Church) that penance should be granted also for sins against modesty. The text has become the object of great discussion, not merely in regard to the question of the power of the keys but also the Primacy of the Roman bishop. The author examines the commentaries of other scholars. He comes to the conclusion that the Roman bishop—who is Callistus—issued a penance-edict, and in justification, referred to the crown witness Mt. 16, 18 ff., and this, with the full conviction that he was a successor of Peter, the prince of the Apostles (see B. Altaner, no. 9).

236 STRATHMANN, H., "Die Stellung des Petrus in der Urkirche. Zur Frühgeschichte des Wortes an Petrus, Matthäus 16, 17-19" — ZST, 20 (1943), 223-283.

With respect to Peter's unique position in the circle of

the Apostles, according to the author there is no such difference as has often been asserted between Mark and the other two Synoptic Gospels. Precisely in the Gospel of Mark, of which it has been said that although written in Rome, it knows no claim for the authority of Peter. The author judges each of the Gospels on the basis of its attitude in the claim of authority for Peter according to the somewhat artificial scheme by which he assumes that it belongs to this or that Church: Mark-Rome-no interest in the Petrine claim; Luke and the Acts—Pauline missionary area—a primacy of Peter for only a limited time; Matthew-Antioch-permanent primacy; John-Asia Minor-anti-Petrine and pro-Johannine tendency.

237 TRICOT, A., "Saint Pierre" — *Dictionnaire de Théologie Catholique*, 12 (1935), 1747-1792.

A comprehensive study of Peter under all aspects.

238 UNDERHILL, F., *Saint Peter*, (New York and Toronto: Longmans Green & Co., 1938), 248 pp.

This is a popular, nontechnical treatment of the Apostle Peter. It contains a chapter (XIII, pp. 201 ff) on St. Peter in Rome in which the author, basing himself on literary and archeological testimony, takes up the question of the historicity of the tradition concerning Peter's life and work in Rome. Chapter XIV (pp. 214 ff.) deals with Peter's tomb at the Vatican and the tradition that links it with San Sebastiano ad catacumbas.

239 VAN CAUWELAERT, R., "L'intervention de l'Église de Rome à Corinthe vers l'an 96" — RHE, 31 (1935), 267-306.

In this scholarly study the author examines the question which history poses: does *I Clement* allow a consciousness of the Roman Primacy? From cumulative evidence that is gathered, his conclusion is in the affirmative. St. Peter's stay in Rome, constituting a delicate discussion pertaining to this period of Christianity, is obviously related with the subject of the origin of Papal Primacy and the Church at Rome.

240 VAN STEMPVOORT, P. A., *Petrus en zijn graf te Rome,* Bibliotheek van boeken bij de bijbel (Baarn: Bosch & Keuning N.V., 1960), 169 pp., 25 plates, 17 figs.

St. Peter's grave in Rome constitutes one of the most delicate subjects of discussion between Rome and the Reformers. The recent archeological excavations under the Vatican are therefore of prime importance so far as other ecclesiastical matters are concerned. The author hopes— by this study—to contribute something to the ecumenical movement.

The book consists of the following three chapters:
1. The Jews and Christians at Rome.
2. Peter's death according to Clement of Rome.
3. Peter's grave.

Herein the author endeavors to utilize new materials of comparison in order to clarify what is already known, and at the same time to present the entire matter in the framework of critical research. He is not concerned with the person of Peter, but with a historical-critical judgement of the small monument that was erected over Peter's grave by the Christian community during the first sixty years of the second century. His conclusions are:

While New Testament information is vague regarding Peter's martyrdom at Rome, yet ancient literary testimony and the evidence of the recent Vatican excavations make it more concrete. Peter was martyred around 64 A.D. in the Neronian circus northwest of the gardens of Agrippina near the Vatican hill, or in the gardens themselves. The most important discovery of the excavations was the *aedicula* dating from the middle of the second century. It is this which has decisive value for the solution of the problem of Peter's stay in Rome, and which can clarify the discussions regarding the fundamental question of Peter's grave. Both archeological and literary testimony have confirmed some of the most outstanding traditions about Peter. Therefore, the "Petrine-legends and myths" of the critics must give way to such historical evidence.

241 VASSALL-PHILLIPS, O. R., "St. Paul and St. Peter" — *The Month,* 157 (1931), 436-442.

In this study the author endeavors to show that as far
as the New Testament reveals, there is no reason to think
that St. Paul was unaware of the privilege conferred by
Christ on St. Peter when He made him the ROCK on
which He built His Church, promised him the keys of the
Kingdom of Heaven, and committed to his pastoral care
all His flock, both sheep and lambs. Peter and Paul are
regarded as twin founders of the local Church at Rome
where they died and rest in death.

242 VELLICO, A. M., "Episcopus episcoporum" in Tertulliani
libro De pudicitia" — *Antonianum*, 5 (1930), 25-56.

In this study the author is concerned with the famous
text that has excited controversy among scholars and
endeavors to examine the apologetic value of the "peremptory edict." Contrary to the Reformers of the sixteenth
century, Catholic writers have employed this text as
classic testimony of the Primacy of the Roman Pontiff.
In this essay the author sets out to prove that this testimony can safely be invoked as referring to the supreme
authority of the Roman bishop, based on the authorship
of the *peremptory edict*. The work has two main sections:
1. A historical exposition of the opinions with regard to
the author of the "peremptory edict."
2. An attempt to reconcile the opposite opinions.

243 VILLIGER, J. B., "Petrusgrab und Papsttum. Eine Erwider-
ung und Richtigstellung" — *Schweizerische Kirchenzeitung*,
120 (1952), 369-371.

This is a reply to the criticism of Vogelsanger against
Kirschbaum's conference in Switzerland. The subject of
Apostolic succession is of prime importance here. The
author feels that the Protestant school's evaluation of I
Clem. has the objective merit of confirming the continued
tradition within the early Christian community.

244 VOGELSANGER, P., "Petrusgrab und Papsttum" — *Reformatio*, 1, 6 (1952), 308-317.

Without substantiating his arguments, the author

criticizes as unscientific, Kirschbaum's conference in Switzerland.

245 VON CAMPENHAUSEN, H., *Die Idee des Martyriums in der alten Kirche*, 1936.

> A passage in *first Peter* (5, 1) deals with the question whether Peter died as a martyr. The author speaks here of himself as a "witness of the sufferings of Christ and a partaker of the glory soon to be revealed." How is this expression to be interpreted? In the technical martyrological meaning? This entire question is the subject of this work in which the author shows that what is involved is a 'martyrological' way of speaking which is here applied to Peter and Paul, and in Eusebius' *Historia Ecclesiastica*, *11, 23,* is used of James.

246 VON CAMPENHAUSEN, H., *Kirchliches Amt und geistliche Vollmacht*, (Tübingen, 1953).

> This study of Peter's apostolic commission endeavors to discredit the Church's traditional teaching. The author's conclusion is as follows: "despite recent attempts to the contrary, there should be no doubt that the Church being founded upon Peter is unthinkable in the mouth of Christ ... The question is merely whether this word stems from the tradition of the primordial community, or whether it originates even later."

247 VON CAMPENHAUSEN, H., Bericht, in: *Verkündigung und Forschung*, 1942-1946 (1956/57), 230.

> The author expresses himself in favor of accepting the Roman stay of Peter based on literary evidence.

248 VON HARNACK, A., *Die Chronologie der altchristlichen Literatur bis Eusebius*, II, 1 (Leipzig: J. C. Hinrichs, 1897), 242; 244, n. 2; 709.

> The fact of Peter's coming to Rome and martyrdom there is maintained by this most competent modern critic who remarks:
> "The martyrdom of St. Peter in Rome was once upon a time disputed by tendentious Protestants and then by

tendentious critical prejudices. That this was an error is now as clear as day to any investigator who does not blind himself. The whole critical apparatus wherewith Baur contested the old tradition is now recognised as worthless" (p. 244, n. 2).

249 VON HARNACK, A., "Ecclesia Petri propinqua. Zur Geschichte der Anfänge des Primats des römischen Bischofs" — SAB, 20 (1927), 139-152.

This study deals with the Primacy of the Roman bishops. In this connection the well-known text of Tertullian which was directed against Callistus and particularly the edict he had issued, is used. Our author identifies the bishop addressed with Callistus. On the expression *ad omnem ecclesiam Petri propinquam*, he says that to take *omnem* as a scribal error for *romanam* is purely hypothetical and is rejected even by most Catholic scholars. A case is made here of whether in Callistus' referring the crown witness —Mt. 16, 17—to himself, with special appeal to Peter's grave, there is to be derived from it the Primacy of the Roman bishop over the entire Church.

250 WILPERT, J., "Pietro, fondatore della Chiesa di Roma e "successore di Cristo come vescovo" secondo del sarcofago 174 e il catalogo filocaliano," BAC, 7 (1937), 2-18.

In this study the author takes up the question of the position of Peter among the other Apostles as seen in the iconographic testimony of a sarcophagus and the literary evidence of the Philocalian catalogue.

251 WINTER, M. M. "St. Peter in Rome" — *St. Peter and the Popes*, (Baltimore, Md.: Helicon Press; London: Darton, Longman & Todd Ltd., 1960), 82-98.

The fact of Peter's coming to Rome, his martyrdom and burial there, is ably defended by the author. Against some few scholars as, for example, Heussi and Guignebert, who are still unwilling to subscribe to the traditional view he takes up an examination of the New Testament evidence. While it is fragmentary, it is clear in its main outlines. He then examines the witness of writers of the early

Church. At the end of the first century the indications
are rather general, but by the end of the second century
the testimonies are explicit and quite detailed. The historical evidence is enhanced by another factor, namely
the complete absence of any rival tradition. In view of
the unanimity of this tradition, throughout the world and
at an early date, the fact of Peter's Roman sojourn and
death must be regarded as established.

Three related but distinct questions are also answered
by the author:

1) Was it possible for the early Christians to obtain the
   body of Peter after his execution?
2) Did they in fact secure it and bury it?
3) What was the subsequent fate of the relics? Have they
   been preserved under the basilica of St. Peter?

Even if it were not possible to give an affirmative
answer to each of these questions, the conclusion of the
historical evidence (namely, that Peter came to Rome and
was martyred there), would not be invalidated. After a
brief inquiry into the liturgical and archeological evidence
the author concludes:

Evidence for the subsequent history of Peter's relics is
not so conclusive, yet it appears probable that his remains
were buried at the Vatican and never moved from there.

252 ZAKRZEWSKI, C., *Kwatalnik historiczny*, 48 (1934), 1-46.

This study examines the traditional fact of Peter's
sojourn and death in Rome.

PART TWO

SAN SEBASTIANO ON THE VIA APPIA AND THE TOMB OF THE APOSTLES

253 AMORE, A., "Cimitero di Catacumbas" — EC, 3 (1949), 1058-1061.

This brief study speaks of the fact that in this region (the cemetery ad catacumbas) there is found the most important and monumental complex of Christian subterranean Rome which has been the object of many studies since 1915, viz., the *Memoria Apostolorum*. The author gives a summary of the archeological findings and admits that scholars are not in agreement as to the scope and nature of the Memoria. Ancient literary tradition (*Liber Pontificalis, Martyrologium Hieronymianum, Itinerari, Passiones*) seems to point to a temporary deposition of the Apostles Peter and Paul here at catacumbas. However, it has not been possible to be more specific in determining the site, nor have the excavations revealed anything positively or definitively. Basing themselves on a study of the literary sources the scholars have conjectured the following hypotheses:

a) The Memoria was in every sense a sepulchral monument where the bodies of the Apostles were temporarily buried, either immediately after their martyrdom and before the completion of the basilicas on the Vatican and via Ostia, or during the Valerianic persecution of 258.

b) The Memoria was constructed to commemorate the place where the Apostles dwelled during their life-time.

c) The Memoria developed as the result of the institution of a liturgical feast in honor of the two Apostles which was inaugurated in 258, when because of the Valerianic persecutions the Christians were forbidden to gather in their cemeteries and hence were not able to venerate the graves of the Apostles in their respective places.

254 ANDREAE, B., "Archäologische Funde im Bereich vom Rom 1949-1956/7."

> See no. 458.

255 ANONYMOUS CC, 46, 2 (1895), 460-471.

> In his evaluation of the results of the excavations at the church of San Sebastiano and the Apostles grave, the author endeavors to broaden an understanding of the investigations by considering the following points:
> a) The Roman tomb of the Apostles 'ad Catacumbas.'
> b) The discovery of the mausoleum of St. Quirinus.
> c) The 'Ecclesia Apostolorum' on the via Appia, later called San Sebastiano. A revindication of the Apostolic sepulchre.
> d) Difficulties arising from the new hypothesis regarding the 'platonia.'

256 ANONYMOUS JRS, 23 (1933), 5-6.

> This brief article calls attention to the discovery of the columbaria of the first and second century A.D., of a house (perhaps a schola of a burial-guild) of the middle of the second century enlarged in the middle of the third century when the columbaria were filled in by the addition of the 'triclia,' the graffiti that were discovered. The question is finally asked: did the Apostles reside here or were they buried here directly or transferred in 258? The theory suggested is that they were brought here directly after their martyrdom though the reason is not known, nor the exact place where they were buried.

257 AUDOLLENT, A., "Iterum "Refrigerare" — *Strena Buliciana*, (Zagreb/Split, 1924), 283-286.

> This is an analysis of the uses of the word "refrigerium." Its frequent occurrence in the graffiti of the triclia at San Sebastiano has aroused interest as to the meaning that should be assigned the word.

258 BARNES, A. S., "A Lost Apostolic Sanctuary" — *The Dublin Review*, 175 (July, 1924), 1-20.

> The author regrets that what was once accepted as the

famous "Platonia" shrine (where Peter and Paul were buried), it now seems to be in shambles because of the archeological campaign. No longer does it seem to be regarded with any interest. Is there any appeal from this sad plight? He then reconstructs the tradition that has always associated this place with the two Apostles under the following headings:

a) Description of the "Platonia."
b) Documentary evidence.
c) The excavations in 1892-3 and the discovery of the monument alleged to have been the resting-place of the Apostles.
d) The "Memoria" of Anacletus.
e) The Sepulchre under the Altar.
f) The fresco of the lunette.
g) The sepulchre of St. Quirinus.
h) A recapitulation.

The author's conclusions are as follows:

1) St. Peter possibly took refuge in a country villa on the via Appia.
2) There he lived and was arrested. After his martyrdom he was brought to the villa while his tomb was prepared on the Vatican.
3) There ad Catacumbas Pope Anacletus built his 'Memoria' over where the sarcophagus had rested.
4) During the persecutions in 258 both Apostles were removed from their tombs and brought to the catacombs. The Memoria was the natural place.
5) Constantine's basilica.

259 BARNES, A. S., *St. Peter in Rome and his Tomb on the Vatican Hill,*

See no. 16.

Chapters V and VI of this excellent work deal with the 'wonderings of Peter's body' and the 'first tombs on the via Appia and the Vatican' (pp. 105-157).

According to the author, the records that have come down to us dealing with the subject of Peter's relics are somewhat scanty, and, as they stand, often contradictory; but they clearly point to one translation at least of the

relics prior to the peace of the Church, and it may be two.
Since several theories have been proposed none of which
are satisfactory to the author, he undertakes a new
examination of the question. He quotes all the documentary and other evidence which bears on this matter, and
then examines the various explanations. He then suggests
a new solution which may satisfy the requirements of the
case more fully than any which has yet been given, and
which therefore may be regarded as probably providing
us with a nearer approximation to the absolute truth. His
conclusion is that the earliest tomb in which Peter was
laid was not on the Vatican, but at San Sebastiano.

260 BARNES, A. S., *The Martyrdom of St. Peter and St. Paul,*
See no. 18.

261 BAUS, K., "Das Petrusgrab" — *Von der Urgemeinde zur
frühchristlichen Grosskirche* I (Freiburg, Basel, Wien: Herder,
1962), 137-140.

In dealing with the subject of Peter's grave the author
examines the literary and liturgical testimony that
associates the grave with the site at San Sebastiano on the
via Appia. The archeological evidence afforded by the
place itself, viz., the graffiti, the Damasian inscription,
etc., point to this place as a cult-center of the Apostles
Peter and Paul. Several theories have been put forward
in an attempt to explain the site.

The author also includes a reference to the Vatican
excavations of 1940-49 wherein he sums up the finds of
the *official report*. Though the riddle of the cult-center on
the via Appia is yet to be solved, great comfort is to be
derived from the fact that research still continues.

262 BELVEDERI, G., "La Tomba di S. Pietro e i recenti lavori
nelle Grotte Vaticane" — BAC, 13 (1943), 1-16.

This is a study on the *Apostolic Tomb* after Constantine's
time according to the testimony of Eusebius of Caesarea
and St. Jerome. In both the texts of Eusebius (Latin
translation: II, 25), and St. Jerome, (*In Ezechielem*, 12, 40)
a reference is made to the tomb (not tombs) of the Apostles

Peter and Paul as still existing in a Roman cemetery. Evidently the bodies of the Apostles were still to be found on the via Appia, where a Christian cemetery existed in the real sense. Jerome speaks of visiting the tomb on Sundays and feast days. The author asks: if the bodies of Peter and Paul had been transferred to their respective basilicas (Peter at the Vatican, Paul on the Ostia) during Constantine's time, how could Jerome be visiting a cemetery, i.e., the catacombs? The author examines the whole question of the association of the Apostles with San Sebastiano ad Catacumbas. He analyzes the two Damasian inscriptions that refer to Peter's tomb, and quotes the various interpretations of the experts. He re-establishes his conclusion based on his reading of the epigrams: the Apostle Peter (and Paul) were buried ad Catacumbas in the very beginning, and that the Vatican excavations have not proven the testimony of the Liber Pontificalis according to which the Emperor Constantine was supposed to have buried Peter beneath the Vatican basilica, and Paul on the Ostia. On the contrary, the excavations beneath San Sebastiano (in our epoch) have demonstrated that Constantine built the *Basilica Apostolorum* on the via Appia for the very purpose of protecting the tomb of the Apostle which was there. This is the only interpretation that can be given the Damasian hymn.

263 BELVEDERI, G., "Depositio Petri in Vaticano, Pauli in Via Ostiensi, Utriusque in Catacumbas" — BAC, 13 (1943), 47-64.

Immediately after the publication of the first study (no. 262) there was a storm of protest among some, scil. Josi (as seen in no. 349) which appeared in the *Osservatore Romano*). The author again takes up his defense. He states the purpose of his first study in BAC, 1942, was to re-examine the question of Peter's tomb according to the Liber Pontificalis, since up until the end of the sixth century, this was the only source to confirm that Constantine placed the body of Peter in the basilica which he erected to Blessed Peter the Apostle.

His conclusion was: that the bodies of Peter and Paul

were buried at the time of their death, at the Vatican and Via Ostia, respectively, at the place of their martyrdom, where they remained until the middle of the third century when they were transferred to the via Appia, "ad cata-cumbas," where Constantine had erected in the first half of the fourth century their tomb, the *Basilica Apostolorum*: and whence in the sixth century they were removed and retranslated to their original resting places on the Vatican and via Ostia. The author continues his study on the question by an examination of the following points:

1. Ecclesiastical writers of the fourth century.
    a) Eusebius.
    b) St. Jerome.
    c) Damasian inscription.
2. The testimony of Ecclesiastical writers of the fifth century.
3. The excavations of San Sebastiano and the "Memoria Apostolorum."
4. Constantine and the Memoria of the Apostle Peter.
    a) Rome and Jerusalem.
5. The basilica on the via Ostia.
6. The liturgical text.

264 BELVEDERI, G., "La cripta di Lucina" — RAC, 21 (1945), 121-164.

In this study the author deals with the crypt of the matron Lucina who, according to the Liber Pontificalis, was associated with Pope Cornelius in the translation of the bodies of Peter and Paul. At her request Cornelius removed the bodies of the Apostles at night. Lucina took the body of Paul and placed it in a plot she owned on the via Ostia. Cornelius took Peter's body and laid it where he was crucified. Our author divides his study as follows:

1. The historical person Lucina.
2. Lucina and the translation of the bodies.
3. Lucina senior and Lucina junior.
4. The cemetery of Lucina on the via Ostia.
5. The translation of the bodies of the Apostles ad Catacumbas.

6. The translation of the bodies of the Apostles ad Catacumbas took place before the year 258.
7. The reason for the translation.
7. The crypt of Lucina in Catacumbas.
9. The crypt of Lucina in ancient topographical documents.
10. Lucina-Cecelia.

265 BELVEDERI, G., *La tombe apostoliche nell'età paleocristiana*, (Collezione "Amici delle catacombe," 12), (Vatican City, 1948), 272 pp.

The vexed question of the temporary burial of the Apostles on the via Appia is the subject of this scientific study. The author deals with the following aspects:
1. The Liber Pontificalis and its testimony regarding the Apostolic tomb.
2. The information with regard to the tomb in the "Vita Petri."
3. The information with regard to the tomb in the "Vita Cornelii."
4. The information with regard to the tomb in the "Vita Silvestri."
5. The information with regard to the tomb in the "Vita Damasi."
6. The Monastery in Catacumbas.
   Part II — The sepulchral topography according to monuments and documents.
1. The first sepulchre of the Apostles Peter and Paul.
2. The "Memoria Apostolorum."
3. The "Basilica Apostolorum."
4. The origin of the basilica on the via Ostia.
5. Literary and liturgical sources.
6. Literary documents of the fourth century.
7. From Appia to the Vatican and via Ostia.
8. Liturgical confirmation.
9. Conclusions.
   The author arrives at the following conclusions:
a) Both Peter and Paul died in Rome, the former in the year 64 on the Vatican hill, the latter in 67 on the via Ostia, and they were buried near the places of their

martyrdom. Shortly after, two "memorie" or basilicas (the "trophies" which Gaius spoke of at the beginning of the fourth century) were erected on these spots.

b) About the middle of the third century their bodies were exhumed from their respective graves (the reason is not known, or obscure), and were transferred to the via Appia 'in catacumbas' where, after the peace of the Church Constantine erected the "Basilica Apostolorum."

c) The same Emperor constructed a large basilica on the Vatican to enclose and protect the ancient 'Memoria' of St. Peter.

d) The same thing was done with respect to Paul's 'Memoria' by the Emperors Theodosius, Arcadius, and Honorius at a later time.

e) The cult of the Apostles is attested to in the basilica (where their bodies rested) by the refrigeria up until the time when the practice was reproved by the Church (end of fourth century) because of abuse.

f) This manner of honoring the deceased was referred to as the feast of the "Cathedra" because a special seat or 'cathedra' was assigned to the deceased where the offerings of food were deposited.

g) From this practice there arose the feast of *the Cathedra of Peter and Paul* which was considered merely as a popular feast, never a liturgical one.

h) During the time of Leo the Great the feast seems to have lost its original significance. It became associated with the *episcopal office*. Hence, the 'cathedra of Peter' became synonymous with the 'episcopacy of Peter.'

i) At the beginning of the sixth century Byzantius asked the Pope for the bodies of the two Apostles. The request was rejected.

j) An attempt was made to carry the bodies away surreptitiously.

k) About the middle of the sixth century their bodies were finally retransferred to their respective burial places on the Vatican hill and the via Ostia.

266 BETTINI, S., "Tusco et Basso consulibus. A proposito della

tomba di S. Pietro" — *Jahrbuch der Oesterreichischen Byzan-tinischen Gesellschaft*, 1 (1951), 67-87.

As in all other accounts of this same nature, this is only a tentative explanation of the place of the Apostle's tomb which has no foundation in an authoritative tradition (according to the author). The author is of the opinion that the year 258 A.D. does not indicate the finding of Peter's body nor the translation 'ad catacumbas.' The Apostles were first buried temporarily on the Vatican and via Ostia and then moved and buried permanently by the via Appia a short while after their deaths, on the spot over which the third-century *Memoria* was afterwards erected.

Gaius's trophy and Constantine's basilica do not sufficiently prove that this was the site of the Apostle's martyrdom. There was a temporary deposition on the Vatican hill which explains the construction of the Vatican basilica. The consular date refers rather to the beginning of his cult and the inauguration of the *Memoria* which had been previously erected.

267 BIRCHLER, L., "Das Petrusgrab," See no. 493.

268 BOEHMINGHAUS, E., "Vom Grabe des hl. Petrus: Funde und Feinde" — *Stimmen der Zeit*, 95 (1918), 251-267.

This is a brief history of the excavational finds at San Sebastiano.

269 BOULET, N., "A propos des fouilles de St. Pierre. Questions historiques et liturgiques."

See no. 494.

270 BUONAIUTI, E., "Gli scavi recentissimi a S. Sebastiano" — *Bollettino di Letteratura Critico-religiosa*, 1915, 375-381.

This is an account of the results of the excavations at that time. The author in explaining the meaning of the *refrigerium* found in the graffiti of the triclia, claims that though an adaptation of the pagan "parentalia," yet it was not absolutely connected with the tomb, but only with the memory of the martyrs and could be celebrated outside the sepulchral precinct.

271 BURGER, J. D., *La tombe de Saint Pierre est-elle identifiée?*

See no. 495.

272 CARCOPINO, J., "Les fouilles de Saint-Pierre."

See no. 503.

272 CARCOPINO, J., "Lezingen en Voordrachten" — *Bulletin van de Vereeniging tot Bevordering der Kennis van de Antieke Beschaving te 's-Gravenhage*, 7 (1932), 33-34.

A rather ingenious solution is proposed here by the author with reference to San Sebastiano on the via Appia being associated with the burial-place of the Apostles Peter and Paul. The monuments of the first two centuries that have been found in the cemetery of San Sebastiano are pagan. The author proposes the idea that the second-century tombs belong to adherents of the Gnostic sects. The inscriptions reveal that many slaves and freedmen of the Emperor were among them. It is true that the Church opposed Gnosticism. But since the Gnostics and Christians were ever in fear of the threat of imperial reprisals, they were united in a common bond of defense. For this reason they may have found it a protection for the relics by burying them in an area where they would have escaped the notice of the police since the proprietors and users of the cemetery were not unknown to the authorities.

274 CARCOPINO, J., "Note sur deux textes controverses de la tradition apostolique romaine" — *Comptes rendus de l'Académie des Inscriptions et Belles-Lettres*, 1952, 424-434.

This is a study of the two controversial texts concerning the Roman tradition of the Apostles' burial at San Sebastiano on the via Appia. The author gives an exact interpretation of the word *trophy* in Gaius's testimony, and *habitasse* in Damasus's epigram found at San Sebastiano. This study is also repeated in *Etudes d'histoire chrétienne*, (Paris, 1953), pp. 251-264.

275 CARCOPINO, J., *Études d'histoire chrétienne.*

See no. 505.

276 CARCOPINO, J., *De Pythagore aux Apôtres. Études sur la conversion du monde romain.*

      See no. 507.

277 CECCHELLI, C., "La tombe di N. S. Gesu Cristo e le "Memorie" Apostoliche" — (Lectures 1952-1953) *Universita degli studi di Roma,* (Rome: editrice F. Ferrari).

      In this series of lectures the author takes up the large and complicated question of the "Memoria ad catcumbas" in which he analyzes the literary and liturgical testimony and ultimately the archeological findings beneath San Sebastiano. He theorizes that it could be said with a serious probability (though not with certainty) that the place where the Apostles were buried was the tomb of the Axe.

278 CELI, C., "La Memoria Apostolica sull'Appia" — CC, 87, 2 (1936), 483-490; 87, 3 (1936), 387-398.

      In line with the previous research on the Memoriae of the Apostles Peter and Paul at Rome, the author now takes up the subject of the famous *Memoria Apostolorum ad catacumbas* on the via Appia. He first examines the inscription of Damasus. Then to clarify the problems raised by the text he deals with the old tradition based on the Philocalian Calendar and the Hieronymianum Martyrology which speak of the celebration of the cult of the Apostles in this place. There follows an examination of the various theories in this regard. He concludes by saying that there is a good probability that the date 258 coincides with the date of the dedication of the place in honor of the Apostles on the via Appia.

279 CELI, C., "Sulle memorie e monumenti dei SS. Apostoli Pietro e Paolo a Roma" — CC, 86, 2 (1935), 247-257; 587-594. 86, 3 (1935), 157-173; 582-589.

      Of all the 'memorie' regarding that Apostles Peter and Paul at Rome the oldest, and without doubt the most important, is their grave at San Sebastiano on the via Appia. In this study the author presents a complete analysis of the literary and archeological evidence with regard to the place. His examination falls under the following headings:

1. The first testimony with regard to the Apostolic grave and its importance.
2. The monument that was erected over the Apostolic grave.
3. The Constantinian sarcophagus and altar of Peter.
4. Observations on the Vatican grave and the work of Pope Damasus.
5. The vicissitudes of Peter's grave from Constantine the Great to modern times.
6. The grave and basilica of Paul on the via Ostia.

280 CHADWICK, H., "St. Peter and Paul in Rome: The Problem of the Memoria Apostolorum ad Catacumbas" — JThSt, 8 n.s., I (1957), 31-52.

The author adopts the theory that the cult of the Apostles on the via Appia was a popular and unofficial cultus that may have originated with a discovery of relics—based perhaps on a special revelation—on June 29th, 258. The Church eventually suppressed this cultus. In reality, the devotion at the via Appia was gradually obscured by the cultus at the Vatican and the via Ostia. The translation-hypothesis is a "bit of highly acute guesswork."

281 CHÉRAMY, M. H., St. Sébastien-hors-les-murs. La basilique Le cimetière ad Catacumbas, (Paris: Maison de la Bonne Press, 1925), 87 pp. with illus.

The results of the excavations that took place between 1915 and 1925 under the direction of A. de Waal and P. Styger are published in this monograph. It is recommended to those who wish to gain a rapid knowledge of the subject without losing themselves in details. The contents are as follows:

I. The Basilica.
   1) Its origin.
   2) The last years of the Roman Empire and the modern age.
   3) Modern times: the Renaissance, the seventeenth

century; transformation of the basilica, the eight-
teenth and nineteenth centuries.
II. The Apostolica Memoria and recent excavations.
    1) The excavations of 1915-1925.
    A group of tombs of the first century. The villa
    and ancient homes. The inscriptions in honor of
    Peter and Paul.
    2) The date of the translation of the bodies of the
    Apostles to San Sebastiano.
III. The Cemetery ad Catacumbas.
    1) The name.
    2) Its origin.
    3) The inscriptions.
    4) The sarcophagi.
    5) Paintings.

282 COLAGROSSI, M., *Sepolcro apostolico dell'Appia nel secolo
III della chiesa*, (Roma, 1908).

283 COLAGROSSI, M., "Di un monumento recentemente scoperto
presso il sepolcro apostolico dell'Appia" — *Nuovo Bollettino
di Archeologia Cristiana*, 15 (1909), 51-61, plates II-VI.

In this study we find a description of a large Christian
hypogaeum with an apse of solid masonry construction
with frescoed walls. It was discovered in the explorations
to the east of the Platonia or Apostolic sepulchre. (At the
foot of the staircase leading down into the room they
found the graffito "Domus Petri" in the stucco of the
wall which was associated with the Apostolic Memorial.
The graffito was not discussed in this work since it was
discovered only later in 1912).

284 CRISTIANI, L., "Saint Pierre inhumé au Vatican."

See no. 546.

285 CRISTIANI, L., "Causerie de l'Ami sur les "Revues," *L'Ami
du Clergé*, 62 (1952), 145-148.

In the second part of the essay the author takes up the
problem of Peter and Paul's transferal ad catacumbas on
the via Appia. He concludes that their relics were buried
here for a time.

286 CUMONT, F., "Un rescrit impérial sur la violation de sépulture" — *Revue historique*, 163 (1930), 241-266.

This is an examination of the famous Nazareth inscription that deals with the high regard of the Romans for burial-places and the severity of their laws against violations of the grave. The juridical conclusions to be derived from this document are of interest for commentators on the problem of the transfer of the bodies of the Apostles to San Sebastiano on the via Appia. A transcription of the text is as follows: "Placet mihi sepulcra tumulosque, quae ad religionem maiorum fecerunt vel filiorum vel propinquorum, manere immutabilia in perpetuum. Si quis autem probaverit aliquem ea destruxisse, sive alio quocumque modo sepultos eruisse, sive in alium loco dolo malo transtulisse per iniuriam sepultorum, sive titulos vel lapides amovisse, contra illum iudicium iubeo fieri, sicut de diis,(ita) in hominum religionibus (Manium sacris?). Multo enim magis decebit sepultos. Omnino ne cuiquam liceat loco movere. Sin autem, illum ego capitis damnatum nomine sepulchri violati volo."

287 DE BRUYNE, L., "Sarcofago cristiano con nuovi temi iconografici scoperto a S. Sebastiano sulla via Appia" — RAC, 16 (1939), 247-270.

A number of Christian sarcophagi had been previously discovered beneath San Sebastiano which revealed a continuous repetition of the same iconographical subjects. One would be inclined to believe that the repertory of themes used in Christian antiquity had been exhausted. However, to everyone's surprise, an unusual sarcophagus came to light in the excavations (1939) which depicted three themes unknown in Christian sculptures up to that time. This study deals with the themes of these artistic representations.

288 DELEHAYE, H., "Refrigerare, Refrigerium" — *Journal des savants*, (Nov. 1926), 385-390.

In this brief study the author examines the uses of the term *refrigerium* and *refrigerare*. He concludes that 'refrigerare' cannot have the two meanings at one and the same time as Grossi-Gondi's interpretation supposes (see no. 329).

289 DELEHAYE, H., "Le sanctuaire des Apôtres sur la voie Appienne" — AB, 45 (1927), 297-310.

In dealing with the problem of the cult of the Apostles on the via Appia the author examines the various explanations which have been proposed by some. He rejects the theory of a translation and shows that the martyrs were many times honored by religious monuments erected in places which were not their tombs, and notably in the places where they lived. The 'Domus Petri' was not a place of burial but the actual dwelling in which the Apostles lived during their lifetime.

290 DELEHAYE, H., "Tusco et Basso cons." — *Mélanges Paul Thomas*, (Belgium, 1930), 201-207.

The oldest calendar of feasts of the Roman Church, the "Depositio Martyrum," enters into its chronology for the year 354 the following text: *III. Kal. Jul. Petri in Catacumbas et Paul Ostiense, Tusco et Basso conss.* (258). The "Hieronymianum Martyrology" records: *Petri in Vaticano, Pauli via Ostiense utriusque in Catacumbas Tusco et Basso conss.* The author analyzes the texts to help solve the riddles which they seem to present regarding the tombs of the Apostles. He believes that the date June 29th, 258 does not refer to the inauguration of a liturgical feast in honor of the Apostles.

291 DELEHAYE, H., "The Martyrdom of St. Peter and St. Paul" — AB, 52 (1934), 69-72.

This is a critique of A. S. Barnes' work by the same title (see no. 18).

Among other things, Delehaye feels that Barnes is incorrect in attempting to find a solution for the text of interminable discussions, scil., *Tusco et Basso cons.* from the "Depositio Martyrum." Barnes asserts that the year 258 in an interpolation of the copyist. But according to

Delehaye, this could not be acceptable. The year is to be retained. (Cf. his study above, no. 290).

292 DELEHAYE, H., *L'origine du culte des martyrs*, (Brussels: Société des Bollandistes, 1933), 417 pp., Cf. pp. 54; 267-268.

In this elaborate treatment on the subject of the cult of martyrs it is interesting to note the author's interpretation (rather novel) with respect to the *Memoria ad Catacumbas*. He rejects any notion of a transfer of the Apostles' relics on account of its juristic difficulties, and he visualizes a cultus without the presence of the bodies.

293 DELFORGE, T., "The Martyrdom of St. Peter and St. Paul" — *Revue Bénédictine*, 47 (1935), 400-401.

This is a critique of A. S. Barnes' work by the same title (see no. 18).

The reviewer feels that Barnes omits mention of the three first-century hypogea beneath the basilica of San Sebastiano which give evidence that this was a burial-place. He does not see how a local veneration could have developed in such a short period. (The bodies of the Apostles were here only nineteen months, according to Barnes). Besides, the graffiti testifying to the "refrigerium" do not seem to furnish clear evidence. However, Delforge does not think that his objections should destroy Barnes' conclusions.

294 DE WAAL, A., "Die Häupter Petri und Pauli im Lateran" — RQ, 5 (1891), 340-348.

In seeking evidence that may point to the separation of the Apostles' heads from the remainder of their relics before the Saracen invasion, the author endeavors to interpret the translation of the heads in the light of the general movement of translation that had developed in the eighth century.

295 DE WAAL, A., "La Platonia ossia il sepolcro apostolico della via Appia" — *Diss. della Pont. accad. rom. di arch.*, 2 (1892), 139-163, plates II-III.

This study deals with a detailed description of the

Platonia—where it was believed that the remains of the Apostles had been laid away—a semicircular building situated behind the apse of San Sebastiano. In 1893 the author proved that the *Platonia* had contained the tomb of Bishop Quirinus of Siscia in Pannonia, a martyr under Diocletian and not those of Peter and Paul as was formerly believed.

296 DE WAAL, A., "Le tombe Apostoliche di Roma, studi di archeologia e di storia" — *Studi e documenti di storia e diritto*, 1892, 321-373.

In this interesting essay the author gives a historical and archeological reconstruction of the Apostolic tomb.

297 DE WAAL, A., "Die Apostelgruft ad Catacumbas" — Supplementheft III (1894), RQ, 7-141.

The problem of a temporary transfer of the remains of St. Peter (and Paul) to the *Memoria ad San Sebastiano* was taken up by the author, who in 1893, after an exhaustive study of all relevant testimony, solved the problem of the so-called PLATONIA, proving it to have been not the temporary resting-place of the Apostles, but a mausoleum raised in honor of Quirinus. Aided by Styger and Fasiolo he began a thorough search under the nave of the present church, and although the excavations at this time lasted only for a few months, the results were gratifying. It was learned that no church, no monumental basilica existed on the site of the present San Sebastiano before the time of Damasus (366-384) and that when this Pope erected the basilica its site was occupied by pagan columbaria of the first century, by a Roman villa with painted walls and crypts, and by a *pergula* or *triclia* with a seat or bench running around at least two sides of the enclosing walls. It was also learned that the grave of St. Sebastian, whose name was given at a later age to the basilica itself, does not occupy any place of honor in Pope Damasus' scheme of the building but only an obscure corner on the left aisle. Lastly, a rough stone coffin was discovered in the center of the church containing the body of St. Fabianus. Graffiti were also discovered on the walls of the triclia which have a direct connection with the main controversy at issue, with the alledged transferal of the bodies of Peter and Paul ad catacumbas. In this lengthy study the author investigates the following points:

a) The primitive grave of Peter at the Vatican.
b) Ancient testimony and an investigation of the story regarding the plundering of the remains of the Apostles Peter and Paul and their salvaging ad Catacumbas.
c) A new attempted explanation.
d) More ancient information regarding the Platonia: its appearance before the most recent excavations, the new opinions gleaned from the same.
e) The most recent excavations in the Platonia and its results.
f) The Church of San Sebastiano in ancient times.
g) The sepulchre of the Apostles and its surroundings.

298 DE WAAL, A., "Die Platonia ad Catacumbas" — RQ, 9 (1895), 111-117.

The author's investigations revealed the fact that about A.D. 400 a martyr named Quirinus had been buried in the Platonia, and he concludes that the Platonia had been constructed at that time and consequently could have had no connection with the burial of the Apostles 140 years earlier.

299 DE WAAL, A., "Zu Wilpert's "Domus Petri" — RQ, 26 (1912), 123-132.

An argument in favor of the Apostle Peter having lived on the via Appia is afforded by the graffito 'Domus Petri' which was found on the wall of a chamber under a little chapel near the Platonia. In this study the author examines the relationship of the Apostle with the 'Domus Petri' based principally on the literary evidence. Could this have been in the beginning a center for the ecclesiastical administration and for the social life of the Roman community? The theory of the Apostle having lived there cannot be considered possible on this testimony since the graffito seems to have been written not earlier than the fifth century.

300 DE WAAL, A., "Gli scavi nel pavimento della basilica di San Sebastiano sulla via Appia" — RQ, 29 (1915), 146-148.

> This is an introductory article to those that follow in this periodical during this phase of the early excavations beneath San Sebastiano. Herein the author briefly reconstructs the history of the Platonia.

301 DE WAAL, A., "Die jüngsten Ausgrabungen in der Basilika des hl. Sebastian zu Rom" — *Der Katholiek*, 6 (1915), 395-411.

> An account of the most recent results of the archeological investigations and its unexpected surprises.

302 DINKLER, E., "Die 'Memoria Apostolorum' an der via Appia" — (Die Petrus-Rom-Frage), TR, 25 (1959), 326-335.

> The author gives an analysis of the critical studies made by others on this very complicated problem.

303 DUCHESNE, L., "La Memoria Apostolorum della via Appia" — *Atti della Pont. accad. rom. di arch.*, 3 ser. 1 (1923), 1-22.

> Found unfinished after the author's death. In this study the author deals with the famous sanctuary of the Apostles under these headings:
> a) The feast of the Catacombs, June 28.
> b) Pope Damasus and the Catacombs.
> c) The basilica of the Apostles.
> d) The mausoleum of St. Quirinus.
> e) Where was the Memoria Apostolorum?
> f) The hypothesis regarding the origin of the tradition.
> g) The translation of Paul the Apostle.
> h) The conclusions:
>> 1) At the III mile on the via Appia there actually was the church of San Sebastiano. From the second century to the beginning of the third, columbaria and funerary structures came into existence.
>> 2) Towards the middle of the third century the area became ecclesiastical property.
>> 3) The graffiti testify to the cult of the Apostles.
>> 4) In the fourth century a large cemeterial church was constructed.

5) In the fourth and fifth centuries a feast was celebrated on June 29th, on the Vatican, the via Ostia,
and both at Catacumbas.

The author supports the theory that Peter was originally
buried at the Vatican, and during the Valeranic persecutions in 258 his remains were transferred to the cemetery
ad catacumbas on the via Appia but very soon returned
to their original resting place at the Vatican. This theory
has the advantage of explaining the cult ad catacumbas in
the second half of the third century.

304 ERBES, K., "Die geschichtlichen Verhältnisse der Apostelgräber in Rom" — ZKG, 43 (1924), 38-92.

In endeavoring to reconstruct the historical relationship
of the Apostles' tombs in Rome with the tradition that
links them from the beginning with *San Sebastiano* on the
via Appia, and Gaius' *trophies of the Apostles*, the author
suggests that this is not to be interpreted in the sense of
"graves." It is to be understood as a place where the
memory of their martyrdom was commemorated. It was
on June 29, 258 when Sixtus II "in order to prepare his
community for the anticipated Valerianic persecution,
commemorated the feast of the martyr-Apostles" because
it was here that provision had been made by a private
individual for such a commemoration.

305 FIASIOLO, O., "La pianta di S. Sebastiano" — RQ, 29 (1915),
206-220, 1 plan, 3 plates.

In February, 1915, Msgr. de Waal entrusted the work
of excavations beneath San Sebastiano to P. Styger and
O. Fasiolo. The results of the work is found here. It is an
illucidation of the plan of the complexus intended to
serve as a guide during the period of excavations to which
has been added the findings of scholars regarding the
topographical and archeological aspects of the Basilica
Apostolorum. However, the work is by no means exhausted. The author himself makes it clear that his objective is to give a topographical plan of the basilica according
to the then-current (1915) excavations.

306 FERRUA, A., "Scavi a S. Sebastiano" — CC, 88, 2 (1937), 361-365.

With the appearance of A. Prandi's important work on the 'Memoria Apostolorum in Catacumbas' the author takes the opportunity to make some observations on the same subject. He treats of the etymology of the word "catacumbas," and makes certain observations on the juridical aspects of Roman burial which can be determined with much evidence uncovered in the excavations at San Sebastiano.

307 FERRUA, A., "Analecta Romana. II. San Sebastiano" — Epigraphica, 5-6 (1943-44), 3-26.

This is a thorough analysis of the pagan inscriptions— not yet edited at this time—that were discovered in the excavations in the necropolis of San Sebastiano.

308 FERRUA, A., "Tre Sarcofaghi importanti da S. Sebastiano" — RAC, 27 (1951), 7-33.

In the most recent excavations at the Basilica Apostolorum many sepulchral discoveries were made in the early Christian cemetery which at the end of the third century to the beginning of the fifth century developed around here. In this study the author speaks of three sarcophagi that were figured and that are of exceptional importance: two because of their consular dates which definitely determine the date of the sculpture, the third because of the grandiosity and singularity of its representations. The three are as follows:
1. Sarcophagus of Flavius Patricius.
2. Sarcophagus of two women.
3. Sarcophagus of Lot.

309 FERRUA, A., RAC, 25 (1949), 212. RAC, 28 (1952), 13-41, 15 figs.

Here we find reports on the excavations beneath the basilica of San Sebastiano, the "Memoria Apostolorum." In the first article there is reference to the latest discovery (the report being made on June 10, 1948) of two ancient mausoleums one of which he believes was Christian and constructed in the fourth century. In the second article the author goes into greater detail to indicate the evidence of funerary laws and other minute details to secure proper respect for the tombs and the evident piety which the ancients had for their dead. He speaks again of the two mausoleums discovered north of the Basilica Apostolorum and gives a description of the archeological findings. In the previous year (RAC, 27 (1951), 7 ff.) he discussed the sarcophagi that were discovered.

310 FERRUA, A., "Recenti ritrovamenti di antichità paleocristiane in Roma e nei dintorni."

See no. 592.

311 FERRUA, A., "Lavori a S. Sebastiano" — RAC, 37 (1961), 203-236, 16 figs.

In this study the author takes up the most recent findings of the excavations beneath San Sebastiano on the via Appia. He discusses the following:
1. The excavations beneath the sacristy.
2. The investigation of the mausoleums.
3. A door of the ancient basilica.

312 FISCHER, B., "Neues von den römischen Apostelgräbern."

See no. 598.

313 FORNARI, F., "Relazione circa un gruppo cimiteriale recentemente scoperte "ad catacumbas" — RAC, 6 (1929), 7-31.

We have here a description of the cemeterial region discovered in the excavations which is of great interest for the cemetery "ad catacumbas."

314 FORNARI, F., "Nelle catacombe Romane. L'attività della P. Commissione d'arch. sacra durante l'anno 1930" — RAC, 8 (1931), 14-16.

This is a report on the excavational work accomplished at San Sebastiano.

315 FORNARI, F., "Il rilievo del complesso monumentale di san Sebastiano sulla via Appia" — RAC, 9 (1932), 201-213.

The author speaks of the results of past excavations beneath San Sebastiano and the findings of the more recent. He distinguishes the various wall-structures, the various plans according to their different levels and the ultimate transformation of the basilica. His objective is to clarify the epoch when the Memoria Apostolorum was constructed as well as the Basilica with all its adjuncts.

316 FORNARI, F., "Il rilievo del complesso monumentale di San Sebastiano sulla via Appia" — *Atti del III Congresso Internazionale di archeologia Cristiana*, Ravenna, Sept. 25-30, 1932 (Roma, 1934), 315-324.

This is an endeavor to fill in the lacunae that were evident in the report of the excavations on the via Appia. With the aid of some excellent plates the author reconstructs:
1) The first plans.
2) The second.
3) The third.
4) Various other sections.
This is truly a detailed analysis of the monumental complexus. The material contained in RAC, 10 (1932), 201-213, is substantially reproduced in this study.

317 FORNARI, F., *S. Sebastiano*, (Collezione "Amici delle catacombe," 4) (Rome, 1934), 69 pp., 19 figs.

We have here a brief but adequate illustration of this sacred monument which represents a valuable treasure for all students of Christian archeology who seek information regarding all those finds brought to light up to the first half of the twentieth century. The book has the following sections:
1) San Sebastiano "extra moenia."
2) The Basilica Apostolorum.
3) The mausoleums.
4) The Memoria Apostolica.
5) The columbaria and hypogea.
6) The Roman villa.
7) The Christian cemetery.
8) The museum.

318 FRANCHI DE CAVALIERI, P., "Note agiografiche" — ST, 27 (1915), 124-125.

In his brief observations here the author brings out some points regarding the problem of the translation of the Apostles' relics to San Sebastiano ad catacumbas. He calls attention to a pseudo-Damasian inscription (no. 82 d Ihm) in which the burial chamber of St. Hippolytus is designated as *domus martyris Hippolytus*. (What about the 'Domus Petri'?). Again, the author feels that under the merciless persecution of Diocletian in 304, the Christians had other things to think about than the translations of martyrs. He expresses himself quite specifically against the assumption of a translation-hypothesis.

319 FREND, W. H., "The Memoriae Apostolorum in Roman North Africa" — JRS, 30 (1940), 32-49.

A certain number of extant inscriptions (and oral traditions still lingering in places as Djebel Nefouca, etc.) indicate that there was a time when the cult of the Apostles Peter and Paul existed in Roman-North Africa. But why in places so far removed? This study is an endeavor to answer the question. The author first quotes the relevant texts and then develops the history of the spread of Christianity with its counterforces and struggles and the ever-prevailing association of the Apostles with the cult of martyrs. We have here an interesting reconstruction of the development of the cult of martyrs in the ancient Church.

320 FUHRMANN, H., "Archäologische Grabungen und Funde in Italien und Libyen" — *Archäologischer Anzeiger. Beiblatt zum Jahrbuch des Archäologischen Instituts*, 56 (1941), 524-530.

The article speaks of some of the excavational findings under St. Peter's, viz., the graves and their inscriptions. It also includes some of the findings under San Sebastiano principally the Sarcophagus with the New Testament theme.

321 GAGOV, G. M., "Il termine "nomina" sinonimo di "reliquiae" nell'antica epigrafia cristiana" — *Miscellanea Francescana*, 55 (1955), 3-13.

Among the various literary sources that are used as testimony for the presence of Peter (and Paul's) body in Rome is the well-known epigram of Damasus. This is a word-study of the terms "nomina" and "reliquiae" as found in ancient Christian epigraphy. The author sees that these terms in epigrams or epitaphs can have the same meaning. To this end he gives a number of examples in African epigraphical usage, and also cites a number of examples found in the Damasian epigrams at Rome. Of the many instances of "nomina" and "reliquiae" quoted by Damasus they are always used to indicate "bodies" or "relics."

322 GERKE, F., "Petrus und Paulus. Zwei bedeutende Köpfe im Museum von S. Sebastiano" — RAC, 10 (1933), 307-329.

This is an unusual and interesting study of the two busts of Peter and Paul in the Museum of San Sebastiano. These might well be considered the prototypes of the oldest portraits of the Apostles.

323 GRÉGOIRE, H., "Le problème de la tombe de S. Pierre."

See no. 613.

In the following four studies the author takes up the question of the Memoria Apostolorum ad catacumbas on the via Appia and its association with the burial of the Apostles. Tradition claimed that the bodies of the Apostles rested here for a while. The author cites many texts containing this idea: *ubi corpora apostolorum jacuerunt*. He searches into the probable origin of the legend, first of all with the Damasian inscription. He concludes that it is certain that from the beginning of the sixth century or even from the end of the fifth century, the Romans believed that the bodies of Peter and Paul were temporarily ad catacumbas.

324 GRIFFE, H., "La légende du transfert des corps de Saint Pierre et Saint Paul ad catacumbas" — BLE, 52 (1951), 195-209.

In this study the author wishes to see in the memoria "ad catacumbas" a *sepulchrum honorarium* in honor of the two Apostles which was supposed to have preceded the elaborate basilicas of the fourth century at the Vatican and the via Ostia. It is divided into three main headings:

In the first, the author speaks of the literary testimony wherein he deals with the well-known letter of Gregory I in 594 to the Empress Constantina. The text speaks of the Apostles' bodies as being buried ad catacumbas. He also quotes the Vita Cornelii as found in the Liber Pontificalis where the same allusion is found. In the second part, the author speaks of the probable origin of the legend. In the *vita Damasi* (Liber Pont.) there is mention of the dedication of the *Platoma ad catacumbas*: "hic dedicavit platomam in catacumbas—ubi corpora Petri et Pauli iacuerunt". Then he takes up the celebrated Damasian inscription: "Hic habitasse." In the third part, he speaks of the cult of the Apostles as found in the Depositio Martyrum and the Martyrologium Hieronymianum, where he feels that there has been a misinterpretation of the consular dates.

325 GRIFFE, H., "La question du transfert des reliques de Saint Pierre "ad catacumbas" — BLE, 54 (1953), 128-142.

Basing himself on the reports of the excavational findings at the Vatican the author takes up the problem of a translation ad catacumbas that some claim took place in 258. He argues his case according to Carcopino's translation-theory which, according to some scholars, does not succeed in removing the difficulties inherent in it.

326 GRIFFE, H., "Hic habitasse prius" (Inscription du pape Damase) — BLE, 58 (1957), 93-101.

An exact word-study of the Damasian poem comparing it with the interpretations found in other epigrams. Among other things he endeavors to prove that this inscription is also of value and interest for the history of monasticism in its beginnings at Rome — a history so little known.

327 GRIFFE, H., "Nouvelle visite "ad catacumbas" — BLE, 59 (1958), 119-122.

The Vatican excavations have once again stimulated interest in the age-old problem of the Memoria Apostolo-

rum on the via Appia. The author cites the studies of
M. Ruysschaert which have endeavored to throw some
light on the matter. Of principle interest is the entirely
new interpretation that Ruysschaert gives to the reading
of the Damasian inscription. *Hic habitasse* is to be read:
hic habitare. In opposition to those texts which speak of
Peter's burial at the Vatican there are those that refer to
his veneration on the via Appia. Ruysschaert inquires
whether there might be any opposition between the
'Vatican-tradition' and the 'via-Appian-tradition.'

Our author makes the following observations:

a) The literary tradition does not favor the hypothesis of
a translation of Peter's body.

b) As regards the graffiti at San Sebastiano, neither
archeology nor epigraphy can clarify the problem.

c) Does the Depositio Martyrum furnish us with a decisive argument for a translation?

d) How to explain the cult of the Apostles ad catacumbas?

He concludes: the 'translation-hypothesis,' while con-
convenient, does not agree with the literary-Vatican-
tradition. The only valid explanation is to attribute a
purely liturgical significance to the site 'ad catacumbas.'
This alone seems adequately to take into consideration
all the data relative to the Appian-tradition.

Such an explanation will serve to restrain a number of
'new ideas' that modern research is attempting to propose.

328 GRISAR, H., "Die Römische Sebastianuskirche und ihre
Apostelgruft im Mittelalter" — RQ, 9 (1895), 409-461.

It is the aim of this study to evaluate the investigations
regarding the Apostolic tomb ad catacumbas which the
author has admirably accomplished. He concludes that
the Apostles were temporarily buried here (for 252 years)
and he propounds his hypothesis basing himself chiefly
on the information gleaned from documents which he had
discovered (dating from the period of Leo X) and which
speaks of the indulgences attached to the shrine of San
Sebastiano. The subject matter is divided as follows:

1) The contents of the documents.

2) Their names and character.

3) The sources.

4) A joining together of both first parts of the documents.

5) The two different traditions in the documents regarding the Apostles' grave.

6) The excavations; the pilgrim itineraries. The very ancient name of the church; the puteus.

7) The disappearance of the old tradition; the prominence of the new.

8) The source of the new tradition, Panvinius' influence. The text of the errors from the year 1521.

329 GROSSI-GONDI, F., "Il "Refrigerium" celebrato in onore dei SS. Apostoli Pietro e Paolo" — RQ, 29 (1915), 222-249.

The graffiti discovered in the spring of the year 1915 beneath the center of the church of San Sebastiano on the via Appia (published for the first time in that same year) offer a wealth of material for research and study on the question of the cultus to the Apostles in this place since tradition speaks of a temporary repose of the bodies of the Apostles ad catacumbas.

The author takes up the question of the meaning to be assigned to the word "refrigerium" in the graffiti of the triclia. Basing himself on the etymology of the term, Scriptural indications, the Fathers, and other literary references to the cultus on the via Appia, he argues at great length insisting on the strictly Christian sepulchral character of the agape-refrigerium.

330 GROSSI-GONDI, F., "Importantissime Scoperte a S. Sebastiano sull'Appia" — CC, 66, 2 (1915), 460-471.

In this study the author examines two extremely important discoveries beneath San Sebastiano:

1. The Memoria Apostolorum.

2. The sarcophagus of Fabianus.

331 GROSSI-GONDI, F., "S. Fabiano Papa e Martyre: la sua tombe e le sue spoglie attraverso i secoli" — CC, 57, 2 (1916), 73-81; 209-218; 685-700.

This study deals with the history of the various sanctuaries—notably the cemetery ad catacumbas—where the body of St. Fabianus had reposed across the centuries.

332 GROSSI-GONDI, F., "La basilica di S. Sebastiano sull'Appia dopo le insigni scoperte degli anni 1915-16" — CC, 68, 2 (1917), 588-598.

One finds here an historical, architectural, and archeological reconstruction of the Basilica Apostolorum after the remarkable discoveries of 1915-1916.

The author gives a brief analysis of the following points:

a) What was known about the monument before 1915.
b) The discoveries made about the middle of the nineteenth century.
c) The curved apse.
d) The matroneum.
e) The three naves.
f) The pilasters.
g) The basilica as it was (supposedly) during the times of Damasus.
h) The excavations of 1915-1916.
i) The area containing the ancient tombs.
j) Their age and that of the basilica.
k) The lower strata, the Christian edifices, pagan columbaria and the Roman villa.

333 GROSSI-GONDI, F., CC, 68, 3 (1917), 519-534.

The author continues his analysis of the Basilica Apostolorum discussing the following:

a) The triclia discovered in the center of the basilica.
b) The graffiti.
c) The refrigerium as a funerary rite at the tombs of the martyrs and of the Apostles Peter and Paul at the III mile along the Appia.
d) The remarkable accord between the present discoveries and documents already known.
e) The 'Domus Petri.'

334 GROSSI-GONDI, F., "La tomba e l'altare di S. Sebastiano nella basilica dell'Appia a proposito del VII centenario della sua consacrazione" — CC, 69, 1 (1918), 235; 338.

This study deals with the tomb and altar of St. Sebastian in the basilica on the via Appia (on the occasion of the 700th anniversary of its consecration) in conjunction with the remains of the two Apostles Peter and Paul and especially the Honorian (III) altar. Erudite investigations and new documents have enlightened us on the subject especially that of March 1672 found in the Codex Vaticano Barberino, lat. 1572.

335 GROSSI-GONDI, F., "La data della construzione della Basilica Apostolorum sull'Appia" — CC, 69, 3 (1918), 230-242

In this brief study the author endeavors to date the construction of the Basilica Apostolorum. A new discovery (an inscription) permits the author to fix the limits with a sureness. He feels that the date at least from 356-357 must be considered as the "terminus post quem non" for its erection.

336 GROSSI-GONDI, F., "Il rito funebre del "Refrigerium" al sepolcro apostolico dell'Appia" — *Diss. della Pont. accad. rom. di arch., 2 ser.,* 14 (1920), 251-277.

A useful accompaniment to the works dealing with San Sebastiano and its association with the Apostles' grave. It is directed against those who maintain that agapes in honor of the martyrs were held at catacumbas absente cadavere. As in his previous study, this is a thorough analysis of the subject "refrigerium" appearing in epitaphs of the triclia. He shows that although the word does not occur in inscriptions of an earlier date than these, it is found in Christian literature as early as 200 and is an exclusively Christian term. The indication is also that the regular funerary feasts were celebrated there where their bodies were buried.

337 GROSSI-GONDI, F., "Di un graffito greco nella tricilia di S. Sebastiano sull'Appia" — *Nuovo Bollettino di Archeologia Cristiana,* 28 (1922), 27-31.

The author examines one of the graffiti and concludes that the refrigerium was celebrated in this place.

338 GUARDUCCI, M., "Interno al graffito Domus Petri in S.

Sebastiano" — *Atti della Pont. accad. rom. di arch., 3 ser., Rendiconti*, 28 (1954-1955; ed. 1956), 3-4.

We find a reference here to M. Guarducci's dissertation about the graffito "Domus Petri" in San Sebastiano. During the excavations in 1909 in the monumental complex of San Sebastiano there came to light, on the wall of a sepulchre datable to the end of the fourth century, this unique graffito in which the expression DOMUS PETRI is read. The many attempts of scholars to solve its significance is finally resolved (according to the author) in this instance. An interpretation is as follows: *Domus Petri—Domus Domini—Domus Patris*. There is an identification between the house of Peter—the home of Christ, i.e., the Church, and of both with the house of the Father, viz., Paradise. All of which demonstrates the firm belief of the early Christians in the primacy of Peter and the supremacy of the Roman Church.

339 GUARDUCCI, M., "Intorno al graffito di "Cosumalu" a San Sebastiano" — *Atti della Pont. accad. rom. di arch., 3 ser., Rendiconti*, 28 (1955-1956; ed. 1957), 156.

The author gives her reading of the graffito "Cosumalu" found among the graffiti of the triclia which is dated at the beginning of the third century. Among the various interpretations she finds in it a reference to the venerated Apostles ad catacumbas beseeching them to obtain (through their intercession) a successful journey for certain children (whose names were lost) and for an older person—Trope Cosumalus by name—who is called the "servant of God." (The journey is a mystic journey). Such a concept was familiar to the early Christians, i.e., "a happy journey in God."

340 GUARDUCCI, M., "Due presunte date consolari a S. Sebastiano" — *Atti della Pont. accad. rom. di arch., 3 ser., Rendiconti*, 28 (1955-1956); ed. 1957), 181-195.

This study deals with the two graffiti:
a) The graffito of "Cosumalu."
b) The graffito of "Celerinus" which were found on the

walls of the triclia ad catacumbas and which expresses the deep religious feelings of the faithful. The theory of two existing consular dates obtained from the interpretation of the graffiti is rejected by the author.

341 GUARDUCCI, M., *La Tomba di Pietro. Notizie antiche e nuove scoperte.*

See no. 630.

342 GUARDUCCI, M., *The Tomb of St. Peter, the new discoveries in the Sacred Grottoes of the Vatican*, (trans. by J. McLellan, New York: Hawthorn Books, 1960), 198 pp., 50 figs., XIII plates. Cf. Chapter VI, "The cult of the Apostles Peter and Paul on the Appian Way," pp. 161-178.

The author's conclusions are as follows:

a) In 258, during the consulate of Tuscus and Bassus, a devotion to Peter and Paul was instituted. June 29 was the date chosen.

b) The devotion was established ad catacumbas.

c) The reason for the site might be attributed to the nearness of the cemetery of St. Callistus where there was a Papal crypt. Since the Valerian edict forbade the Christians to meet in their own cemeteries they had to choose a place nearby for their devotion to the two Apostles.

d) There was a cemetery here ad catacumbas owned by Christians who covered it over to build a shrine to the Apostles on the new level.

e) The new devotion had a funerary aspect that was seen by the refrigerium.

f) This aspect can be explained without recourse to the thesis—very improbable and certainly not proved—of a transfer of the Apostles' bodies from their original graves.

g) The material center of devotion must have been various "relics" of the Apostles kept in a typical monument with two small arches.

h) The devotion did not last long—from 258 to about 320 A.D.

i) At the latter date the triclia was buried over to erect Constantine's basilica.

j) In the ninth century the basilica was given the name of St. Sebastian because of the tomb of this Saint which had been buried there at the beginning of the fourth century and which had attracted many pilgrims.

There is not sufficient reason to prove that the remains of the Apostles were kept for some time in Catacumbas on the site of the present church of San Sebastiano—though the region can claim the merit for giving impetus to the devotion to the Apostles.

343 GUIGNEBERT, C., "La sépulture de saint Pierre."

See no. 138.

344 HERTLING, L. and KIRSCHBAUM, E., *The Roman Catacombs and Their Martyrs*, (trans. M. J. Costelloe, Milwaukee: Bruce, 1957), 196 pp., 8 figs., 44 plates. Cf. Chapter V, "The Tombs of the Apostles," pp. 66-86.

The authors examine the various accounts that speak of the bodies of the Apostles being buried at San Sebastiano ad catacumbas. As far as they are concerned all such accounts are only tentative explanations. Some, in fact, are contradictory. They enumerate five theories and conclude that they all have weak points and that the present state of the question makes it impossible to decide in favor of any one of them with certainty. According to them we must read the notice of the calendar of 354 as follows: "the 29th of June. The feast of Peter is celebrated 'in catacumbas" and not in his basilica on the Vatican, (which perhaps was not yet completed), "and the feast of Paul on the Ostian Way." The reason for this regulation is "the year 258."

345 HUDEC, L. E., "Recent excavations under St. Peter's basilica in Rome."

See no. 637.

347 JONES, H. S., "Memoria Apostolorum on the via Appia" — JThSt, 28 (1926), 30-39.

With a cessation of the work of excavations beneath San Sebastiano, the author feels it opportune for a provisional interpretation of the results obtained in the light of traditions connected with the sight. He examines the literary testimony that indicate the existence of a liturgical cult in this region. The meaning of "habitasse" in the Damasian epigram means *resting place*. He finds a parallel example in another epigram. Further, as regards the obscure line in the same Damasian poem (those who came from the Orient, etc.) he says it is impossible to dissociate the lines from the well-known legend that a band of eastern Christians attempted to remove the bodies of the Apostles (from this place) but were frustrated through a convulsion of nature. He then takes up a cursory survey of the excavational findings: the graves, graffiti, etc., and asks where the site of the actual resting place was. The indication seems to be a chamber adjoining the triclia where three sarcophagi were found. He concludes by saying that he sees no valid objection to the interpretation of the documentary and archeological evidence which indicate that the bodies of the Apostles were temporarily in this place.

346 JONES, H. S., JRS, 14 (1924), 286.

We have here a brief interesting notice. In reply to a Professor Merrill who sought to prove that the tradition of St. Peter and his Roman sojourn had every mark of being mythical, the author draws attention to the recent discoveries on the via Appia. From the excavational results, viz., the well-preserved tombs one of which bore traces of Christianity and close by one that was definitely Christian—showing that Christians were buried in that region in the early third century; the group of chambers; a roofed-in space; the graffiti to Peter and Paul; all of this seems to indicate that their bodies rested here temporarily. His conclusion is: "the archeological evidence fitted in better with the belief in the residence of the two Apostles in Rome than with any other theory."

348 JOSI, E., "Rilievi archeologici sugli scavi di San Sebastiano"

— *Atti del III Congresso Internazionale di archeologia cristiana,
Ravenna, Sept. 25-30, 1932*, (Roma, 1934), 325-326.

With the termination of the exploration beneath the
central nave at San Sebastiano, the author now takes up
a brief consideration of the excavations under the lateral
naves and describes the finds under the left nave in
particular.

349 JOSI, E., "I sepolcro di S. Pietro in Vaticano e di S. Paolo
sull'Ostiense" — *L.Osservatore Romano*, July 3, 1943, p. 3.

The author takes exception to G. Belvederi's studies
that appeared in the *Bollettino degli Amici della Catacombe* (1942-43) (On these see nos. 262, 263, 487). Josi
claims that Belvederi, by his new theory, has shaken the
very solid basis for the venerated tradition of the Apostles'
burial place in Rome: the "Memoria Apostolorum ad
catacumbas." For this reason he once again examines the
problem and concludes: When Constantine erected both
basilicas (Vatican and via Ostia) both Apostles were
buried ad catacumbas. How long were their bodies there?
At least until the sixth century when they were returned
to their respective graves. It is true that this theory has
also aroused some criticism. However, Josi endeavors to
clarify the issue which he feels Belvederi has obscured.

350 JOSI, E., "Pietro."

See no. 158.

351 JOSI, E., "Ipotesi sulla traslazione delle sole teste degli
apostoli in Catacumbas in seguito all editto di Valeriano del
258," RAC, 29 (1953), 94-95.

Among the various hypotheses proposed in regard to
the explanations of the Memoria Apostolorum ad catacumbas, the author puts forth an interesting new version
of the translation-theory which avoids many difficulties
of the older ones. He cites a text from the third-century
Roman jurist, Julius Paulus, to the effect that legally
the grave is reckoned to be where the head is. Following
the edict of Valerian in 258, only the Apostles' heads were
translated ad catacumbas.

352 KIRSCH, J. P., "Arthur Stapylton Barnes: St. Peter in Rome."

See no. 165.

353 KIRSCH, J. P., "Das neuentdeckte Denkmal der Apostel Petrus u. Paulus "in catacumbas" an der Appischen Strasse in Rom" — RQ, 30 (1916-22), 5-28, 1 plate.

In this study the author treats of the most important results of the excavations in timely connection with Styger's report in 1915. In this framework he demonstrates and discusses the opinions which were brought forth in an attempt to solve the questions about the real character of the Memoria Apostolorum. He divides his study as follows:
a) The 'Memoria Apostolorum' (the triclia).
b) The Roman tombs and the remains of the old Roman buildings.
c) The tombs in the deep-grooved hallow under the basilica.
d) The character and origin of the *Memoria Apostolorum* ad catacumbas.

He concludes that it is incomprehensible how the bodies of the Apostles were exposed to a desecration in their original and generally-known tombs because, according to law, Christian tombs were protected from all violation and there is no example in Rome of any such profanation. Therefore, it is not easy to assume that a translation of the bodies did occur.

354 KIRSCH, J. P., "Die Memoria Apostolorum an der Appischen Strasse zu Rom und die liturgische Festfeier des 29. Juni" — JL, 3 (1923), 33-50.

In the first section of this study the author examines the literary evidence of the Depositio Martyrum and Episcoporum, and the Martyrologium Hieronymianum, with regard to the liturgical feast of June 29 and its association with the Memoria Apostolorum on the via Appia. In the second section he takes up the archeological evidence, and concludes with a consideration of the liturgical Acts.

355 KIRSCH, J. P., "Die stadtrömische christliche Festkalender

im Altertum" — *Liturgiesgeschichtliche Quellen, VII-VIII, Münster-in-W., 1924.*

The author deals with the notice of the Jerome Martyrology which connects the martyrdom of Peter with the Vatican hill and Paul with the via Ostia, and also mentions the "catacombs."

356 KIRSCH, J. P., "Die beiden Apostelfeste Petri Stuhlfeier und Pauli Bekehrung im Januar" — JL, 5 (1925), 48-67.

The author opposes the theory of a translation of Peter's body as proposed by Duchesne and Lietzmann and others since there is no trace of it in the Roman liturgy nor any mention of it in the martyrology, although the Jerome Martyrology does speak of Paul's translation on Jan. 25, viz., "Romae translatio *Pauli* Apostoli."

357 KIRSCH, J. P. "Le feste degli Apostoli S. Pietro e S. Paolo nel Martirologio Geronimiano" — RAC, 2 (1925), 54-83.

The common feast that commemorates the martyrdom of Peter and Paul at Rome is celebrated June 29, and this is the feast assigned to this date according to the so-called Jerome Martyrology. However, we also find other days when a common feast is commemorated. This is a critical examination of the respective text in the Martyrology which is important not only for the history of this liturgical feast in honor of the Apostles, but also for the study of the development of the Jerome text according to a form derived from the more ancient manuscripts. The study has the following sections:
1. The feast of June 29.
2. The feast of the Cathedra of St. Peter.
3. The conversion of St. Paul.
4. St. Peter in chains.

358 KIRSCHBAUM, E., "Petri in Catacumbas" — *Miscellanea Liturgica in honorem L. Cuniberti Mohlberg*, 1 (1948), (= Bibliotheca "Ephemerides Liturgicae," 22), Rome, 221-229.

Peter's body, linked by tradition with Paul's in the cult of the two Apostles, is brilliantly deduced from new research—at the basilica of San Sebastiano ad catacumbas.

The line of argument used by the author regarding the notices cited from the Depositio Martyrum concerning June 29 referring to the cult veneration—why Peter is mentioned here only with the catacombs and why he alone is mentioned, the author states: at the time when the Roman calendar originated (that is, in the year 354), the basilica which Constantine had begun to build for Peter at the place of the Vatican 'trophy' was not yet complete. So for a time the only cult-site at which Peter was venerated was still the place in the catacombs; while in the case of Paul, the basilica outside the walls (which was much smaller) and therefore took less time to complete, was already dedicated to the cult.

359 KIRSCHBAUM, E., "Petri in Catacumbas et Pauli Ostense, Tusco et Basso consulibus," nella Depositio Martyrum," RAC, 25 (1949), 199.

> This is a resumé of a communication delivered on Feb. 13 regarding the cult of the Apostles connected with the notice of the Depositio Martyrum. See above.

360 KIRSCHBAUM, E., *The Tombs of St. Peter and St. Paul*, (trans. J. Murray, New York: St. Martins Press, 1959), 242 pp., 57 figs., 44 plates. Cf. Chapter VI "Peter and Paul on the Via Appia," pp. 196-200.

> In his usual scholarly way the author gives here a brief survey of the Basilica Apostolorum and its association with the two Apostles based on some of the archeological and literary evidence. He mentions in a cursory way some of the hypotheses which attempt to explain the origin and significance of the apostolic cultus on the via Appia. The specialists are divided into two groups: one supposes a translation of the apostles' bodies, the other rejects any sort of translation. Against the first it is objected that no credible spot has been discovered beneath San Sebastiano on the via Appia, where the Apostles could have been buried. As for the second group there is the difficulty of imagining how a cultus centre of the Apostles could have arisen in early Christian Rome at a distance from their

graves or place of martyrdom. Cultus centres are normally associated with the place of burial or of the actual martyrdom. There are no exceptions to this in all of Rome. Basing himself on an hypothesis of E. Josi (quoted above) our author concludes that the simplest explanation of all is that a "bone-deposit" in the *graffiti wall of the Vatican* was made for the remains of the Apostles when they were brought back from the via Appia. In his reconstruction there was a first transfer which was concerned only with part of the Apostles' relics, viz., the head. This seems quite compatible with the existence of other portions of the remains (results of the Vatican excavations) beneath the Red Wall, and seems to fit best with the new archeological data brought to light under St. Peter's.

361 KLAUSER, T., *Die Römische Petrustradition im Lichte der neuen Ausgrabungen unter der Peterskirche,*

See no. 674.

362 KLAUSER, T., "Die Deutung der Ausgrabungsbefunde unter S. Sebastiano und am Vatikan" — JAC, 5 (1962), 33-38.

This is a reply to A. von Gerkan's observations in his study: *Petrus in Vaticano et in Catacumbas* (see no. 450).
The author concludes as follows:

1. The triclia could have been a cult-room since at that time there were no specific features differentiating cult-chambers from other rooms. They didn't even have fixed altars.

2. He agrees with Von Gerkan's conclusions with regard to the corrections of the architectural features.

3. He has reservations regarding the testimony of liturgical and ecclesiastical history.

4. Delahaye's arguments against the translation-theory have not yet been disproven. In the year 258 there was no need, nor a possibility, nor idea of translating the relics of the Apostles.

5. The dates recorded in liturgical calendars indicated only the celebration of the feast. They did not give the reason for the institution of the feast. It seems that February 22nd is the more original feast of Peter.

6. The graffiti in the passageway near the triclia do not prove the temporary presence of the relics there. They are of a later date, and fewer in number than those in the triclia.
7. The break beneath the aedicula at the Vatican is no argument for or against the translation-theory.
8. There hasn't been any reliquary found in which the relics could have been deposited and translated by Constantine.
9. Klauser still holds to the two-fold tradition regarding the burial place of Peter at Rome, scil.
   a) That of the orthodox who claimed that Peter was buried at the Vatican.
   b) That of the dissenters who claimed that Peter was buried ad catacumbas.

363 KÜNZLE, P., "Sul carme damasiano "Hic habitasse" — RAC, 27 (1951), 192-193.

In this brief study the author thinks that the words 'hic habitasse' in the famous Damasian epigram should read: *hic habitare* which is more logical and makes the reading easier. This also seems to be confirmed by many codices.

364 KÜNZLE, P., "Bemerkungen zum Lob auf Sankt Peter und Sankt Paul von Prudentius (Peristeph. 12)" — *Revista di Storia della Chiesa in Italia*, 11 (1957), 309-370.

This interesting study treats of the famous hymn by the Christian poet Prudentius which celebrates the martyrdom of the two Apostles and refers to the feasts celebrated in their honor at the Vatican and the via Ostia. It seems significant, however, that Prudentius does not mention the feast on the via Appia. How is this silence explained?

365 LAMMERT, F., "Τρόπαιον" — *Real Encyclopädie der classischen Altertumswissenschaft, ser. II*, vol. 7 (*neue Bearbeitung*), par. I, (1939), 663-673.

In this study the author gives a detailed explanation of the meaning of the word *trophy*.

366 LANCIANI, R., *Pagan and Christian Rome*.

See no. 174.

367 LANCIANI, R., "The Memoria Apostolorum on the Appian Way" — *The Dublin Review*, 158 (1916), 220-229.

This is a discussion of the problem of the alleged temporary transferal of the bodies of Peter and Paul to the catacombs on the via Appia. The author describes briefly the remarkable excavational findings of the first campaign (undertaken by De Waal, Styger and Fasiolo). Based on this early evidence he proposes the following probable hypotheses which he feels can be accepted without hesitation:

1. There is no doubt that at (or very near) the spot where the church of San Sebastiano now stands there existed a *Memoria Apostolorum*—a hall or shrine connected with some act or event in their lives.
2. There is nothing known of the origin, nature, or the *raison d'etre* of the Memoria at San Sebastiano.
3. The suggested translation of relics may be accepted as possible, if not probable, for Peter, for the reason given in the *Vita Heliogabili*; but would be absurd to claim the same for Paul.
4. There is a marked preference in the graffiti for Paul's name over that of Peter. These invocations cannot be taken as proof of their translation to the via Appia.
5. The true solution is to be found in the Damasian epigram. The verb *habitasse* must be taken in the literal sense: here Peter and Paul *lived*. The *Memoria* must have been a private house or hostelry made sacred by the temporary residence of the Apostles.
6. The great veneration in which the *Memoria* was held is shown by the number of private tomb-chapels which crowd the site of San Sebastiano.
7. When the church was built, towards the end of the fourth century, no special importance was attached to the fact that St. Sebastian's body had been included in the area. The church was exclusively dedicated to the memory of the Apostles.

368 LANCIANI, R., "La memoria apostolorum al III miglio dell'-
Appia e gli scavi di San Sebastiano" — *Diss. della Pont.
accad. rom. di arch.*, 2 ser., 14 (1920), 57-111, plates VIII-IX.

> The author holds the same opinion in general as Wilpert
> (see "Domus Petri" no. 452). He does not accept the
> hypothesis of a translation of the bodies of Peter and Paul
> to this place. Instead, he claims that a commemoration of
> the Apostles was celebrated here at the III mile on the via
> Appia (since the cemetery had been confiscated), in which
> region a house had stood where the Apostles had lived
> for a time, and which was replaced by a church.

369 LA PIANA, G., "The Tombs of Peter and Paul ad Catacumbas"
— *Harvard Theological Review*, 14 (1921), 53-94, 3 plates.

> This is a discussion in the light of the most recent
> excavations at Rome (1921) on the several hypotheses
> which have been put forward in regard to the ancient
> tradition connected with the church of San Sebastiano at
> Rome and the Apostles.
>
> Analyzing the literary testimony and the archeological
> findings the author controverts the view that a trans-
> lation of the relics of Peter and Paul ad catacumbas, (that
> is, to the site of the later basilica of San Sebastiano) took
> place on June 29, 258. He defends his opinion that what
> took place in the year 258 was only the inception of a
> memorial festival in honor of the two Apostles. This
> solution satisfies the wording of the Martyrologium Hiero-
> nymianum.
>
> The origin of a translation is implicitly excluded by
> the assumption that the 29th of June is the *dies natalis*
> of the Apostles. It cannot be denied that the verb *habitare*
> is found in the epigraphic terminology in the meaning
> 'to be buried.' While it is, to be sure, not impossible to
> interpret 'habitasse' in its primary meaning *to dwell* of a
> living person, the author rejects Wilpert's use of the graf-
> fito *Domus Petri* in one of the excavated chambers.

370 LAST, H., "St. Peter the Excavations under his Basilica in
Rome and the Beginnings of Western Christendom."

> See no. 682.

371 LAST, H., *Journal of Roman Studies*, 44 (1954), 112-116.

> See no. 683.

372 LECLERCQ, H., "Saint Pierre."

> See no. 686.
>
> The phrase *hic habitasse sanctos* by Damasus strikes him as being legendary. He explains the legend as having arisen from the later habitual combination of the two Apostles as a pair—"a binomial like Castor and Pollux." He theorizes that Peter might have dwelled ad Catacumbas, while Paul was added later by legend. He also sees in the verses that follow a coloring of the antagonism which divided Rome and the East in the time of Damasus and which came to a climax in 381.
>
> Further, if the translation of the bodies (presuming there was one) had taken place after Constantine, such a great event would certainly have left some trace in the records of time. From this he draws the conclusion:
>
> Even if there was a translation ad catacumbas (either in 64 or 258)—it makes no difference—the bodies in any case "remained ad catacumbas for a very brief time—one or two years." It has to be admitted, therefore, that the refrigeria were held ad catacumbas *absente cadavere*, and so as mere commemorative meals in honor of the Apostles, contrary to the usual meaning of the term.

373 LEOPOLD, H., "Le memorie apostoliche in Roma e i recenti scavi di S. Sebastiano" — *Bilyenis*, Sept. 30, 1916, 172 ff.

> The ever-vexing problem with its various solutions prompted the author to seek for some satisfactory explanation. In the general framework of the findings and questions newly aroused by other scholars he endeavors a further analysis. He treats the subject as follows:
> a) The origin of the basilica later called the church of San Sebastiano.
> b) The origin and purpose of the 'platonia.'
> c) The so-called 'Domus Petri.'
> d) The triclia or dining-room.
> e) The stratum of the classic remains of the villa etc.

f) The tradition with regard to the hiding of the bodies of Peter and Paul 'ad catacumbas.'

He concludes that the triclia was a wayside tavern which the Christians used because of some vague traditional assiciation of the site with the Apostles. There is no question here (the Memoria Apostolorum) of a place of burial, but of an actual dwelling, the house in which the Apostles lived during their life-time. The graffito *Domus Petri* discovered in 1912 in one of the old side chapels of the basilica is commonly used to support this theory.

374 LIETZMANN, H., *Petrus und Paulus in Rom. Liturgische und archaeologische Studien.*

See no. 177.

375 LIETZMANN, H., "The Tomb of the Apostles ad Catacumbas" — *Harvard Theological Review*, 16 (1923), 147-162 with 2 plates.

In the first part of this study the author answers the objections raised by G. La Piana (*Harvard Theological Review*, 14 (1921), 53-94, see no. 369) against the theory proposed with regard to the ancient tradition connected with the church of San Sebastiano in Rome and the Apostles. As in his original work—*Petrus and Paulus in Rom* (1915), the author again defends his opinion that a translation of the relics of Peter and Paul to the catacombs took place on June 29, 258. In reply to La Piana's query as to why he assumes a translation which Philocalus does not mention and against which many arguments can be used, Lietzmann replies:

1. Because of the testimony of Damasus.
2. Because of the archeological facts.
3. Because of the general principle that in antiquity, church festivals were not instituted by an arbitrary decree, but arose out of some tangible liturgical act, which in this case is most easily conceived as a translation.

He then takes up the interpretation of the epigraphic terminology in Damasus' verse and in parallel texts to show that Damasus intended to express the idea "buried here." Another one of the decisive arguments that favors the theory of a translation in 258 is the "meals for the dead" that presupposes in theory the presence of the relics of the martyrs venerated. The author finally turns to the examination of the archeological facts wherein he includes a brief history of the site with obvious points favoring his theory.

His conclusion is that while we are still far from having the positive proof of a translation, yet he believes that the recent excavations have increased the probability of his view.

376 LUGARI, G. B., "I varii seppellimenti degli apostoli Pietro e Paulo sull'Appia, confirmati e chiariti dagl'ultimi scavi" — Bess, 2 (1897), 317-330.

According to tradition the bodies of the two Apostles were laid here on two occasions: in the first century and again in the third. The latest excavations (at that time) give full support to the ancient tradition. In this study the author examines the literary and archeological evidence which (he feels) confirms the fact that there were two temporary translations of the bodies of the Apostles to this place.

377 MACKENDRICK, P., "Caesar and Christ."

See no. 699.

378 MANCINI, M., "Scavi sotto la Basilica di S. Sebastiano sull'Appia antica" — *Notizie degli Scavi, ser. II*, 20 (1923), 3-79, plates I-XVI, 25 figs. in text.

This is the main report of the Italian Government excavations conducted by our author and Fornari. Here Mancini speaks of the first beginnings of the excavations, its discoveries at that time and those that followed. There is a very detailed description of the Basilica Apostolorum wherein he deals with the following:
1. The tombs that were discovered.
2. The columbaria.
2. The constructions annexed to the place of the ancient tombs: the atrium and triclia.
4. The graves.

5. A resume and conclusions.

The author says that if the Apostles had really been deposited here in 258 and removed at the end of the third or beginning of the fourth century, some trace would have remained considering that the basilica was constructed only a few years later.

379 MANCINI, M., *Diss. della Pont. accad. rom. di arch., 2 ser.*, 14 (1920), 302.

We have here a communication w·th regard to the results of the excavations at San Sebastiano. The author gives a brief history of the explorations by De Waal and Styger and the important results of their most recent campaigns. He speaks of further discoveries: three sepulchres, that of M. Clodius Hermes, that of the Inno- centes, and a third unnamed. All the testimony points to the fact that there was a Memoria Apostolorum in this place where the bodies of the Apostles were temporarily buried (in 258 A.D.) during the Valerianic persecutions.

380 MANCINI, M., "La depositio dei SS. Pietro e Paolo ad Cata- cumbas" — *Atti del I Congresso nazionale di studi romani*, 1929, 195-201.

This brief study deals with the date of the deposition of the Apostles ad catacumbas. The author gives a brief survey of the excavational findings up to that time and he analyzes the interpretation of the *Depositio Martyrum* and the *Liber Pontificalis* (life of Cornelius) in an endeavor to find the possible time when the Apostles might have been buried here.

381 MANCINI, G., & PESCI, B., "San Sebastiano fuori le mura" — *Le Chiesa di Roma Illustrata* 48 (Roma: Marietti, 1959), 80 pp., 12 plates, 1 plan.

This is an excellent brochure recommended for those who do not wish to become involved in details. It contains a historical reconstruction of San Sebastiano with descrip- tive remarks (and illustrations) of the various aspects of the basilica and sepulchral discoveries.

An earlier edition of the same work by G. Mancini was published in 1928.

382 MARICHAL, R., "I graffiti della triclia in Catacumbas" — RAC, 29 (1953), 91.

Mention is made here of the report of Oct. 2, 1952 concerning R. Marichal's examination of the graffiti of the triclia ad catacumbas and the new reading of the Celerinus text. Marichal concludes that the greater part of the graffiti are anterior to the peace of the Church. This same idea is found in the following study.

383 MARICHAL, R., "La date des 'graffiti' de la basilique de Saint-Sébastien à Rome" — *Comptes rendus Académie des Inscriptions et Belles-Lettres*, 1953, 60-68.

A proposed new reading of one of the graffiti from the walls of the triclia. The author maintains that a consular date of Aug. 9, 260 may be found among these graffiti, and this seems to confirm an interpretation that San Sebastiano had been a center of devotion about 258, if the reading is accepted.

384 MARICHAL, R., "La date des graffiti de la basilique de Saint-Sébastien à Rome" — NC, 5 (1953), 119-120.

This brief study speaks of the date of the graffiti scrawled on the walls of the triclia discovered beneath the basilica of San Sebastiano. The author thinks they cannot be dated before 244 or after 356. He concludes that the date 258 marks the beginning of the cult of the Apostles ad catacumbas which is confirmed by the graffito of Celerinus. The paleography of all the graffiti indicates that they are before the fourth century. Therefore, the triclia would have ceased to be well-frequented before the new basilica made access to it impossible.

385 MARUCCHI, O., "Osservazioni intorno al cimitero delle Catacombe" — RQ, 6 (1892), 275-309.

An inquiry by one of the very early experts into the tradition which relates the burial of the Apostles with this place. The author makes the following observations:

a) A preliminary survey wherein he speaks of the Philocalian calendar.
b) The Apostolic sepulchre of the catacombs in which he
   includes documentary testimony. He concludes that
   the examination of all the documents in the light of the
   excavations proves beyond doubt the veracity of the
   fact, that is, that in this place the bodies of the Apostles
   were temporarily buried.

386 MARUCCHI, O., "Scavi nella Platonia" — *Notizie degli scavi*,
    1892, 90 ff.

387 MARUCCHI, O., "Scoperta di un graffito presso le catacombe
    di S. Sebastiano" — *Nuovo Bollettino di Archeologia Cristiana*,
    15 (1909), 218-219.

> A reference is found here to the inscription DOMUS
> PETRI mentioned by Colagrossi. The author's opinion is
> that it is not anterior to the beginning of the fifth century
> or perhaps the end of the fourth. According to him, this
> would seem to indicate that a devout visitor traced this
> on the wall to express a broad interpretation of the phrase
> in the Damasian inscription: "hic habitasse prius sanctos,"
> etc.

388 MARUCCHI, O., "Nuovo osservazioni sulla questione teste
    ridestata della Memoria di S. Pietro nella regione Salario-
    Nomentana" — *Nuovo Bollettino di Archeologia Cristiana*, 22
    (1916), 159-191; 238-240, plates I-IV.

> In dealing with the question raised by the evidence of
> a Memoria to St. Peter in the Salaria-Nomentana region
> the author treats of the following:
> a) A detailed history of the present controversy.
> b) A critical examination of the question by considering
>   the prejudicial questions and documents.
> c) The cathedra in the Major cemetery of St. Agnes on the
>   via Nomentana cannot refer in any way to the memoria
>   of the cathedra of St. Peter.
> In the second section of the study the author takes up
> the excavational findings beneath the basilica of San
> Sebastiano.

An interesting development is to be seen in the following works of O. Marucchi, all of which have been based on the excavational campaigns beneath the Memoria Apostolorum. They were interrupted in 1916, resumed in 1917, and again in 1919 with important results.

In the light of the new data Marucchi thinks the question is finally solved, viz., that the translation of the Apostles ad catacumbas in 258 or even earlier is an established historical fact.

389 MARUCCHI, O., "Le recenti scoperte presso la basilica di S. Sebastiano" — *Nuovo Bollettino di Archeologia Cristiana*, 22 (1916), 1-61, plates I-V.

This study contains the following sections:
1) The state of the question regarding the studies made on the Memoria before the most recent excavations.
2) The discovery of some important graffiti. They confirm the existence of a sepulchral memorial to the Apostles. Certain observations are made with regard to a translation.
3) Even before the discovery of the historical graffiti one must continue to acknowledge a commemorative monument to the Apostles in the platonia. It must also be admitted that the sepulchre of St. Quirinus is in this same room.
4) Particulars regarding the position of St. Quirinus' grave.
5) An illustration of the historical graffito which commemorates the translation of St. Quirinus' body from Rome.

The author concludes that the ancient tradition is confirmed. There was no mere undetermined or vague memoria here—actually there was a translation of relics.

390 MARUCCHI, O., "Ulteriore studio sulle recenti scoperte nelle catacombe di S. Sebastiano" — *Nuovo Bollettino di Archeologia Cristiana*, 23 (1917), 47-87, plates II-VII.

Basing himself on the excavational findings in the catacomb of San Sebastiano the author presents the following study wherein he treats of:

1) The historical question of a sepulchre or a dwelling place of the Apostles.
2) The commemorative monument of the Apostles in the catacombs.
3) The date of the construction of the Basilica Apostolorum.

391 MARUCCHI, O., "Alcune osservazioni sui recenti scavi nella basilica di S. Sebastiano sulla via Appia" — *Diss. della Pont. accad. rom. di arch.*, *2 ser.*, 13 (1918), 265-271.

In this communication (April 29, 1916) in view of Styger's and De Waal's discoveries, the author takes up the subject of the Memoria Apostolica and endeavors to show how the discovery of the graffiti invoking the Apostles affords important confirmation to the ancient tradition. However, he suspends judgment on one point, namely, whether such a memoria is to be seen in the center of the basilica. He then takes up the subject of the graffiti found in the triclia and speaks briefly of the platonia (behind the apse of the basilica).

392 MARUCCHI, O., "La Memoria apostolica degli Apostoli sulla via Appia" — *Diss. della Pont. accad. rom. di arch.*, *2 ser.*, 14 (1920), 249-260.

The author's scope in this study is to make certain observations about the famous "Memoria" by demonstrating that it was in reality a sepulchral Memoria (as was always believed) and not a place where the Apostles were supposed to have resided during their lifetime (as some have attempted to claim). He then takes up the opinions already developed by others. After an analysis of the literary testimony—the Feriale of the fourth century and the Damasian inscription—he concludes that this important tradition was substantially admitted officially in the Roman Church up until the first half of the fourth century when, that is, the events and memories of those first centuries were still very much alive.

393 MARUCCHI, O., "La Memoria sepolcrale degli Apostoli sulla via Appia secondo il risultato delle ultime ricerche" — *Nuovo Bollettino di Archeologia Cristiana*, 26 (1920), 5-31, plates I-IV.

This is the first in a series of three studies by the author which appear in this periodical in successive years. Here he gives an analysis of the following:

1) A general survey of the excavations.
2) The discovery of the venerated platonia beneath the left nave of the basilica and its importance.
3) The latest observations on the form of the monument called the platonia.

Among his observations the author gives an ingenious suggestion with regard to a flight of steps on the south side of the court which lead to a depth of four meters below the level of the valley into a horizontal passage leading to an old well. At a certain point the wall of the passage is entirely covered with stucco on which are graffiti with invocations of the Apostles. At this point the author thinks the passage was closed by a cross-wall, and in the time of Nero the bodies of the Apostles were temporarily concealed here.

394 MARUCCHI, O., "L'ipogei con i graffiti degli Apostoli Pietro e Paolo scoperto sotto la Basilica di San Sebastiano" — *Nuovo Bollettino di Archeologia Christiana*, 27 (1921), 3-14; 112-117, plates I-VI.

In this second study the author gives a descriptive analysis of the graffiti which testify to the celebration of the refrigerium.

395 MARUCCHI, O., "Gli ultimi scavi nella Basilica S. Sebastiano e la Memoria Sepolcrale degli Apostoli Pietro e Paolo" — *Nuovo Bollettino di Archeologia Cristiana*, 28 (1922), 3-26, plates I-III.

This is the conclusion in the three series of articles by the author. On the basis of the archeological findings he deals with the following points:

1) The original graves of the Apostles were at the Vatican and the via Ostia respectively. Their deposition on the via Appia took place later.
2) The determination of the place for their sepulchral memoria on the via Appia and the conclusions reached after the excavations of 1922.

3) Particulars regarding the hypogaeum of the graffiti. The refrigerium was celebrated there.

4) The abandonment of the hypogaeum of the graffiti and the honorary momument to the Apostles in the so-called platonia. The inscription of the martyr Quirinus and the latest writings by De Rossi on the subject.

396 MARUCCHI, O., "Di un' iscrizione storica che puo attribuirsi alla Basilica Apostolica sulla via Appia" — *Nuovo Bollettino di Archeologia Cristiana*, 27 (1921), 61-69.

Here the author treats of the famous inscription of Damasus—"Hic habitasse"—which he analyzes and compares with that of another (found in the Basilica of John and Paul) to show the relationship and concept of both epigrams.

397 MARUCCHI, O., "Scavi ed ulteriori esplorazioni sotto la Basilica di S. Sebastiano" — *Nuovo Bollettino di Archeologia Cristiana*, 27 (1921), 112-117.

The author gives a brief study of several inscriptions that came to light in the excavations at San Sebastiano.

398 MARUCCHI, O., "Note sulle memoria cristiana esplorate nelle scavi di S. Sebastiano" — *Notizie degli scavi*, ser. II, 20 (1923), 80-103, plates XVII-XVIII.

This is a report on the excavations adjacent to the church which were conducted by the Pontificia Commissione di archeologia in conjunction with the Government. The author first evaluates the documents which deal with the tradition of a Memoria Apostolica on the via Appia, and in this framework he endeavors to broaden the testimony in great detail by an appraisal of the discoveries that came to light.

399 MARUCCHI, O., "Cimitero di S. Sebastiano "ad catacumbas" — *La Catacombe Romane*, (posthumous ed by E. Josi, Roma: La Liberaria dello Stato, 1932), 251-281.

The author discusses the historical monument of the Apostles at San Sebastiano ad catacumbas. The testimony of the Apocryphal Acts, the Philocalian Calendar, St.

Damasus and St. Gregory, confirm the tradition that
Peter and Paul were buried here for a short time. The
circumstances, however, are obscure. Some (Baronius,
Pagi, Papebrocj, Bianchini, Borgia, Duschesne) are of
the opinion that there was only one translation. Others
(Panvinio, Vignoli, Marangoni, Marchi, Lugari) admit of
two. The author feels that the first opinion is more probable. The remainder of the essay deals with a description
of the excavational findings.

400 MARUCCHI, O., *Pietro e Paolo a Roma.*

See no. 188.

401 MAURICE-DENIS, N., & BOULET, R., "A propos des
fouilles de Saint-Pierre. Questions liturgiques et historiques."

See no. 708.

402 MOHLBERG, L. K., "Petri ad Catacumbas. Una parola per
la soluzione del problema della considdetta "Memoria Apostolorum" alla via Appia" — *Atti della Pont. accad. rom. di
arch., 3 ser., Rendiconti,* 15 (1939), 16.

This is a communication delivered to the meeting of
May 25, 1939.
Concerning the tradition that associates Peter with
San Sebastiano ad catacumbas the author proposes a new
hypothesis as to the origin of the Memoria Apostolica on
the via Appia. He examines the documents that contain
references to the Memoria. He points out that the *Depositio Martyrum* and the *Depositio Episcoporum* contained
in the so-called *Chronograph* of 354 do not represent the
Feriale Romanae Ecclesiae and do not have any official
character. In fact, by combining the data of both Dpeo-
sitiones, a list of the Roman bishops is obtained that
begins with Hipollytus-Callistus without any mention of
Pope Cornelius, the foe of the Novations. Furthermore,
there isn't even an indication of a commemoration of the
feast of Peter at the Vatican where his body reposed from
the beginning of the third century. Other elements seem
to indicate that the document was edited by Novatianist
sympathizers. Further proof of his hypothesis is that the

sanctuary on the via Appia originated immediately after
326 (the year after the Council of Nicea) when the Novatians were granted terrenial concessions, churches and
other privileges. It was only at the beginning of the fifth
century that the sanctuary began to decline when the
Novatians were opposed by Innocent I. The graffiti in
the triclia beneath the church have no connection with
the feast of June 29, but rather with that of February
22, the feast of the Cathedra, which seems to have been
substituted for the pagan feast commemorating the memory of the dead.

403 MOHLBERG, L. K., "Historisch-kritische Bemerkungen zum
Ursprung der sogenannten "Memoria Apostolorum" an der
Appischen Strasse" — *Colligere fragmenta. Festschrift Alban
Dold*, Beuron, 1952, 52-74.

The author suggests that the late third and early fourth
century so-called *Memoria* of the two Apostles and the
Basilica Apostolorum which was built over this shrine later
on did not belong to the Catholic Church in Rome, but
to the Novatianists, whose founder Novatian, was an
anti-pope and who led his followers into schism. He
further maintains that the building in which the graffiti
were discovered was not a true *Memoria*. There has been
no evidence to prove that it was either a tomb, a reliquary
of the Apostles, the place where they were martyred, or
even the site of property which they personally might
have owned.

It was merely a cult-center which might have been
initiated by the Novatianists some time after 251 to
counteract the Catholic cult of Peter and Paul on the
Vatican hill and via Ostia respectively. The date 258
recorded in the calendar might refer to the inauguration
of the cult on the via Appia, although the triclia might
have been built only several decades later.

The *Depositio Martyrum* and the *Depositio Episcoporum*
omit the name of Pope Cornelius. This would indicate that
they were edited by Novatianists. With regard to the
Basilica Apostolorum, it was built at a time when the
Novatianists (who accepted the decrees of the Council

of Nicea) were not yet regarded as formal heretics and were allowed to possess churches and other property.

It was only in the early fifth century—under Innocent I and Celestine I—that the Novatianist schism was finally suppressed.

It was at that time that the schismatic cult of the Apostles on the via Appia was followed by that of the martyr St. Sebastian.

404 MOHLBERG, L. K., "Osservazioni storico-antiche sull'iscrizione tombale di Novaziono" — EL, 51 (1957), 242-249.

In this study the author deals with the problem of the tomb of Novatian discovered on the via Tiburtina— a possible solution to the problem of the *Memoria Apostolorum* on the via Appia.

A reference is first made to the discovery of the tomb of Novatian on April 1, 1932. Could this have been the martyr? Archeologists are not in agreement. After a cursory survey of the various hypotheses of the experts he takes up a critical examination of the documentary sources relative to Novatian.

The conclusions are:

1) Novatian was exiled before 258.
2) He died in exile and hence was considered a martyr. In this wise he was also reconciled with the Church.
3) Toward the end of the third century, about 266 or after 270, his relics were transferred to the catacombs on the via Tiburtina.
4) After the peace of the Church—between 326 and 354, Leo who acquired the area above the catacombs erected a small basilica in honor of Novatian.
5) The relics were transferred from the catacombs to the new basilica.
6) In 389 a campaign was inaugurated against the Novatian Leo and the Novatianists.
7) Under Innocent I and Celestine I the Novatianists were despoiled of their goods and the basilica of Novatian was consecrated by Pope Simplicius to eradicate the memory of Novatian.

The author concludes by saying that both the Novatian

inscription and tomb (discovered on the via Tiburtina) can be of important assistance in solving the problem of the Memoria Apostolorum in Catacumbas.

405 MOHRMANN, C., "A propos de deux mots controverses de la latinité chrétienne, "tropeaum-nomen."

See no. 717.

406 MURPHY, F. X., "Saints Peter and Paul" — *The American Ecclesiastical Review*, 140 (1959), 27-31.

In this brief study the author gives a rather general idea of the significance of the Vatican archeological discoveries for settling the problem connected with the celebration of a feast of the Apostles at San Sebastiano on the via Appia.

407 NEWBOLD, W. R., "Five transliterated Aramaic inscriptions" — AJA, 30 (1926), 295-329.

The author discusses three inscriptions found beneath the church of San Sebastiano in Rome during the excavations made there since 1915. He feels that these inscriptions would read more intelligibly if they were read in Aramaic. The one inscription implies beliefs as to the experiences of the soul after death which at that time were widely held by Christians and non-Christians. The other is concerned with Damasus' inscription (the main topic of this study) which is confirmed by the traditions preserved in the apocryphal martyrdoms, in Gregory of Tours and Panvinio, and by the archeological evidence unearthed by Styger and Mancini.

After a thorough analysis of these three inscriptions he concludes that they prove that the relics of the Apostles once rested at San Sebastiano, and they also prove that the "legend of the oriental thieves" is true. Such arhceological evidence is a cardinal contribution to history.

408 NORTH, R., "Domus Petri, Domus Domini, Domus Patris" — *Biblica*, 36 (1955), 156-157.

A reference is made here to the well-known inscription "Domus Petri" discovered in a private sepulchre in the

catacombs of San Sebastiano and which has been the
object of much discussion. The question had often been
asked whether the allusion confirms the apparent meaning
in the Damasian epigram that the Apostles once "lived"
here, or is this "domum" to be taken metaphorically—an
eternal dwelling or a temporary grave? The author gives
Guarducci's interpretation, i.e., Ecclesia Petri est ecclesia
Christi et regnum Dei.

409 PACINI, G., *La Basilica degli Apostoli sulla via Appia*, (Roma:
Tipo-Litografico. V. Ferri, 1951), 34 pp., 16 figs.

In this monograph the author deals with the history
of the basilica in the light of recent excavations. He
speaks of the literary testimony relating to the site and
includes the various works written by expert authors.
There follows a summary of the excavational findings:
a) Beneath the central and side naves.
b) The mausolea A, B, E, F, G, H, I, L, M, N, O, P, Q.

410 PARIBENI, R., "Le tombe degli Apostoli Pietro e Paulo in
Roma e i recenti scavi."

See no. 745.

411 PARROT, A., "Le "refrigerium" dans l'au-dèla" — *Revue de
l'Histoire des Religions*, 114 (1936), 69-92; 158-196. 115 (1937),
53-89.

This is a detailed examination of the uses of the term
refrigerium.

412 PESCI, B., "La cripta del martire S. Sebastiano ad Catacumbas" — BAC, 8(1938), 2 ff.

413 PESCI, B., "Un atto notarile del 29 Marzo 1672 relativo all'altare di San Sebastiano nelle chiese omonima della via Appia"
— *Antonianum*, 15 (1940), 125-154.

An interesting study of a discovery made of a document
relative to the basilica of San Sebastiano which was published for the first time in 1920 by Achille Ratti (later
Pius XI). It was a copy of the inventory of the basilica
and its annexed monastery. The original up to this period

of writing had not been discovered. It was inserted in the cod. Vat.-Barber.-Lat. 1572. This document throws light on the subject of the Honorian altar of San Sebastiano and at the same time it allows one to follow with precision the ultimate phase or arrangement of the place of cult reserved to the martyrs in the basilica on the via Appia. Of extreme importance is the reference made in the text to the fact that the bodies of Peter and Paul were placed beneath the basilica after they were stolen by the Greeks. The text is quite lengthy but of extreme interest for the history of the basilica and its traditions.

414 PRANDI, A., *La Memoria Apostolorum in Catacumbas. Libro 1° Illustrazione del rilievo e studio architettonico del complesso monumentale.* (Roma sotterranea cristiana, vol. II) Vatican City, Pontifical Institute of Christian Archeology, 1936, xvi-62 pp., 23 figs., 11 plates.

From 1914 on archeologists began to interest themselves in the Memoria of the Apostles Peter and Paul which had then been discovered beneath the sanctuary of San Sebastiano. Later excavations revealed some outstanding findings. This is a detailed technical study of the monumental complex. The author deals exclusively with all the details of the ruins which he studied and examines the architectural and chronological rapport that these parts might have between themselves.

However, despite all this, no definite solution is reached on the question. The plans and illustrations which the author gives us are very clear and very minute. The work will continue to be useful in subsequent research.

415 PRANDI, A., "Sulla ricostruzione della Mensa Martyrum nella Memoria Apostolorum in Catacumbas" — *Rendiconti della Pontificia Accademia Romana di Archeologia*, 19 (1944), 345-353 with 7 figs.

This study was inspired by Josi's announcement on Jan. 16, 1936 of a very important discovery in the ruins of the Memoria Apostolorum ad catacumbas, viz., a "mensa martyrum." Its function in the complex and relationship with the rite of the refrigerium was evaluated.

In this we see consequential evidence regarding the
traditional view that the Apostles were here at Catacumbas
—if only temporarily. The author reconstructs the unique
form of the *mensa* and endeavors to see if some rapport
could be established with other testimony.

416 PROFUMO, A., "La Memoria monumentale in Catacumbas
degli Apostoli Pietro e Paolo" — *Studi Romani*, 2 (1914),
415 ff.

417 PROFUMO, A., "La Memoria di San Pietro nella regione
Salaro-Nomentana" — RQ, (supplem) 31 (1916).

418 QUENTIN, H., "Tusco et Basso consulibus" — *Rendiconti
della pontificia Accademia Romana di Archeologia*, 5 (1927), 145-
147.

This study treats of the liturgical source—the Depositio
Martyrum—in which we find the famous text (June 29):
III Kal. Jul. Petri in catacumbas et Pauli Ostense, Tusco
et Basso consulibus.
The author endeavors to prove that the consular date
does not refer to the Apostles. He traces the mention of
the two consuls back to a copyist's error.

419 RATTI, A., (Pius XI) "Di un documento relativo alla basilica
di San Sebastiano in Roma" — *Diss. della Pont. accad.
rom. di arch.*, 2 ser., 14 (1920), 139-146.

This is an important addition to the evidence collected
by Styger in "Gli Apostoli Pietro et Paolo, etc." (Römische
Quartalschrift, 29 (1915), 149-205; cf. also *Diss. della
Pont. accad. rom. di arch.*, 2 ser., 13 (1918), 3-112) which
deals with the history of the local tradition in great detail.
Grisar also dealt with a document in 1895 (Römische
Quartalschrift, 9 (1895), 409-461) which consisted of a
privilege granted by Leo X to the church of San Sebastiano. Grossi-Gondi (La Civiltà Cattolica, 69, 1 (1918),
340 ff.) speaks of a document which enlightens us on the
vicissitudes of the altar of San Sebastiano consecrated by
Honorius III in the crypt of the martyr. According to our
author, the relationship between the document treated
by Grisar and this at hand leads him to believe that we

are dealing here with two things—which have come by
different ways—but derived from the same source. Both
documents precede and reflect the state of the Basilica
of San Sebastiano before its reconstruction in 1612. The
document is found in the cod. Vat.—Barber.—Lat. 1572,
ff. 288-297, in which, among the many other interesting
items it contains, speaks of the bodies of Peter and Paul
being buried beneath the basilica after they were stolen
by the Greeks.

420 RIMOLDI, A., "L'Apostolo San Pietro."

> See no. 217.

421 RUYSSCHAERT, J., "La tradition romaine des tombes
apostoliques et Eusèbe de Césarée."

> See no. **775.**

422 RUYSSCHAERT, J., "Vaticano: III. Autenticità della tomba
di S. Pietro."

> See no. 777.

423 RUYSSCHAERT, J., "Les documents littéraires de la double
tradition romaine des tombes apostoliques" — RHE, 52
(1957), 791-837.

> This is a study of the literary sources pertaining to the
> theories of a translation of the relics of the Apostles. The
> author rejects the modern hypothesis that speaks of a
> translation in the third century. According to him the
> relics were never moved from the original tombs at the
> Vatican and via Ostia, but that the worship of the Apostles
> was conducted at the via Appia, at a period when the
> tombs did not offer the same facilities for the liturgy.
> After the completion of the Constantinian basilicas it was
> natural that the cult-centers should focus on the tombs,
> embellished as they then were with the magnificent tombs.
>
> In explaining the cult without having recourse to a
> translation-theory he observes that in the first place the
> Philocalian Calendar, in addition to Christmas and the
> feast of the Cathedra Petri, contains three feasts of non-
> Roman martyrs. In other words, the Roman Church was

already celebrating the cult of martyrs whose relics were not in the city. Therefore, it is possible to admit the cult at the via Appia did not demand the presence of the relics of the Apostles. The idea of a temporary deposition ad catacumbas arose from a misunderstanding of the Damasian inscription. On the principles of textual criticism, the author shows that it should be read not as *hic habitasse* but as *hic habitare*. The word *prius* should, moreover, refer not to *habitare* but to *requiris*. These corrections provide a reading of the text indicating that their present memory lives on: "Before you seek the fame (nomina) of Peter and Paul, you should know that the Saints live on here" (i.e. the memory of the people and in the continuance of their liturgical cult). The possibility of a partial translation, e.g. the skulls, is not ruled out by the author. But this remains no more than a hypothesis.

424 SCHÄFER, E., "Das Petrusgrab und die neuen Grabungen unter St. Peter in Rom."

See no. 783.

425 SCHÄFER, E., "Die Bedeutung der Epigramme des Papstes Damasus I. für die Geschichte der Heiligenverehrung" — EL, 46 (1932), 154-163.

In this study of the significance of the Damasian inscriptions for the history of the veneration of the Saints, the author examines the well-known *hic habitasse* epigram of Pope Damasus. He examines this and other literary testimony that form the basis for the tradition that associates the Apostles Peter and Paul with San Sebastiano on the via Appia. He includes the archeological findings and the various hypotheses that attempt to explain the tradition.

426 SCHNEIDER, A. M., "Die Memoria Apostolorum an der via Appia" — (= *Nachrichten der Akademie der Wissenschaften in Göttingen. Philologisch-Historische Klasse*, 1951, 3), 15 pp.

A comparatively recent study of special importance on the ever-recurring problem of San Sebastiano ad catacumbas, and the theories proposed in its regard. The author sees a translation-theory as improbable. The mysterious entry into the *Calendar* under the year 258, "III Kal. Jul. Petri ad Catacumbas" might well refer to the inception of a Novatianist cult of the Apostles on the via Appia site at that date, although the triclia itself may have been built several decades later. A tradition that the Apostles had at one time lived and/or been temporarily buried on the via Appia site might account for a Novatianist choice of it for the setting of Pope Damasus' inscription in the vicinity. It is indeed possible that the Catholic Church took over the cult-center on the via Appia long before the final suppression of the Novatianists — perhaps as early as the beginning of the fourth century and that the Basilica Apostolorum itself was of Catholic origin.

427 SCHUSTER, Card. I., "Domus Petri" — Ambrosius, 14 (1938), 157-163.

428 SCIVOLETTO, N., "Pietro e Paolo nel quartiere ebraico dell'- Appia" — *Giornale italiano di filologia*, 13 (1960), 1-24.

429 SEPPELT, F. X., "Das Petrusgrab."

See no. 288.

430 SHEEN, F. J., "Ad Catacumbas" — *This Is Rome*, (New York: Hawthorne Books, 1960, Image ed.), 85-90.

We have here an interesting account—written in a popular style—in which the author reconstructs the history of the early excavations at San Sebastiano and the tradition associating the grave of the Apostles Peter and Paul at this place.

431 SIGRIST, F. A., *Petrus der erste Papst.*

See no. 232.

432 STERN, H., "Le calendrier de 354. Étude sur son texte et ses illustrations" — (= *Institut français d'archéologie de Beyrouth. Bibliothèque archéologique et historique 45*), Paris, 1953.

A monograph on the Philocalian calendar with its literary history and iconographical questions. The text presents some riddles. Is there a reference here to the tombs of Peter and Paul ad Catacumbas, or only a cult? (There is an obvious connection between cult and place of burial).

433 STEVENSON, E., "Studi intorno all a basilica di S. Sebastiano ed alla Platonia" — *Diss. della Pont. accad. rom. di arch.*, *2 ser.*, 5 (1894), 367.

A reference is made of a communication on the architectural observations which are of great value for establishing the chronology of the sanctuary.

434 STYGER, P., "Scavi a S. Sebastiano" — RQ, 29 (1915), 73-110, plates I-IV.

This is a preliminary report on the results of the author's excavations. Among the many finds beneath San Sebastiano on the via Appia are the graffiti scratched on the walls of the pergula which have a direct connection with the main controversy regarding the temporary transferal of the bodies of the Apostles to this place. The author undertakes the very difficult and heavy task of describing and translating them one by one. There are hundreds of them nearly all pointing to the same fact that at this precise spot of the *Queen of roads* there was something which reminded the faithful and pilgrims of the presence, or life, or passion or burial of Peter and Paul in Rome. This was the *Memoria Apostolorum* which throughout the Middle Ages was believed to be under the floor of the church. In the thirteenth century a rival tradition appeared which placed it in the so-called 'platonia'—a large, partly subterranean chamber situated outside the apse of the church, and in the seventeenth century this later tradition completely displaced the older one.

The study has the following sections:
1) A summary of the earlier excavations.
2) The graffiti.
3) The period of the 'formae' graves.
4) A list of seals in the formae.
5) The discovery of St. Fabian's body.

6) The ancient means of communication between the crypt of St. Sebastian and the basilica.

7) The discovery of an ancient Roman villa behind the basilica.

435 STYGER, P., "Gli Apostoli Pietro e Paolo ad Catacumbas sull'Appia" — RQ, 29 (1915), 149-205.

The excavations undertaken thus far have furnished the first monumental proof of the temporary deposition of the bodies of Peter and Paul here ad catacumbas. The author undertakes a new examination of all the traditional sources alluding to the Apostles' death and burial in Rome and the history of the local tradition. In his reconstruction he considers the following:

1) The Memoria of Sts. Peter and Paul. (the monument)
2) The Sepulchral Memoriae.
3) The banquets of the faithful at the tombs of the martyrs.

With regard to the documentation pertaining to the tradition:

1) The Liber Pontificalis.
2) The Damasian inscription.
3) The Legendary accounts.
4) The Monument itself—when were the bodies placed here; when were they transported to their original graves; on what occasion?

Regarding the Memoria ad catacumbas in the Middle Ages:

1) The information gleaned from the Acts of St. Sebastian and St. Quirinus.
2) The Apostolic sepulchre according to Panvinio's description and of Hugonius; the privileges and indulgences of the later guide-books.

The author concludes that throughout the Middle Ages the Memoria Apostolorum was believed to be under the floor of the church where the bodies of the Apostles were buried.

436 STYGER, P., "Il Monumento apostolico dell'Appia" — *Diss. della Pont. accad. rom. di arch.*, 2 ser., 13 (1918), 3-112, plates I-XXVI, 2 plans, 61 figs.

This is the main report of the excavations conducted by himself and Fasiolo. The latest results of the excavational work done beneath San Sebastiano down to April, 1915 are contained in this fundamental publication. It is replete with careful descriptions, abundant plans and plates. Some of the observations presented are as follows:

1) The sepulchres beneath the Basilica.
2) The construction pertaining to the *Memoria Apostolorum* and the graffiti.
3) The complexus of classical structures: the columbaria and villa.

In the framework of No. 1 (above) he considers:

a) The various pavements of the church.
b) The graves, inscriptions, sculptures, stamps on tiles, money, etc.

In No. 2 (above):

a) The triclia, graffiti and a paleographic examination of same, the courtyard.

He concludes that the burial-place of the Apostles should perhaps be sought in a room whose structure appeared on first investigation to be a rebuilt sepulchral monument originally of the first or second century. The triclia (which was explored very thoroughly as well as the graffiti) seems to indicate that they (the graffiti) might have been written during the second half of the third century and not very long before the destruction of the triclia. The word *refrigerium* could not have any other meaning than *funereal*, i.e., in the meaning that it was celebrated at the grave of Peter and Paul.

437 STYGER, P., "Katakumbas. Nach Ursprung und Sprachgebrauch" — *Schweizer Rundschau*, 21 (1921), 132-142.

Substantially the same material is contained in this study as found above (*Diss. della Pont. accad.* 13 (1918), 3-112). This also appeared in an article in the *Kölnischen Volkszeitung*, no. 525, July 13, 1921.

438 STYGER, P., "Die erste Ruhestätte der Apostelfürsten Petrus und Paulus an der via Appia in Rom" — ZkTh, 45 (1921), 543-572.

This study is a good summary of the work of later excavations at San Sebastiano. The site is described as follows:

A row of columbaria was constructed on the flat top of the cliff (last quarter of first century A.D.).

At the same time three burial chambers were cut off in the cliff. They were used as pagan burials. To the right, other structures were found. Despite all pagan characteristics, Christian features were found.

At about the time of Hadrian a villa was built above a tomb extending back as far as the row of columbaria and with its east wall extending, resting partly on the facade of tomb (32). Part of the columbaria had to be destroyed because of one of its rooms.

These rooms were not the dwelling rooms of the villa but pagan meeting-places of a sepulchral character.

In the middle of the third century the villa was destroyed. Its lower rooms and the valley were filled in, and the low rear wall of the columbaria as well as the wall of the building (17) were used to form the back of a colonnade opening toward the south-west and of an enclosed court (22) roofed over on the north side.

This court extended also over the demolished walls of the villa.

The triclia—a reconstruction by the Christians for funeral banquets. Subsequently the Basilica Apostolorum was built covering up the remains of the earlier structures. There were many surprises in the excavations as there were disappointments.

439 TAILLIEZ, F., "Notes conjointes sur un texte fameux d'Eusèbe I. La tombe de Saint Pierre. Correction au texte de H.E. II, 25."

See no. 806.

440 TESTINI, P., "Noterelle sulla "Memoria Apostolorum in catacumbas" — RAC, 30 (1954), 209-231.

The author's hypothesis is that the Apostles were originally buried here and then retransferred to their final resting places on the via Ostia and the Vatican basilica, an opinion expressed previously by many others.

441 TESTINI, P., "Le 'presunte' reliquie dell'Apostolo Pietro e la traslazione 'ad catacumbas' *Actes du Ve Congrés international d'archéologie chrétienne"* — (=Studi di antichità cristiana, 22), Vatican City, 1957, pp. 529-538.

In the light of the various theories that have been proposed to explain the cult of both Apostles 'ad catacumbas' the author holds that after their martyrdom each was buried on the Vatican hill and the via Ostia respectively. However, their relics were temporarily transferred 'ad catacumbas' in 258 and after a period of time were retransferred to their original resting places.

442 TOLOTTI, F., "Ricerche intorno alla memoria Apostolorum" — RAC, 22 (1946), 7-62, 5 plates; 23-24 (1947-1958), 13-116, 12 plates.

This is a study on the latest excavations beneath San Sebastiano ad catacumbas. The author gives a very thorough and accurate description of the complexus. The excavations have brought to light an *arenario* which had been used as a place of sepulture and then later destroyed by the cemetery courtyard (piazzuola) which was developed above it.

He therefore distinguishes with clearness the four principle landmarks that followed in succession at the site:
1. The arenario.
2. The courtyard.
3. The Memoria.
4. The basilica.

In the second article the author discusses:
1. The praedium funerario.
2. The area and the sepulchres.
3. The staircase to the well.
4. A very ancient memoria.
5. The filling in of the courtyard.
6. The final aspects of the Memoria.

443 TOLOTTI, F., *Memorie degli Apostoli in Catacumbas: relievo critico della Basilica Apostolorum al III miglio della via Appia* (Collezione "Amici delle catacombe," 19), (Vatican City, 1953), 285 pp., 8 plates, 60 figs.

> This is a valuable and most recent large-scale contribution to the study of this baffling question. For acuteness and precision of observation, few other studies can compare with it. His description of the site is most thorough in every detail. The author deals with his subject under the following aspects:
> 1. What was believed and known about the Memoria Apostolorum ad catacumbas.
> 2. The distinction of the ruins.
> 3. The quarry and reservoir in the arenario.
> 4. The construction of the courtyard.
> 5. The Memoria in the second century.
> 6. The filling-in of the courtyard.
> 7. The final aspects of the Memoria.
> 8. The basilica and mausoleums.
> 9. Interpretation of the basilica and conclusions.
>
> The author thinks the memoria was built to commemorate the temporary burial of the Apostles ad catacumbas immediately after their martyrdom, and their burial was focused on this spot. The original choice of the site was dictated by the fact that the Apostles' residence—which they used in their lifetime, was nearby.

444 TORP, H., "The Vatican Excavations and the cult of St. Peter."

> See no. 812.

445 TOYNBEE, J. M. C., and PERKINS, J. B., *The Shrine of St. Peter and the Vatican Excavations.*

> See no. 821.

446 TOYNBEE, J. M. C., (Review of F. Tolotti's: Memorie degli Apostoli in Catacumbas, etc.), *Antiquitaries Journal*, 35 (1955), 104-106.

> According to the reviewer, the author summarizes the

problem. He states the literary sources and the theory, especially of Duchesne—who linked the date 258 with the shrine at the catacombs and concluded that it refers to the inauguration of this last-mentioned cult center, since at the time of the Valeranic persecutions in 258, the bodies of the two Apostles were removed from their graves and taken to safety to the via Appia, and they were not returned till the reign of Constantine. The purpose of the book is to offer a solution to the problem.

447 TOYNBEE, J. M. C., (A review of J. Carcopino's De Pythagore aux Apôtres), *Gnomon*, 29 (1957), 261-270.

Carcopino's work consists of the following detailed studies:
1) The Porta Maggiore of the subterranean basilica.
2) The hypogaeum of the Aurelii on the viale Manzoni.
3) The debate on San Sebastiano ad catacumbas, and a history of Christian devotion through the ages on the spot leading to the stories current in medieval times of its association with Peter and Paul. These traditions of a one-time burial are based on fact—a fact that explains the original dedication of the Church as Basilica Apostolorum. The concluding section is devoted to the Damasian inscription erected here. According to Carcopino, the relics did not arrive here till after c. 199-217 since they were on the Vatican and via Ostia when Gaius spoke of "trophies." Carcopino agrees with C. Mohrmann in interpreting these "trophies" neither as tombs nor commemorative monuments, but as *relics—bodies*.
See no. 507.

448 VON GERKAN, A., "Basso et Tusco consulibus."

See no. 847.

449 VON GERKAN, A., "Die christlichen Anlagen unter San Sebastiano" — H. Lietzmann, *Petrus und Paulus in Rom*, (2nd ed. Berlin, 1927), 248-301.

This is a report of the excavations undertaken in 1915

on the Appian way under San Sebastiano. It is an added appendix to Lietzmann's famous work.

After a careful analysis of the findings, the author challenges Lietzmann's hypothesis of a translation of the relics of Peter and Paul from their burial places to the via Appia. Even in the acceptance of such a theory he does not believe that there is any evidence whatsoever that there ever was any tomb near the triclia. He imagines the development of the cultus in the following way:

1. The triclia was constructed with no specific religious purpose whatsoever and in a neutral site.
2. After the presence of the bodes was announced (however that may have happened), the Christian pilgrimages were initiated and lasted until the Basilica was erected above.

450 VON GERKAN, A., "Petrus in Vaticano et in Catacumbas" — JAC, 5 (1962), 23-32.

This is a short summary of the present results of research on the burial-places of Peter (at the Vatican and ad catacumbas) based on the author's two previous studies. The author concludes as follows:

1. According to R. Marichal it has been proven that one acclamation in the triclia can be dated 260 A.D. The necropolis was originally pagan (from about the beginning of the second century A.D.) though we find the Christian graffito ITXΘYS (about 200 A.D.). The triclia (which originated after 250 in the course of private construction enterprise) was constructed on a higher level and its western wall was windowless.
2. There are only two indications of consular dates in the Roman-feast calendars. When particular feasts were instituted specific dates were never recorded. Von Gerkan presumes a translation to the triclia and prefers to interpret the text in the Martyrologium Hieronymianum: "from the year 258 on."
3. There is no indication of any heretical or Novatian influence here. Therefore, the translation-theory has to be accepted. Roman law at that time must have made it necessary that the translation take place in 'secrecy.'

4. The triclia was a rural tavern owned by Christians who had been entrusted with the task of secreting the relics of the Apostles. The subterranean passageway (where the relics had been deposited between the newly erected walls) served to supply the water for the triclia.

5. After 313, the place was remodeled for private religious worship, and a memoria was erected above the ground, something like the aedicula at the Vatican. However, the Pope had already planned the retranslation of the remains to their original burial-places (Vatican and the via Ostia) at that time.

6. It cannot be claimed that the Philocalian calendar of 354 is a distortion of the original text. It is very likely that St. Paul's basilica (the smaller one) had been completed and his relics had been retranslated there, while Peter's relics remained ad catacumbas because the larger basilica of St. Peter required thirty more years to complete.

7. The Basilica Apostolorum (erected above the triclia) might have been constructed before 340 since there are tombstones dating from 349-356/7. It was not constructed to house the relics but was intended as a memorial recalling the fact that the Apostles were venerated here for some seventy years.

8. The 'rm' wall and the east wall of mausoleum Q (at the Vatican) were joined just above the presumed tomb of the Apostle without any concern for the latters grave. The aedicula came later. Only the upper niche N_3 is original. Its window illuminated the clivus. The aedicula is to be dated between 185 and 200.

9. The break in the foundation of the 'rm' wall can only be explained by a translation in 258. The Christians knew where Peter's tomb was. However, since there was no visible evidence, the exact spot was unknown to them.

451 VON GERKAN, A., "Noch einmal Petrus in Vaticano et in catacumbas" — JAC, 5 (1962), 39-42.

This is a reply to T. Klauser's contribution in this discussion (see no. 362). The author's reply is as follows:

1. The area around the triclia proves that it must have been in existence in 258.
2. It was not a place for the refrigeria, nor any other type of cult.
3. The passageway is even older than the triclia. It seems, perhaps, to have been thought of as starting point for a cemetery.
4. Peter's tomb was in a pagan necropolis that developed after Nero's gardens had been abandoned. There was no actual tomb, though it was known where the place of burial was, and also, that an aedicula had been constructed above it.
5. The first translation took place in secrecy.
6. Since the triclia was constructed as a private enterprise, the cemetery was no longer in use.
7. Since one of the reasons for the Valerianic persecutions was attributed to the fact that the Christians were celebrating the deposition of their martyrs, the liturgical calendar must date back to that time. There was a new deposition to be celebrated because of the translation.
8. The architectural features of the passageway seem to indicate that a vault was there. The graffiti date after 258.
9. Peter must have been buried (and Paul also) on the spot where they died, because it was very unlikely that the Christians could have asked for his body since he was not a 'civus Romanus.' Peter was probably buried by the soldiers who executed him.
10. The only testimony we have for a two-fold burial-tradition is from the Philocalian calendar, and this does not prove anything.

452 WILPERT, J., "Domus Petri" — RQ, 26 (1912), 117-122.

The author first examines the meaning of the Damasian inscription and relates it to the graffito DOMUS PETRI. He denys a translation-theory and explains the consular date in the Chronograph in this way: since the cemetery was confiscated the commemoration of Peter and Paul could not be celebrated at their graves, therefore, it was on this day and in this year that it was celebrated at the III mile on the via Appia where it was believed that a house stood in which the Apostles lived for a time and which was replaced by a church.

453 WINTER, M. M., "Archeological and Liturgical Evidence Relative to St. Peter's Presence in Rome" — *St. Peter and the Popes*, (Baltimore, Md.: Helicon *P*ress; London: Darton, Longmann & Todd Ltd., 1960), 99-112.

In this work which has as its main objective to supply an answer to the question of the Papacy in the Roman Church, the author includes an excursus on the archeological and liturgical evidence pertaining to Peter's presence in Rome and death there.

He first examines the testimony that links Peter (and Paul) with San Sebastiano on the via Appia. After a cursory analysis of the various hypotheses he concludes: The theory of a total translation of the relics in 258 must be ruled out. "All the relevant evidence can be accounted for much more satisfactorily by the theory that the liturgy, and not the relics, was transferred to the via Appia in 258. The possibility of a partial translation, for instance the skulls of the Apostles, is not ruled out, but it remains no more than an hypothesis."

The author also presents a cursory survey of the Vatican excavations. With regard to the aedicula which came to light and the conclusion that was drawn, he accepts the sober judgement of Toynbee-Perkins:

"Although it is not certain that the monument marks the site of an earlier grave, the hypothesis that it did so explains much that is otherwise obscure; and although there is nothing to prove that this grave was that of St. Peter, nothing in the archeological evidence is inconsistent with such an identification."

454 ZEILLER, J., "Les récentes fouilles des cryptes de Saint-Pierre de Rome."

See no. 865.

455 ZEILLER, J., "A propos de l'inscription damasienne de

la catacombe de Saint-Sébastien" — BAC, 6 (1933), 272-277.

See same in *Melanges Jorga*, 1933, 803-808.

456 ZIHLER, J., "Zur Diskussion um das Petrusgrab. — Orientierung."

See no. 867.

PART THREE

THE VATICAN EXCAVATIONS

457 ALTENDORF, H. D., "Die römischen Apostelgräber" — TLZ, 84 (1959), 731-740.

This is a critique of E. Kirschbaum's famous work: "Die Gräber der Apostelfürsten" (Frankfurt, 1957; in English: "The Tombs of St. Peter and St. Paul," New York, 1959).

Basing himself on A. von Gerkan's arguments, the author criticizes the report of the excavations beneath St. Peter's basilica in Rome. He adds a number of detailed critical observations of his own. While endeavoring to undermine the established hypotheses of others, at no time does he establish any of his own. He further objects to the inexact methods used in the excavational procedure.

458 ANDREAE, B., "Archäologische Funde im Bereich von Rom, 1949-1956/57" — JDAI, 72 (1957), 207 ff.

In evaluating the archeological finds during this period the author first speaks of the excavations undertaken in the last ten years in Rome in the necropolis under the Vatican. He mentions in particular, the various scholarly publications in a number of languages: their author's and the particular aspect treated. Emphasis is given Magi's work at the time preparations were being made to build a Vatican garage (1956-57) and another necropolis came to light which was in use from the first to the third and fourth centuries. A report is also found here with regard to some of the discoveries made up to the present time beneath San Sebastiano on the via Appia (cf. pp. 225 ff.).

459 ANICHINI, G., "Le sacre Grotte Vaticane e le recenti scoperte" — BAC, 11 (1941), 49-61., 6 figs.

The discoveries in the Sacred Grottoes assume a scientific and religious significance of the highest order. In this study the author endeavors to present a complete picture, basing himself on the information supplied by the competent authority. The sensational reports of the daily journals at the time had aroused a legitimate curiosity regarding the discovery of a necropolis beneath the Vatican and Peter's tomb. He intends this information to be presented in a more reliable fashion. To this end he answers first of all what is meant by the designation "Sacred Vatican Grottoes." The designation was used since the end of the seventeenth century to specify the area which extends beneath a good part of the subterranean region beneath the central portion of the basilica. He then distinguishes between the "Grotte Antiche" and the "Grotte Nuove." He finally takes up a consideration of the first works of excavation initiated by Pius XII, and the archeological findings, scil., the necropolis, mausoleums, the decorations, epigraphs, sarcophagi.

460 ANICHINI, G., "I recenti scavi nelle Grotte Vaticane" — VP, 33 (1942), 183-188.

In this study the author assesses the excavations based on new factors: the discoveries in the Sacred Vatican Grottoes. He distinguishes between the *Grotte Nuove* and the *Grotte Vecchie*—what was originally known about them. He then speaks of the particular discoveries in the *Grotte Vecchie*, viz., the mausoleums, the sarcophagi. According to him all the archeological discoveries prove that we have evidence on the Vatican hill that in the first century—and even before—there was a pagan necropolis over which developed a Christian cemetery. Here, in its very center Pope Anacletus constructed a *memoria* or sepulchral chamber destined to conserve the relics of the Prince of the Apostles. There remains, however, the question of the via Cornelia: the excavations have not revealed any trace of it, nor can it be held that it flanked the wall of the Neronian or Gaianum circus.

461 ANICHINI, G., "Di una singolare scultura scoperta nelle Grotte Vaticane" — BAC, 12 (1942), 6-10.

The author speaks of an outstanding sarcophagus that

came to light during the excavations beneath the Vatican Grottoes which depicted two new iconographic motifs: Joseph being sold by his brothers and the coming of the Magi to adore the Christ child.

462 ANONYMOUS *Memorie Storiche delle Sacre Teste dei Santi Apostoli Pietro e Paolo e della loro solenne ricognizione nella Basilica Lateranense,* (Roma: coi tipi di Giovanni Ferretti, 1852).

This is a well-studied account with a historical reconstruction of the discovery of the famous relics of the Apostles Peter and Paul in the Lateran Basilica. An essential study for supplementing the subject of the excavations. It includes the following:
1. An appraisal of the Lateran basilica.
2. The antiquity of the cult of the heads.
3. The existence of Paul's head at Rome.
4. The cult under Boniface VIII.
5. The discovery of the heads by Urban V.
6. The heads in their new reliquaries.
7. Valuable donations made to the relics.

463 ANONYMOUS "The search for the bones of St. Peter" — *Life Magazine,* March 27, 1950, 65-78 (American edition); April 19, 1950, (International edition).

This article gives a series of excellent photographs (the majority in color) with a partial description of the tombs discovered in the Vatican excavations. Noteworthy is the picture of the mosaic on the vault of the Christian mausoleum which depicts the chariot of the sun (Christ-Helios). It was through the kindness of the Administrator of the Fabbricca of St. Peters, Msgr. L. Kaas, that these photos were released to the world for the first time. An article is also found by Msgr. Kaas (pp. 79, 82, 85) under the title: "Bold adventure gets rich return," wherein he speaks of the history of the excavations and mentions some inaccuracies that had been published by certain ones. At the same time he promises to publish the *official report* some time in the near future.

464 ANONYMOUS *The Illustrated London News*, March 9, 1946, p. 267; September 7, 1946, pp. 276-277.

> We have here a partial account (written for the ordinary reader) of the pagan necropolis discovered in the Vatican excavations. A number of photographs accompany the description.

465 ANONYMOUS "Billet de Rome: Le tombeau de S. Pierre" — NC, 4 (1952), 325.

> A reference is found here to the inscription ΠΕΤ discovered by M. Guarducci and the studies in its connection.

466 ANONYMOUS *Paris Match*, n. 67, July 1, 1950, pp. 18-19.

> We find here a brief history of the Vatican excavations.

467 ANONYMOUS *The New York Times*, December 24, 1950, p. 1; 27.

> The Pope confirms the discovery of Peter's tomb in the Vatican. His long-awaited announcement bore out a report in the New York Times, August 22, 1949 (see no. 518) that some bones, believed to be Peter's had been found. Has Peter's tomb really been found? The Pope said—"to this question the answer is beyond all doubt: yes. The tomb of the Prince of the Apostles has been found." A second question: have the relics of Peter been found? At the side of the tomb the remains of human bones have been found. However, it is impossible to prove with certainty that they belong to Peter. This still leaves intact the historical reality of the tomb itself.

468 ANONYMOUS "Beneath St. Peter's: the expected announcement about the excavations" — *The Tablet*, 195 (April 15, 1950), 295.

> Mention is made here of a formal announcement expected to be made by Pope Pius XII regarding the discovery of Peter's tomb beneath the Constantinian basilica. There is also a brief summary of the first beginnings of the excavations in 1940—what occasioned the project—and

how a Roman cemetery was subsequently discovered which led to the discovery of the Apostle's grave.

469 ANONYMOUS "Excavations under St. Peter's" — *The Tablet*, 198 (Dec. 15, 1951), 456.

> This contains the important announcement that soon the *official report* of the excavations (which had taken place during the previous ten years) would be made known. It consists of two volumes of which only 1,500 copies have been printed. There is no claim in the *report* that the bones of Peter have been identified. However, it is definite that his tomb has been found beneath the Confessio, and from it an urn has been removed containing some human bones and a fragment of a purple shroud. (These are believed to be Peter's). The urn is now beneath the altar in the Pope's private chapel. There is also a reference to the Pope's Christmas allocution of the previous year (1950) wherein mention was made of the Vatican excavations. It is expected that he may do the same again in the present year.

470 ANONYMOUS "Beneath St. Peter: the archeological reports are published" — *The Tablet*, 198 (Dec. 29, 1951), 496.

> In this brief account mention is made of the historic episode when the summary of the *official archeological report* in two volumes is presented to Pope Pius XII. It also describes the contents of the article that appeared on the entire front page of the official Vatican newspaper: "Osservatore Romano" for Dec. 20, 1951, which reported the event.

471 ANONYMOUS "Tomb of St. Peter: the report on the excavations beneath the Vatican basilica" — *The Tablet*, 200 (Aug. 23, 1952), 145.

> This is a rather brief account written in a popular style describing the excavations initiated beneath the Vatican. The experts to whose care the project was entrusted are also mentioned. In one page the writer endeavors to summarize the chief results and to envisage some of the problems that still await a final answer.

472 ANONYMOUS *Universitas*, 7 (Stuttgart, 1952), 1112-1114.

> This is a review of the well-known *official report*: *Esplorazioni sotto la Confessione de San Pietro in Vaticano esequite negli anni 1940-1949* (see no. 477). The solid literary tradition regarding Peter's tomb on the Vatican hill is greatly substantiated by the archeological excavations.

473 ANONYMOUS "Shrine of St. Peter: replies" — *The Tablet*, 202 (Oct. 17, 1953), 378.

474 ANONYMOUS "Saint Pierre est-il au Vatican" — *Ecclesia*, 95 (1957), 115-122.

475 APPOLLONJ GHETTI, B. M., "Il mausoleo dei Cetenni nella necropoli vaticana" — *Roma*, 21 (1943), 80-81.

> This brief study is concerned with the first tomb of the Caetennii (Tomb F), the first mausoleum to be cleared by the Vatican excavators. Those whose names it recorded practiced cremation. A Christian is also buried here: *Gorgonia*.

476 APPOLLONJ GHETTI, B. M., "Il mausoleo di Cetennia Hygia nella necropoli vaticana" — *Bollettino del Centro nazionale di studi di storia dell'architettura*, (Sezione di Roma), 4 (1945), 1-3.

> As in his previous essay the author gives here a description of the tomb of the Caetenii (Tomb F). No tomb is epigraphically and architecturally richer nor more informative about the persons who made its history.

477 APPOLLONJ GHETTI, B. M., FERRUA, A., JOSI, E., KIRSCHBAUM, E., * *Esplorazioni sotto la Confessione di San Pietro in Vaticano eseguite negli anni 1940-1949*, 2 vols. (Vatican City, 1951). Vol. I: xi-275 pp., 171 photos and designs, 10 plates; Vol. II: 17 pp. and 109 plates.

> This is the *official report*. It is the most recent and detailed archeological material giving the results of the excavations under the altar. The authors restrict themselves to the general region beneath the high altar in the Vatican (the *Confessio*) since this is the region that has

aroused the interest of historians in the world. The contents is as follows:

Pars I. THE CEMETERY
1. The Vatican in antiquity.
2. The Vatican cemetery.
3. The 3 first mausoleums of the Caetenii L, of the Ebuzi N, of the Julii M.
4. The mausoleum O of the Matucci.
5. The mausoleum T of Trebellena Flaccilla and that adjacent U.
6. The mausoleum U and the piazzole in front of the Ebuzi.
7. The mausoleum S at the south-east corner of the Confessio.
8. The mausoleum R at the south-west.
9. The area of inhumation Q and the passage of approach.

Pars II. THE MEMORIA
1. The central graveyard P.
2. The Memoria Apostolica.
3. Chronological reconstruction.

Pars III. THE BASILICA
1. Constantine's basilica.
2. The Constantinian monument and presbyterium.
3. The semicircular Confession and elevated presbyterium.
4. The niche of the pallia.
5. From the old to the new basilica.

The conclusions are as follows: the excavations give:
a) Evidence that St. Peter's tomb has been found where it has always been believed to be.
b) Constantine in building his basilica gave more solemn and external form to the cult of Peter. The excavations show that he created a monument out of a little shrine and adorned it with marble. He did not erect an altar, but a memorial to Peter, situated in the center of the apse of the basilica.
c) Constantine did not have to invent the place of Peter's burial, but he had before him the "trophy" of Gaius built about 160 A.D. on the Vatican hill.

This is the *official report* (though not to be regarded as definitely finished), and a masterpiece of scholarly scientific work. For such a study there is no substitute. *While this study is referred to as the *official report* (both here and in many other titles), the implication contained therein is that it represents the report of the "official excavators."

478 APPOLLONJ GHETTI, B. M., "La tomba e le basiliche di san Pietro al Vaticano" — *Le Meraviglie del Passato*, (1954), 619-636, 24 figs.

This is a simple, concise and clear summary of what has already been given in the *official report* regarding the uninterrupted series of monuments which were constructed over Peter's grave from the most simple tomb to those constructed by Clement VIII and Paul V. The 24 reproductions are taken from the *official report*.

479 ARMELLINI, M., *Le chiese di Roma*, 2 vols. (2nd. ed. Rome, 1942: R.O.R.E. di N. Ruffolo), vol. 2, 859-913.

In the second volume of this valuable history of the Churches of Rome is found an account of the Vatican excavations undertaken in 1939-1941. The author then relates the successive events in the various stages of the construction of St. Peter's basilica. This is both interesting and essential information on the basilica as such which takes the incontestable archeological evidence of the very *first* excavations as its starting point, viz., when the Bernini columns were erected for the baldachino and some graves were discovered.

480 AUDIN, A., "Le memoria de Saint Pierre au cimitière du Vatican" — *Byzantion*, 24 (1954), 265-294, 2 figs.

The recent publication of the excavations beneath St. Peter's enables one to form an opinion on the results. The authors of the *Esplorazioni* have their own ideas but they express them with an objectivity that leaves room for various conclusions. In this framework our author examines the following points:
a) The Vatican necropolis—the various mausoleums and their chronology.
b) Area P from 150-190.

c) Area P towards 190-200.
d) Area P after 200.
e) The Memoria.
f) The grave.
g) The Memoria in the third century.
h) Gaius's *trophy*.

The author claims that with regard to Gaius, every material object recalling Peter's mission at Rome constituted a TROPHY. Such an object existed but he does not see how this is Peter's tomb or the Memoria in area P. He further concludes:

The renowned reputation of the place (area P) which started around some ancient tombs at the beginning of the third century, enables us to admit that there was a very ancient and revered Christian cemetery on this site in Rome where Peter's successors were buried. A shrine was erected here but it was not a tomb—not a subterranean reliquary. It was obviously constructed to receive some object to enhance it as well as to be enhanced. The author further presents the hypothesis (which he feels can meet with some of the objections of the critics) that we can say that they have not found the site of Peter's tomb in the Vatican, but that they have perhaps found the site of his *cathedra*. At Peter's death his disciples could easily have kept some object which would not have attracted the attention of the persecutors. What trophy could be more venerable? This is the TROPHY of Gaius if we distinguish between the *cathedra* (the *trophy*) and the Memoria, which came later.

481 BAIRD, N., *The Tomb of St. Peter. Recent excavations and discoveries*, (Glasgow, the Catholic Truth Society: 1953), 47 pp. with illus.

A popular and quite uncritical and inaccurate approach published by the Catholic Truth Society of Scotland.

482 BALIL, A., "El mausoleo de san Pedro y las excavaciones de la basilica vaticana" — *Zephyrus*, (Salamanca), 5 (1954), 223-226.

The author endeavors to give a schematic assessment

of the excavations beneath St. Peter's basilica and some of the problems that have resulted.

483 BARNES, A. S., *St. Peter in Rome and His Tomb on the Vatican Hill*.

See no. 16.

484 BARTINA, S., *Ecclesia*, (Madrid), Feb. 14, 1953.

In this article the author deals with the inscription in the tomb of the Valerii traced in red and done over in black together with the portraits—which was discovered and photographed and deciphered by M. Guarducci. Among his observations he adds an interesting hypothesis: The Christians buried around Peter were probably the first Popes.

485 BAUCH, A., "Das Petrusgrab im Lichte neuster Forschung" — *Klerusblatt. Organ der Diözesan-Priestervereine Bayerns* (Eichstätt), 30 (1950), 173-176; 197-200.

This is an evaluation of Vatican excavations in the light of the latest research. A clear account of a very complicated problem.

486 BELVEDERI, G., "La tomba di s. Pietro e i recenti lavori nelle Grotte Vaticane" — BAC, 12 (1942), 35-56, 10 figs.

This is an analysis of the excavational findings beneath the Vatican which the author relates with the Memoria Apostolica ad Catacumbas. He first speaks of the Pope's radio-message announcing to the world that Peter's tomb had been found. He asks the question: where was the tomb? According to tradition it was beneath the Papal altar. He examines the Constantinian tomb according to the Liber Pontificalis. Basing himself on Grisar he rejects the value of this information, though he concludes that in the middle of the sixth century when the Liber Pontificalis was compiled, Peter's body was in the Confessio at the Vatican. But where was his body while the Emperor was building the basilica? He then takes up the question of San Sebastiano ad catacumbas and analyses the excavational findings and liturgical evidence and quotes the theories in its regard. He concludes that just as Constantine erected a martyrial basilica on Calvary to consecrate the place sanctified by the Sacrifice on the Cross, so in Rome, he erected the two basilicas (of Paul's also) on the Vatican and via Ostia—on the site sanctified by their martyrdom and at the place of their original burial; whereas he erected their mausoleum on the via Appia in the "Basilica Apostolorum."

487 BELVEDERI, G., "All'Osservatore Romano" — BAC, 13 (1943), 43-46.

This is a reply to Prof. Josi's article in the *Osservatore Romano* wherein the author was labeled as having upset the very solid basis of a venerable tradition by the studies he wrote in the BAC with regard to Peter's tomb. It is particularly involved with the value of the Liber Pontificalis' testimony in this regard. According to Belvederi: at the time when the tomb of the Apostle in Rome was known only from the evidence of the Liber Pontificalis, Protestant theologians were vehemently denying Peter's death and burial at Rome. When, however, the "Memoria Apostolorum" was discovered (at San Sebastiano), even the more rigid Protestant-rationalistic schools had to change their opinions and they even accepted the Catholic thesis. The Catholic tradition does not say about Peter that his body was buried at the Vatican or ad Catacumbas, but rather that the Apostle Peter suffered martyrdom in Rome where he was, and where his tomb is.

488 BELVEDERI, G., "La Tomba di S. Pietro e i recenti lavori nelle Grotte Vaticane."

See no. 262.

489 BELVEDERI, G., "Depositio Petri in Vaticano, Pauli in Via Ostiensi, Utriusque in Catacumbas."

See no. 263.

490 BERNARDI, J., "Le mot Τρόπαιον appliqué aux martyrs" — VC, 8 (1954), 174-175.

This is a brief summary of J. Carcopino's analysis of the

famous text of Eusebius ("Études d'histoire chrétienne," Paris, 1953, pp. 99-101; 251-258) relative to the monuments of Peter and Paul. The famous term used here is TROPAON which Carcopino seeks to establish could not merely refer to a cenotaph, but that it really refers to the bodies of the martyrs themselves. He then quotes a well-known passage of Prudentius (*Perist.* XII, 7-10) which carries this same meaning. He further substantiates his hypothesis by a comparison of the usage of the word TROPAON with the usages found among the Christian writers in the Greek language: Gregory of Nyssa, (*Or. II in Laud. quadrad. mart.*: P.G. 46, 769); St. Basil (*Or. XIX.*: P.G. 31, 521); St. Gregory Nazianzus (*Or. XXXXV,* P.G. 36, 257).

491 BERRA, L., "Le Grotte Vaticane" — *Arte Cristiana,* 29 (1941), 49-56.

This study which deals with the Vatican excavations takes up two essential points: 1) the tomb of Peter; 2) the ancient Constantinian basilica. The author first considers the basilica and its corresponding subterranean arrangement. The excavations confirmed the fact that a sepulchral area existed along the north wall of the Neronian circus, whence there later arose the hypothesis that Peter was martyred nearby and buried in a private hypogeum. The excavations also verified the fact that the via Cornelia ran more to the north of the circus of Nero, hence, the *forma Urbis* of Lanciani stands to be corrected. In the framework of these conclusions the author then considers Peter's tomb. In the light of critical history and scientific archeology, there is no doubt of the existence of the venerated body of Peter in a tomb beneath the basilica.

492 BERRA, L., "Vaticano: II, La tomba di S. Pietro alla luce degli ultimi scavi" — *Dizionario Ecclesiastico,* 3 (Turin, 1958), 1274.

In the light of the most recent excavations beneath the Vatican the author gives a historical reconstruction of Peter's martyrdom and burial and tomb in its successive development.

493 BIRCHLER, L., "Das Petrusgrab" — *Schweizer Rundschau*, 60 (1960), 308-315.

The interest aroused by the sensational announcement of the discovery of Peter's grave which appeared in the Catholic German press prompted the author to give a recapitulation of the contents of a number of articles in a cursory fashion. He speaks principally of the findings reported by Guarducci, Prandi and Galeazzi without neglecting to mention the *Esplorazioni*. He then speaks of his own experience when he inspected the excavations in 1949 (the cemetery and its mausoleums, Gaius's trophy and its subsequent development). This is concluded with the age-old question "was Peter in Rome" and the famous efforts of Cullman and Lietzmann to answer it. There is also included some comment on San Sebastiano and its association with Peter and Paul according to Damasus and the graffiti. P. Styger is acredited with much of the work of the early excavations.

494 BOULET, N., "A propos des fouilles de St. Pierre. Questions historiques et liturgiques" — RSR, 34 (1947), 385-406.

Basing himself on the finds that had been published (between 1940-1946), the author treats of the historical and liturgical questions connected with the excavations. In the first section he deals with the date of the Constantinian basilica and the reason for its construction. In the second part he considers the Confessio, the character and plan of the first basilica, and finally the translation of the relics of Peter and the Memoria ad catacumbas.

495 BURGER, J. D., *La tombe de saint Pierre est-elle identifiée?* (Les Cahiers de 'foi et vérité,' 27), Geneva, 1954, 31 pp.

Basing himself on the Papal pronouncement regarding the discovery of Peter's grave and the theological views on the Petrine-Roman tradition expressed by Heussi, Cullman, Lietzman, the author takes up the following points of consideration:
1. Peter's sojourn and martyrdom in Rome.

2. The tradition with regard to his burial.
3. The Vatican excavations.
4. A discussion of the results.
5. Conclusions.

The author feels that Peter's tomb has not been discovered. Moreover, it appears as though it is a rather useless attempt to look for it. Is the Petrine monument the *trophy* that existed in Gaius' time? It could possibly be. However, the absence of any inscription leaves doubt. It seems rather rash to affirm more than history can prove.

496 BUSCH, K., "Das Petrusgrab" — *Das Münster*, 5 (1952), 313-321.

In endeavoring to solve some of the problems connected with Peter's tomb, the author reconstructs the religious-political situation of the second century.

497 BYVANCH, A. W., "De opgravingen onder de Pieterskerk te Rome" — *Bulletijn van de Vereeniging tot bevordering der kennis van de antieke beschaving te 's-Gravenhage*, 27 (1952), 19-24.

498 CAGIANO DE AZVEDO, M., "L'origine della necropoli vaticana secondo Tacito" — *Aevum*, 29 (1955), 575-577.

This study deals with the interesting theory as to the possible way in which the first cemetery may have developed around the Vatican.

According to Tacitus, when Rome was burning, Nero offered the Vatican gardens as a lodging place to the destitute. Being public property, a cemetery developed which may have been the forerunner of the one discovered.

499 CALDERINI, A., "A recent discovery in the Holy Grottoes of the Vatican" — *Italy's Life*, Sept.-Oct., 1948, 50.

500 CAMPICHI, M., "S. Pierre et son martyre," *Revue de l'Université d'Ottawa*, 22 (1952), 249-273.

See no. 31.

501 CAPOCCI, V., "Gli scavi del Vaticano. All ricerca del sepolcro di S. Pietro e alcune note di diritto funerario romana" — *Studia et documenta historiae et iuris*, 18 (1952), 199-212.

This is a summary of an address delivered before the Roman Pontifical Accademy of Archeology. A jurist himself, the author presents here a very interesting study of the juridical aspects of Roman burial and translation in connection with the question of Peter's grave.

The first part deals with the literary testimony which speaks of Peter's death. Then, basing himself on the *official report* which announced the finding of Peter's grave, the author endeavors to explain some of legal sepulchral problems involved according to Roman law.

It is presumed that the Christians made a special request to the Roman authorities asking for Peter's body, a *peregrinus* and a common felon in the eyes of the law. (otherwise his body, as that of a criminal might have been thrown into the Tiber). Speaking of the *locus petri*, Roman law prohibited any violatio sepulchri. This would not only make the removal of a body illegal but also protect it from harm. Even a felon's permanent grave would have been safeguarded as a *locus religiosus* if not a *pleno iure religiosus*.

What about the Red Wall? What would have happened to the body? According to Roman law a new burial or new structure might be superimposed upon an existing burial provided the body in the first grave had not been tampered with. But in certain special circumstances when there were cogent reasons for it, permission to disturb the bones of the original burial could be obtained. If permission was granted to open the tomb to remove the remains, this had to be done at night and accompanied by the sacrifice of a black sheep. This was a purely pagan rite which obiously would have been repugnant to the Christians. However, circumstances must have forced them to accept it merely as a matter of formality.

502 CAPOCCI, V., "Sulla concessione e sul divieto di sepoltura nel mondo romano ai condannati a pene capitale" — *Studia et documenta historiae et juris*, 22 (1956), 266-310.

Almost in the same vein as the above title. This is an interesting study on the juridical aspects of Roman burial and its concessions to criminals. The privilege which the Roman law allowed to graves, even of criminals who had undergone capitol punishment made it easy for the Christians of the age of persecutions to keep them in good order and with absolute impunity. For the study of the Vatican excavations and the tomb of Peter such information is indispensable.

503 CARCOPINO, J., "Les fouilles de Saint-Pierre" — *La Revue des Deux-Mondes*, 1 (Oct. 15, 1952), 588-610; 2 (Nov. 1, 1952), 77-93; 3 (Nov. 15, 1952), 213-245; 4 (Dec. 1, 1952), 412-428; with illus.

The purpose of these studies is to give the most significant aspects of the Vatican excavations. It is, however, unfortunate that critical references are lacking. Herein the author describes the gigantic task of the excavations and the numerous surprises revealed by the discoveries beneath the Vatican basilica. He holds the theory of a re-translation of the relics from the via Appia (where they had been transferred in 258) to the Vatican Confessio in 356, which was eventually transformed.

504 CARCOPINO, J., "Note sur deux textes controversés de la tradition apostolique romaine" — *Comptes rendus de l'Académie des Inscriptions et Belles-Lettres*, 1952, 424-434.

See no. 274.

505 CARCOPINO, J., *Études d'histoire chrétienne*: Le christianisme secret du carré magique, Les fouilles de Saint-Pierre et la tradition, (Paris; éditions Albin Michel, 1953) 291 pp., 14 figs., 11 plates. (2nd. ed. 1963).

The two studies under the above mentioned titles are combined in this volume. The first which appeared earlier and which examines the problems raised by the cryptogram SATOR AREPO ... is substantially the same here, though brought up to date. The square is shown to be crypto-Christian, and the author corroborates his theory with a number of reasons. This renders it all the more interesting since it brings into full light the fluctuations between the contrary opinions in view of the new discoveries.

The second part of the book (pp. 97-286), the larger part, is occupied with the excavations beneath the Vatican basilica and the traditional views regarding St. Peter in the course of which the author develops some new views. He believes that Peter's body was buried when he died on the spot marked by the *trophy* which came to light during the excavations. It was in 258 that Peter's remains together with Paul's (from the via Ostia) were surreptitiously removed to San Sebastiano ad catacumbas. Peter's relics were returned to the Vatican in 336 A.D. when Constantine's basilica had been sufficiently completed. They remained in front of the *trophy* up until the 6th century when Gregory the Great, fearing Gothic invasions, placed them in a less conspicuous *loculus* in wall 'g.' In the 9th century the Saracens invaded the *loculus* and scattered its remains. The author does not think that the bones found beneath Niche I of the trophy could seriously be regarded as Peter's. By good fortune he also deals with the subject of the 'golden cross' mentioned in the Liber Pontificalis and the graffiti, etc., discovered after the publication of the *official report*. The volume is written in the author's usual learned and scholarly style.

506 CARCOPINO, J., "Vatican" (Fouilles du) I-VI. — DACL, 15 (1953), 3291-3310.

Justice is done to the unparalleled interest in the subject by our author. We find here a summary of the excavational results (1940-1949) beneath the Vatican Grottoes with the additional research concluded by Christmas of 1952. The study is based on scientific data only and bears solid witness to the early history of the church.

507 CARCOPINO, J., *De Pythagore aux Apôtres. Études sur la conversion du monde romain*, (Paris: Flammarion, 1956), 380 pp. with illus. and plans.

This interesting study takes up the following points:
1) The Porta Maggiore of the subterranean basilica;
2) The hypogaeum of the Aurelii on the viale Manzoni;
3) The debate on San Sebastiano ad catacumbas.

The last begins with a description of the modern scene ad catacumbas and a history of Christian devotion through the ages on the spot which led to the stories current in medieval times of its association with Peter and Paul. The author presents the archeological findings also and gives his views concerning the tradition about a translation of Peter's relics from the Vatican to catacumbas on the via Appia. In the first section of Chapter 3 the author deals with the recent discoveries under the Vatican basilica. Here he gives a reading of the "red wall" Greek graffito: ΠΕΤΡ(ος) ΕΝΔ for ΠΕΤΡ(ος) ΕΝ Ι (ρήνη); and he invites this reconstruction ΠΕΤΡ(ος) or ΠΕΤΡ(ον) ΕΝΔ (εί), a reconstruction that fits his translation-theory ad catacumbas. He also reiterates his view already published in Études d'histoire chrétienne, (1953), that the absence of Peter's name from the wall 'g' graffiti implies that the relics were elsewhere in the latter third and early fourth centuries. He also notes that the year 333 to which Seston called attention apropos of violatio sepulcri marks, not the beginning of work on Constantine's basilica, but the end of the first stage, the filling up of the mausoleums upon which the Church was erected, and which is most acceptable.

508 CARCOPINO, J., "Qu'ont prouvé les fouilles de Saint-Pierre?" — Historia, (Paris, July, 1956, n. 116), 73-79.

As the title indicates, the author inquires about the results of the excavations beneath St. Peter's. His conclusion is that the excavational research has reconfirmed the Roman tradition of Peter's presence and burial, thanks to the providential initiative of Pope Pius XII.

509 CARCOPINO, J., Encore "tropaeum" et "nomen." — Studi in onore di A. Calderini e R. Paribeni, I (Milan, 1956), 385-390.

A repetition of a subject previously treated by the author: a word-study on these two famous words. He agrees with C. Mohrmann in interpreting "trophies" (which Gaius spoke of) neither as tombs nor commemorative monuments, but as 'relics,' 'bodies.' As for the word 'nomina' it is no fault of his that the monuments which use the word in the sense indicated are from Africa.

510 CARCOPINO, J., *The Vatican*. (trans. by C. Smith, L. Sawyer and advisors of the National Arts Foundation). (New York: Abradale Press, 1960), 224 pp.

511 CARLETTI, S., "Le pietro hanno parlato" — *L'Osservatore della Domenica*, Dec. 30, 1951.

> The archeological excavations beneath the Vatican are incontestable evidence of the Roman tradition of Peter's sojourn and burial.

512 CARLETTI, S., "Gli scavi nelle Grotte Vaticane" — *Roma nobilis*. L'idea, la missione, le memorie, il destino di Roma, (ed. I. Cecchetti, Rome: Edas, 1953), 278-288.

> An interesting account of the archeological finds beneath the Vatican Grottoes.

513 CARNATIU, P., "Mormantul Stântului Petru" — *Suflet Românesc*, 4 (1952), 64-71.

514 CARY-ELWES, C., "Reflections on the Finds under St. Peter's" — *The Dublin Review*, 228 (1954), 151-160.

> This is an endeavor to bring to the attention of those concerned with the Vatican excavations, the findings of the Abbe Ruysschaert which appeared in the *Revue d'histoire ecclésiastique* for 1953 and 1954.

515 CASTAGNOLI, F., "La tomba di S. Pietro" — *Studium*, 48 (1952), 30-36. (cf. also 1-7).

> This is a brief summary of the results obtained from the excavations around the Apostolica Memoria at the Vatican. It is based on the *official report* and also contains some of its illustrations. The author, in adding some personal observations, clearly indicates that he disagrees with those views expressed by Lemerle, Goguel and Gregoire.

516 CASTAGNOLI, F., "Probabili raffigurazioni del ciborio intorno alla memoria di s. Pietro in due medaglie del IV secolo" — RAC, 29 (1953), 98-101, with 2 figs.

The author deals with two medals which probably contain figurations of a ciborium similar to that erected by Constantine over the Memoria of Peter.

517 CASTAGNOLI, F., "Il circo di Nerone in Vaticano" — *Rendiconti della Pont. Accademia Romana di Archeologia, 3 ser.*, 32 (1959-60), 97-121, with 23 figs.

This is a scholarly study on the subject of the circus of Nero in the Vatican. Recent excavations have uncovered the foundation of the obelisk presently standing in the center of the piazza in front of the Vatican basilica. Hence, the "Gaii et Neroni principium" (*Nat. Hist.*, 36, 37), has been found at the south of the Constantinian basilica, where, according to tradition, it had always been indicated.

518 CIANFARRA, C. M., "Bones of Saint Peter found under altar, Vatican basilica" — *The New York Times*, Aug. 22, 1949, p. 1; 3, 4 fig.

One of the first reports to appear on the excavations from which one can fairly reconstruct what was expected to be found: Peter was buried in the cemetery which was in use in Nero's time. A regards the secrecy which surrounded the excavational campaign the writer reports: "The secrecy is evident. The pontiff gave orders to his archeologists to gather proof so incontrovertible that no one would be able to challenge its authenticity. . . . the Pontiff gave approval to the proposal that the world's leading archeologists be invited to check the findings . . . After the members of this neutral committee have closed their investigations, the *official publication* will appear."

519 CECCHELLI, C., *Saint-Pierre et les Palais du Vatican*, (Paris: édition Nilsson, 1927).

A popularly written account of the Vatican basilica including Peter's tomb, Constantine's basilica, the work of Bramanti and Raphael, the transformation of the ancient basilica, with added items of interest pertaining to the Vatican.

An Italian edition appears entitled:

Il Vaticano (Milano-Roma: Bestetti & Tuminelli, 1928), 105 pp., 448 plates.

The following chapters are included in this interesting account:

1. The Vatican
2. Rome (the city)
3. San Pietro in Vaticano (the church).

520 CECCHELLI, C., "Alla scoperta del sepolcro di s. Pietro" — *Capitolium*, 17 (1942), 173-180.

Basing himself on the speech of Pius XII delivered May 13, 1942, (on the occasion of his twenty-fifth episcopal consecration) wherein he particularly noted the discoveries beneath the Vatican Confessio, and quoting the same Pontiff (Osservatore Romano of May 14, 1942) where he speaks of the existence of a pagan cemetery with monuments from the end of the first century, the author gives a schematic summary of the discoveries of the following years (viz., coins, graffiti, mausoleums, etc.). He further observes that neither the remains of the circus Gaii nor the via Cornelia have been uncovered. However, all the evidence points to the fact that the memoria of Peter was located in the heart of an area destined for burials. (Paul was also buried in a pagan necropolis). Mention is made of the Memoria Apostolica ad catacumbas where the graffiti testify to the invocations to the Apostles. The author compares these with the graffiti to be seen at the Vatican. They are all sepulchral in character. He then asks: why was Peter buried here in the Vatican—a pagan cemetery? How explain the first Constantinian memoria with the many obstacles that had to be overcome in order to construct it? Obviously, Peter was buried here. There is a reference also to the Liber Pontificalis that speaks of a golden cross with an inscription of Constantine and Helena that adorned the Apostle's tomb. He concludes that we know for certain that an authentic sepulchral memoria existed in the Vatican and that Peter was buried here.

521 CECCHELLI, C., "L'obelisco vaticano "Miliarium Aureum"

della Roma cristiana" — *Capitolium*, 25 (1950), 53-71, with 14 plates.

This study deals with the problem of the connection between the circus of Nero and the obelisk. The location of the circus has constituted one of the problems connected with the Vatican excavations and the tomb of Peter. Its precise position is essential for a knowledge of the ancient topography of the entire Vatican and of great interest for the question of Peter's tomb. The author proposes a new theory that the surviving obelisk is not that mentioned by Pliny as being the one in the circus of Nero but is instead another. On this hypothesis the author claims that the obelisk must have been torn down when the circus was abandoned and still awaits discovery. Whereas the surviving obelisk, as we know from identical inscriptions carved near the foot of what were, in its original position, the east and west sloping faces, was dedicated by Gaius to the memory of his two imperial predecessors, and as a funerary monument, was respected by Constantine. He also suggests that the rotunda of Sant'Andrea is to be identified with the temple of Apollo which is mentioned in the Liber Pontificalis as existing in the Vatican.

522 CECCHELLI, C., "La tomba di S. Paolo" — *Capitolium*, 25 25 (1950), 115-131, with 13 figs.

The author examines the historical testimony regarding the Apostle's burial in the framework of the dimensions of the Constantinian basilica and subsequent constructions. He concludes that the tomb is located in its original site, and that the case of Peter's tomb and that of Paul's are very similar; in fact, one corroborates the other.

523 CECCHELLI, C., "Documento per la storia antica e medioevale di castel S. Angelo" — *Archivio della Società Romana di storia patria*, 74 (1951), 27-67.

This study examines the Vatican surroundings and the mausoleum of Adrian—essential knowledge for the topography of the Vatican region and the excavations. It is replete with documentary evidence of the various works executed (pp. 46-67).

524 CECCHELLI, C., *Il Tempo*, December 11, 1952.

> The author makes an interesting observation here. It is of great surprise to him that no one, in his studies of the tomb of St. Peter, has yet exploited the passage of Julian the Apostate where he speaks of "the tombs of Peter and Paul." This is valuable literary evidence supporting the Roman tradition.

525 CECCHELLI, C., *La Tomba di N. S. Gesù Cristo e le "Memorie" Apostoliche*, (Lectures delivered at the Università degli studi di Roma) (Rome; Libreria Editrice F. Ferrari, 1952-53).

> In pages 133-169 the eminent scholar, basing himself on the literary evidence, speaks of St. Paul's coming to Rome, his martyrdom and the construction of the subsequent basilicas. He then takes up the large and complicated question of the "Memoria ad catacumbas" (pp. 170-246) in which he analyzes the literary and liturgical testimony and finally the archeological excavations at San Sebastiano. In pp. 247-303 he gives a survey of the historical evidence pertaining to Peter's coming to Rome and his death and burial and concludes with the Vatican excavations and its findings.

526 CECCHELLI, C., "Le vicende della tomba di s. Pietro" — Grande scoperte archeologiche (Quaderni della Radio, 35), Turin, ERI, (1954), 155-167.

527 CECCHETTI, I., "Il ritrovamento della tomba dell'Apostolo" — *Roma Nobilis*. L'idea, la missione, le memorie, il destino di Roma, (ed. I. Cecchetti, Rome: Edas, 1953), 288-19/23).

> This study was a follow-up of the Pope's Christmas message, Dec. 23, 1950 (AAS, 43 (1951), 51-52) wherein he announced the discovery of Peter's tomb. Based on the *official report* (and 10 of its reproductions) the author discusses the following points:
> 1. The discovery of Peter's tomb.
> 2. The tomb of the prince of the Apostles.
>   a) The archeological exploration,
>   b) The Constantinian foundation,

c) Documentary illustrations,
Early Christian sarcophagi near the tomb of Peter.

528 CERRATI, M., "Tiberii Alpharani De Basilica Vaticanae antiquissima et nova structura" — ST, 26 (1914), 148 pp.

All documentation and research on St. Peter's basilica is contained in this valuable and accurate account which was published towards the close of the sixteenth century. The author has left to posterity a carefully drawn plan in which all points of interest are carefully included. Herein we also find the very ancient tradition which claims that the Constantinian basilica was erected, at least in part, over the demolished circus of Nero.

529 CERRATI, M., "Il tetto della basilica Vaticana rifatto per opera di Benedetto XII" — MAH, 35 (1915), 81-117.

While this is to be classified as general information on St. Peter's basilica, it is of value in the work of excavations.

530 CHÉRAMY, M. H., *St. Pierre de Rome*. (Paris: E. Flammarion, 1933), 213 pp.

General historical information with regard to the Vatican basilica. There is also included a very interesting chapter (I) which deals with the tomb of Peter.

531 CHERUEL, J., "Les fouilles de Saint-Pierre de Rome" — *L'Union*, (Paris), n. 694 (1954), 39-59.

The interest aroused in the excavations prompted the author to supply some general information which he writes in a popular style basing himself on the archeological findings and historical facts. He lists also in a cursory fashion the various studies that have already appeared on the subject. The article contains the following sections:
1. Beneath the nave of St. Peter's.
2. Beneath the apse.
3. The Confessio and the grave.
4. The "red wall" and the early trophy.
5. Probabilities and certitudes.

532 CHRISTIE, J., "The Shrine of St. Peter" — *The Tablet*, 202 (Oct. 10, 1953), 354.

533 COLINI, A. M., "Il sepolcro di S. Pietro" — *Capitolium*, 27 (1952), 1-16, with 19 figs.

> In this study the author gives a descriptive synthesis of the excavations with some criticisms. It is admirable in objectivity and clarity. It covers the results of the Vatican excavations conducted during the first ten-year period. He also includes a conclusion that the more probable opinion with regard to the year 258 is that there was a translation ad catacumbas.

534 CONTE, C., "Où en est la question de la tombe de S. Pierre?" — *Ecclesia* (Paris), n. 39 (June, 1952), 75-84.

535 CORTE, N., *Saint Pierre est-il au Vatican?*

> See no. 37.

536 COPPO, A., "Gli scavi della necropoli vaticana in una recentissima pubblicazione" — EL, 74 (1960), 128-132.

> Reference is made here to M. Guarducci who has made many scholarly contributions on behalf of the archeological investigations under the Vatican basilica and the tomb of Peter. The author observes her particular endeavors to interpret the inscriptions on wall "g" (which were discovered in the excavations) according to a cryptographic system. While some arguments might be deduced in this method, it does not lack its difficulties and some quite serious. The author then gives a review of M. Guarducci's work: *La Tomba di Pietro, notizie antiche e nuove scoperte*, (Rome: Studium, 1959), 228 pp., 48 illus., 13 plates. While it could not be said that the subject-matter in general deals with the principal question—the apostolic tomb in the Vatican necropolis—nevertheless he feels the knowledge and experience of M. Guarducci has helped considerably in shedding some light on the work of the excavations.

537 COPPO, A., "De inscriptionibus cryptographicis basilicae vaticanae" — EL, 77 (1963), 115.

> A reference is made here to M. Guarducci's cryptographic reading of the inscriptions found on wall "g" and

A. Ferrua's objections to these interpretations. The author feels that much more research is to be done with these inscriptions, viz., they are to be studied individually with regard to chronology, etc., This is a necessary conditio sine-qua-non before one can consider such interpretations without danger of error.

538 CORISH, P. J., "The Vatican Excavations" — *The Irish Theological Quarterly*, 23 (1956), 273-277.

After giving a short history of the first beginnings of the Vatican excavations (its problems, its objectives), the author takes up a brief analysis of the famous book: "The Shrine, etc." by Toynbee-Ward Perkins. The author feels that we have here an account of the excavations as a whole, and not merely of the problems raised by the question of Peter's tomb. Toynbee-Ward Perkins have presented the evidence of the discovered necropolis of the first century of the Christian era which is a matter of great interest for students of history and culture of the time. In most matters the authors agree with the findings of the *official report* This work (according to Corish), is scholarly, well documented, and a sober introduction to the story of the excavations which will be a boon to all English-speaking people who wish to have an informed interest in its discoveries.

539 COSSIO, A., *The tomb of St. Peter and its artistic representation on ancient monuments of Christian art*, (Città di Castello, 1913).

540 CRISTIANI, L., "Causerie de l'Ami sur les "Revues" — *L'Ami du Clergé*, 62 (1952), 145-148.

The author gives a brief summary of the articles written by two scholars whose authorship enjoys incontestable authority. He quotes from P. Romanelli (*Osservatore Romano*, Dec. 20, 1951), and two studies by A. Ferrua (*Civiltà Cattolica*, Jan. 5, 1952, and *Études* of Jan. 1952).

The first part of this summary deals with Peter's tomb —what was known before recent excavations. The pious pilgrim inquiring as to the place of the Apostle's tomb was given a vague answer though it was always known that Peter was buried beneath the main altar in the Vatican. What does the *trophy* mean? The excavations have identified it with Peter's tomb on the Vatican. In the second part the author takes up the problem of Peter and Paul's transferal ad catacumbas on the via Appia where, he concludes, their relics were buried for a time.

541 CRISTIANI, L., "Les fouilles de St.-Pierre du Vatican" — *L'Ami du Clergé*, 63 (1953), 49-62.

The source for this article is the two-volume commentary published by M. Carcopino following the *official report*. The author prescinds as far as possible from the controversy regarding the tradition of a translation of Peter's body ad catacumbas. He endeavors rather to present the archeological findings and the historical indications as presented by Carcopino.

The article deals with:
1. The value of the publication concerned with the results.
2. The immensity of the excavational project and the perils involved.
3. The results.
4. A history of the tomb of Peter and its origin from Constantine.
5. The graffiti-wall.
6. M. Guarducci's discovery.
7. Constantine's basilica.
8. The relics of St. Peter.

The author also adds a postscript which speaks of the testimony of Julian the Apostate and which he quotes from an observation made by C. Cecchelli in *Il Tempo*, Dec. 11, 1952.

542 CRISTIANI, L., "Les fouilles de Saint-Pierre à Rome" — *L'Evangile et la vie*, 34 (1953), 237-256.

543 CRISTIANI, L., "Sur les fouilles de Saint-Pierre" — *L'Ami du clergé*, 63 (1953), 229-231.

The author speaks of the three studies by scholars in conjunction with the Vatican excavations, viz., J. Daniélou in *Études*, (Feb. 1953), I. Congar in *Vie intellectuelle*,

(Feb. 1953), and S. Bartina in *Ecclesia* (Madrid, Feb. 14, 1953).

The first two studies deal with the recent work about St. Peter by the famous Protestant theologian Cullmann, whose scientific acumen, loyalty and sincerity they eulogize. The third study by Bartina speaks of M. Guarducci's discovery in the tomb of the Valerii: the portrait of the two heads and the accompanying inscription. It also adds an interesting hypothesis (by Bartina) viz., the Christians buried near Peter were probably the first Popes.

544 CRISTIANI, L., "Excavations at the Vatican" — *Theology Digest*, 2 (1954), 33-38.

This present study is the same—in digested form—as that appearing in *L'Ami du Clergé*, 63 (Jan. 22, 1953), 49-62.

545 CRISTIANI, L., "Réflexions sur les fouilles de Saint-Pierre" — *L'Ami du Clergé*, 64 (1954), 536-541.

This is the same title as that published in the *Revue d'Histoire ecclésiastique*, 3-4 (1953) and 1 (1954) by J. Ruysschaert. Its purpose is to explain the present (at that writing) state of the question—the Vatican excavations— while at the same time it is intended to formulate a reasonable and certain opinion on the subject of the various opinions formulated by critics who dealt with the question. The author gives the following sections in the framework of J. Ruysschaert's conclusions.

1. Archeological data:
    a) General observations;
    b) Is the monument funerary or commemmorative?
    c) The date of the monument;
    d) The subterranean tomb;
    e) An urn or tomb of inhumation;
    f) The date of the tomb;
    g) The decisive argument;
    h) The objections;
    i) The discovered bones;
2. Epigraphical and literary data:

a) The Greek *Petros*;
b) The graffiti on the wall "g;"
c) The inscription of the mausoleum of the Valerii;
d) The literary witnesses before the sixth century;
e) The biography of Pope Anacletus and general conclusions.

546 CRISTIANI, L., "Saint Pierre inhumé au Vatican" — *L'ami du Clergé*, 66 (1956), 369-370.

This brief account is interesting for the general reader. It is a cursory survey of J. Carcopino's report of the excavations as appeared in his writings.

The article begins with the cult 'ad catacumbas' and then takes up the discoveries at the Vatican. Carcopino's conclusion is quoted as follows: "One cannot think with Renan that the only indication of Peter's being buried in Rome is based on the fact that he came to Rome. On the contrary, one ought to say that Peter's coming to Rome stems from the certitude now had that he had been buried at the Vatican in Rome. Such is the truth which the excavations of 1939-1949 have manifested. The historian who seeks only for the truth and who tries to explain in the face of all opposition cannot help but be deeply grateful to Pius XII whose faith has obtained for him (the historian) the evidence of this truth."

547 CRISTIANI, L., *Saint Pierre est-il au Vatican?*

See no. 37.

548 CULLMANN, O., *Journal of Eccl. History*, 7 (1956), 238-240.

This is a critique of the well-known work by Toynbee-Perkins: "The Shrine of Peter and the Vatican Excavations", (see no. 821). Cullmann mentions that among the number of studies it was unfortunate that A. M. Schneider A. von Gerkan, P. Lemerle, H. Marrou and H. Torp arrived at a negative conclusion with regard to the finding of Peter's tomb. As to his own position he concludes that nothing in the archeological evidence is inconsistent with such an identification. However, he feels that the archeological evidence, since it does not go back further than the end of the second century, must be supplemented by literary and historical consideration.

549 CUMONT, F., "Rapport sur une mission à Rome" — *Comptes-rendus de l'Académie des Inscriptions*, 1945, 386-420.

In the first part of this study the author doubts that the results published regarding the excavations beneath the Vatican Confessio are trustworthy. He then treats of the pre-Constantinian mausoleums and their decorations.

550 CUMONT, F., "Epitaphe d'un fonctionnaire impérial de la Belgique romaine" — *Bulletin de l'Académie royale de Belgique, Classe des Lettres, 5 ser.,* 32 (1946), 160-162.

This brief study is concerned with the inscription of Gaius Poplius Heracla of mausoleum A (uncovered in the Vatican excavations) which has social, legal and topographical interest. Two other inscriptions are mentioned.

551 DANES, G., "La tomba di S. Pietro. Un ventennio di ricerche archeologiche" — RivB, 8 (1960), 144-165, 13 figs.

The results of the excavations (which were contained in the *official report* and many other scholarly works that were written by experts) were not wholly accepted by skeptics who rejected them either in part or in whole. Since many problems have resulted, the author endeavors to give here a reply to the new questions which the excavations have aroused and also to fill in the gaps left by the report of the first campaign and the one that followed. He gives:

1. A summary of the exploration 1939-49. Its principle discoveries, the significance of the monuments, the names of the tombs.
2. The second phase of excavations:
   a) The *red wall* and adjacent constructions.
   b) Cemetery P.
   c) Testimony of the graffiti.
   d) Some objections.

Conclusions: Was the tomb found? One of the first explorers said "the trophy of the second century was found." The Apostolic tomb in the proper sense was not found but proven as having existed there. There were a series of indications to prove this. However, the material elements as such no longer existed.

552 DE AZEVEDO, M. C., L'origine della necropoli Vaticana secondo tacito" — *Aevum*, 29 (1955), 575-577.

The cemetery that came to light in the excavations under the Vatican basilica has a bearing not only on the Apostles' tomb, but also on the history of the topography of the region. In this study the author examines the text of Tacitus *Ann. 15.39.2* and *15.44* to clarify some obscure points regarding the events that immediately followed the Neronian conflagration, and also to possibly clarify—on a juridical and historical basis—Peter's martyrdom and burial in the Vatican.

553 DE BRUYNE, L., "Importante coperchio di sarcofago cristiano scoperto nelle Grotte Vaticana" — RAC, 21 (1944-45), 249-280.

This is a discussion of a very interesting Christian sarcophagus-lid found beneath the Confessio. The general character and especially the artistic details argue for a late Constantinian date, about 340 A.D. The lid shows the adoration of the Magi, the Blessed Virgin, the Cross and scenes to the left of the panel hitherto unknown in the repertory of early Christian-sarcophagus-decorators, scil., two episodes from the story of Joseph in the Old Testament.

554 DE BRUYNE, L., "La tomba apostolica in Vaticano" — RAC, 27 (1951), 218-224.

This study deals with the most important and long-awaited announcement by the Pontifical Institute of Christian Archeology (Rome), namely, the publication of the *official report* regarding the results of the Vatican excavations which task was the privileged assignment of a group of its expert professors. The study gives the following tripartite summary:
1. The pagan necropolis.
2. The Memoria Apostolica.
3. The basilica itself.
The conclusions can be seen in no. 477, *Esplorazioni* etc.

555 DE CAVALIERI FRANCHI, P., "Constantiniana" — ST, 171 (1953), 119-120.

Data is found here with regard to the Constantinian basilicas of St. Peter and that of St. Paul. The matter of the Apostles being buried at these places respectively and at San Sebastiano ad catacumbas is briefly reviewed by the experts. With regard to the date of the construction of the Vatican basilica, the author theorizes that the year 333 was the beginning of the work, and he places its completion at a very long period after Constantine's death.

556 DE LABRIOLLE, P., "Refrigerium" — *Bulletin d'ancienne littérature et d'archéologie chrétienne*, 1912, 214-219.

This is a scholarly examination of the use of the word "refrigerium" as seen in various authors—the Fathers— in inscriptions, etc.

557 DELVOYE, C., "Les fouilles de la Basilique Vaticane et la prétendue découverte du tombeau de Saint Pierre" — *Les Cahiers du libre examen*, 14 (Brussells, 1953), 51-64.

558 DEROUAU, W., "Les récentes fouilles à Saint-Pierre de Rome et la découverte du tombeau de Saint-Pierre" — *Les Études Classiques*, 21 (1953), 145-155, with 6 figs.

This is an objective presentation of the history of Peter's tomb in the light of recent excavations beneath the Vatican.

559 DE VISSCHER, F., "A propos d'une inscription nouvellement découverte sous la basilique de Saint Pierre" — *L'Antiquité classique*, 15 (1946), 117-126.

This is a communication with regard to the inscription found in one of the ancient mausoleums (A) discovered during the excavations—of great importance for the topography of the Vatican region, and of interest for its general aspects. It contains a clause of a certain Poplius Heracla imposing upon his heirs the condition of con- structing for him a tomb "in Vaticano ad circum." The inscription is still in situ, and therefore has topographical value of undoubted significance. The author comments on the legal points raised by this text.

560 DE VISSCHER, F., "Une inscription nouvellement découverte sous la basilique Saint-Pierre" — *Bulletin de l'Académie royale de Belgique. Classe des Lettres . . .*, 5 ser., 32 (1946) 67.

> This is a resumé of the above communication.

561 DE VISSCHER, F., "Locus religiosus" — *Atti del Congresso internazionale di diritto romano e di storia del diritto*, (Verona, Sept. 27, 28, 29, 1948) vol. 3, (Milan: Giuffrè), 181-188.

> An interesting study on the Roman law which safeguarded the grave of even a common criminal since it was considered a *locus religiosus*.

562 DE VISSCHER, F., "Un texte négligé dans les controversés autour de la tombe de l'apôtre Pierre" — *Studia et documenta historiae et juris*, 26 (1960), 362-365.

> In constructing the basilica of St. Peter, Constantine the Great was absolutely convinced that the remains of the Apostle occupied the place of the TROPAION mentioned by Gaius in the second century. This study deals with the *Codex Theodosianus*, 9, 17, 7.

563 DINKLER, E., "Die Petrus-Rom-Frage" —

> See no. 117.

564 DOUGHERTY, E. O., "The Tomb of St. Peter" — *The American Ecclesiastical Review*, 128 (1953), 438-444.

> This is a rather unpretentious account of the results of the Vatican excavations. The author is acquainted with the *official report* and also the essay in *Biblica*, 33 (1952), 165-168; 306-309 of which it is also a summary. This study is intended merely for popular reading as is seen from a lack of critical references.

565 DOWNEY, G., "The Shrine of St. Peter and the Vatican Excavations" — AJA, 62 (1958), 247-248.

> This is a review of the well-known work by J. Toynbee-

J. W. Perkins (see no. 821). According to the reviewer, the work is based on the *official report*, though it presents its own conclusions. The Vatican authorities should congratulate themselves that these two scholars have provided a monograph of this kind. Scholars will consult it rather than the *official report*. If the conclusions reached in the present volume are less far-reaching than those set forth by the officials of the Vatican, the reader is free to form his own opinion.

566 DUSCHESNE, L., edited: *Liber Pontificalis* (Bibliography of Pope Sylvester), I, 124 ff.

It is possible to use its statements by comparison with the facts of the discoveries in the Vatican excavations since it is made up of elements which take us back almost to the beginning of Christian life in Rome. Duchesne is responsible for bringing order into the present text.

567 DUSCHESNE, L., "Naumachia, Obelisque, Terebinthe" — *Diss. della Pont. accad. rom. di arch.*, 2 ser., 8 (1903), 135-148.

This study is concerned with the topography of the Vatican region—of extreme importance for a knowledge of the Vatican excavations. The author clearly states that some points are quite certain while others are not. Hence the undoubted value here with regard to the Apostolic tomb. Traditional evaluations are not always in agreement. The legend of the passion of Peter which speaks of his death and burial mentions also the three topographical designations, i.e., the Numachy, Terebinth, and Obelisk. However, these three names are not always attached to the same objects in the same region. For this reason the author endeavors in this study to identify their sites.

568 DUSCHESNE, L., "Vaticane" — MAH, 35 (1915), 3-13.

The author here considers a number of elements which are of value for a knowledge of the excavations. He traces the course of tradition for many of the aspects pertaining to the archeological explorations.

569 DUFRESNE, D., *Les cryptes Vaticanes*, (Paris: Desclée
Lefébure, 1902), 128 pp.

> Interesting information on the history of the Vatican
> crypts: the *Grotte Nuove* and the *Grotte Vecchie*, beginning
> with the tomb of St. Peter, inscriptions, and a description
> of the successive burials here.

570 EGGER, H., "Quadriporticus Sancti Petri in Vaticano" —
Papers of the British School at Rome, 18, n.s. 5 (1950), 101-103.

> The author gives us an account of the atrium as it was
> planned for Constantine's basilica of St. Peter.

571 EGGER, H., "Das Goldkreuz am Grabe Petrus" — *Anzeiger
der Akademie der Wissenschaften, Wien, Phil.-hist. Klasse,
1952*, 182-202.

> This study is concerned with the famous 'gold cross'
> that tradition claims was placed over Peter's bronze
> casket by Constantine and Helena.

572 EGGER, H., "Das Armengrab des Petrus" — *Wort und
Wahrheit*, 13 (1958), 371-377.

> This is a brief analysis of E. Kirschbaum's latest
> research on the Vatican excavations (*Apostelfürsten*, etc.,
> see no. 672) in which the author agrees essentially with
> Kirschbaum's findings.

573 EHRLE, E., "Ricerche su alcune chiese nel borgo S. Pietro" —
Diss. della Pont. accad. rom. di arch., 2 ser., 10 (1910), 3-64.

> An interesting historical reconstruction of the Con-
> stantinian basilica and its neighboring churches in the
> eleventh century when the area was divided into three
> district groups:
> 1. The oldest consisted of four monasteries which sur-
>   rounded the basilica and which took care of the choral
>   duties at the tomb of Peter.
> 2. The national churches.
> 3. The pilgrim churches.

574 EHRLE, E., *La pianta di Roma di Leonardo Bufalini nel
1551*, (Roma, 1911).

575 EHRLE, E., "Dalle Carte e dai disegni di Virgilio Spade (m. nel 1662): Cod. Vat. Lat. 11257-258" — *Atti della Pont. accad. rom di arch., 2 ser., Memorie, II,* Rome, 1928, 1-98.

This is valuable information for a knowledge of the history of Virgilio Spada's work and his building-activity in conjunction with the basilica of St. Peter, the arrangement of the piazza and Bernini columns, etc.

576 EHRLE, E., *La pianta di Rome di Antonio Temptesta del 1593,* (Roma, 1932).

577 ELGSTRÖM, A. L., "Apostlgraven under Peterskyrkan" — *Credo,* 35 (Stockholm, 1956), 28-34.

578 ELTESTER, W., "Epimetron: Die Gebeine des Petrus" — ZNW, 43 (1950/51), 280.

One of the surprising finds of the Vatican excavations was the so-called "Tropaion." The fact has been confirmed that St. Peter was venerated at the Vatican during the last decades of the second century. Did the Tropaion stand over his grave? It seems that its foundation was discovered in the condition known to the early Christians. It is possible that the bones which were discovered in the excavations could be Peter's. However, no certainty can be expressed in this respect.

579 FERRUA, A., "Nelle grotte di S. Pietro" — CC, 92, 3 (1941), 358-365; 424-433.

In these studies and those that followed the author announced a series of excavations that had been initiated in the grotto beneath St. Peter's by pure accident. When Msgr. L. Kaas was seeking a place for the tomb of Pius XI, he came across a number of walled-over alcoves beneath the western section of the present transept of the basilica. Several ancient tombs were found therein. When a later attempt was made to lay a foundation for a sarcophagus which contained the remains of the Pope, the top of an ancient Roman mausoleum was unearthed. This proved to be one of the double row of monuments running beneath the basilica. These studies constitute the most detailed description (the results between the early years of the excavations) of the discoveries that were made beneath the central nave of St. Peter in the Vatican.

580 FERRUA, A., "Nuove scoperte sotto S. Pietro" — CC, 93-4 (1942), 73-86, with 2 figs.; 228-241.

In the first study the author observes some of the critical and erroneous reaction to the Pontiff's announcement to the world of the excavational findings.

In the second study he deals with the mausoleums and the epigraphs and their proprietors. His conclusion is that it is certain that from the end of the second century, and even before, the Christians had their own sepulchral area. But when Constantine erected his basilica over Peter's tomb, this was in a pagan area. Why so? In view of this circumstance, as well as the immense difficulties he had to overcome to build the basilica, the answer could only be—despite contrary opinions—that he knew that Peter was buried here.

581 FERRUA, A., "Lavori e scoperte nelle grotte di S. Pietro" — *Bollettino della Commissione Archeologica Comunale di Roma*, 70 (1942), 95-106.

This is a description—though partial— on the findings in the pre-Constantinian necropolis: its graves, sarcophagi, and pagan mausoleums with their furnishings, etc.

582 FERRUA, A., *Epigrammata damasiana*, (Vatican City, 1942).

We have here a compilation of the Damasian epigrams. Among its contents are found those that refer to tombs of Peter and Paul in Rome, (pp. 139-144, n. 20).

583 FERRUA, A., "La donazione della contessa Matilde" — CC, 94, 1 (1943), 212-223.

Among the many valuable relics in the history of ancient art that came to light during the Vatican excavations were the fragments of a marble slab whereon the very interesting information was incised testifying to the benefactions made the Holy See by the Countess Mathilda.

The complete text is reconstructed in this study: (*Cartula Comitisse Mathilde*).

584 FERRUA, A., "Nuovi frammenti degli Atti degli Arvali" — *Epigraphica*, 7 (1945), 27-34.

> During the recent excavations beneath the Vatican grottoes (precisely the "Grotte vecchie") there came to light beneath the central nave of the basilica two large fragments of the Acts of the Arval brethern (though other fragments had previously been discovered). In this study the author gives an analysis of the fragments, reconstructs their text and endeavors to establish a chronology.

585 FERRUA, A., "Fratelli Arvali" e i loro "Atti" — CC, 97, 1 (1946), 41-49.

> This study is somewhat similar to the above. It concerns the Arval brethern—a sacerdotal college of twelve persons dedicated to a special cult of the goddess Dia. Of special interest here is the fact that the Vatican excavations brought to light marbles whereon were incised the ceremonies practiced by this sect.

586 FERRUA, A., "Un mausoleo pagano ultimamente scavato sotto S. Pietro" — *Atti della Pont. accad. rom. di arch., 3. ser., Rendiconti*, 22 (1946-47, ed. 1948), 6-7.

> This is a resumé of a communication of Feb. 27, with regard to the most recent discovery of a pagan mausoleum under St. Peter's. The same is described in the study below.

587 FERRUA, A., "Un mausoleo della necropoli scoperta sotto S. Pietro" — *Atti della Pont. accad. rom. di arch., 3 ser., Rendiconti*, 23-24 (1947-49, ed. 1950), 217-229.

> The author describes the mausoleum discovered beneath the Vatican grottoes, approximately beneath the middle of the central nave of the basilica. He speaks of its structure and decorations.

588 FERRUA, A., "Lavori e scoperte in catacombe e basiliche paleo-cristiane" — *Fasti Archaeologici*, 4 (1949, ed. 1951), 557., figs., 134-139.

This is a rather cursory survey of the excavations in several of the catacombs. It also deals with the excavations beneath St. Peter's basilica and several other basilicas.

589 FERRUA, A., "Il sepolcro di San Pietro è certo nella basilica in Vaticano" — *IL Messaggero*, Jan. 16, 1952, n. 16, p. 3.

As testimony to the fact of Peter's certain burial beneath the Vatican basilica, the writer commemorates the famous early Christian inscription discovered in the tomb of the Valerii which accompanied the sketch of the head of Peter. This was dealt with at great length by the eminent M. Guarducci.

590 FERRUA, A., "A la recherche du tombeau de Saint Pierre" — *Études*, 285 (1952), 35-47.

Though presented in a slightly different form, the present study is substantially the same as the one mentioned above. Interesting to note is the author's suggestion that the *loculus* in wall "g" was cut by Constantine to receive Peter's relics which were re-translated to the Vatican after a temporary sojourn on the via Appia.

591 FERRUA, A., "La storia del sepolcro di san Pietro" — CC, 103, I (1952), 15-29.

This is one of the first studies published after the release of the *official report* on the excavations. Many studies by others have been based upon this publication. The author again recalls how Pius XII took the courageous step to commission the excavations under St. Peter's which were conducted between 1940-1950. In this study he finds it opportune to give a history of Peter's tomb in the framework of the excavational findings. He deals with Peter's death and burial based on the literary testimony of the Liber Pontificalis. He then gives an analysis of the graveyard—the site of the *locus Petri*, the scrawled Greek inscription with the truncated name of Peter, the surrounding graves, the niches, the shrine, the cult. He concludes that the excavations prove that a cultus existed in this place already in the second half of the second century.

While it is difficult to say whether it was of a liturgical nature, it was at least similar to that "ad catacumbas." Here we also have a clear example of an ancient "martyrium" or "aedicula" erected over the tomb of a martyr (contrary to Delehaye's theory). The concrete facts that we have make this point incontestable. Other particulars (not found in the *Esplorazioni*) are treated, thereby rendering this study a valuable contribution for the knowledge of the problems connected with Peter's tomb. Of interest also is the mention of the theory once held that the Apostles were buried together from the beginning and only later transferred to their respective graves. Scholars have now given up this theory after reconsidering it in conjunction with the unsolved riddles presented by the Vatican excavations.

592 FERRUA, A., "Recenti ritrovamenti di antichità paleo-cristiane in Roma e nei dintorni" — *Atti del I Congresso nazionale di archeologia cristiana*. Siracusa, Sept. 19-24, 1950, Roma (1952), 149-156.

On pp. 153-155 the author speaks of the principle work of the Roman Pontifical Commission of Archeology (in these last two years) at San Sebastiano on the via Appia where the excavations of a large early complexus had been terminated.

On pp. 155-156 he commemorates the tremendous importance of the discoveries under St. Peter's in the last ten years. Its results proved that we have discovered the ancient arrangement of Peter's tomb which was venerated by the Christians in the center of an essentially pagan necropolis over which Constantine constructed his basilica.

593 FERRUA, A., "La criptografia mistica ed i graffiti Vaticani" — RAC, 35 (1959), 231-247, with 2 figs.

This is an appraisal of M. Guarducci's: "I graffiti sotta la Confessione di San Pietro in Vaticano," 1958, 3 vols., (see no. 625) which endeavors to demonstrate a cryptic play on the letters she reads in the Vatican graffiti. Ferrua claims that Guarducci's hypothesis forms a new concept of early Christian epigraphy which she herself terms: "mystic cryptography." It is an attempt to prove that there are very many symbolic values to be read in early Christian epigraphy which were previously unknown. They consist mainly in abbreviations and suspensions, i.e. B and V equals *v(ita)*, etc. Our reviewer takes up a number of her examples to demonstrate this theory. Thus, phrases are formed from this vocabulary through the medium of a new syntax—quite novel, to say the least. Our reviewer concludes by saying that he feels M. Guarducci is deserving great praise for her untiring efforts. However, all this does not warrant our accepting a work which is fundamentally erroneous. "We still think we do honor to the five years of her labors by applying the famous words of St. Augustine: *"magni passus extra viam."*

594 FERRUA, A., "Scoperte fatte nel Lazio e nell'Italia meridionale" — *Actes du V Congres international d'archéologie chrétienne*, (Studi di antichita cristiana, 22), Rome, 1957, 147-158.

On pp. 152-153 the author deals with the graffito ΠΕΤΡ scrawled on the "red wall."

595 FILSON, F. V., "The Grave of Peter" — *The Biblical Archeologist*, 17 (1954), 23-24.

A full summary of O. Cullmann's famous work: "Peter: Disciple, Apostle, Martyr."

596 FINEGAN, J., "San Pietro in Vaticano" — *Light from the Ancient Past*, (Princeton, N. J., 1959), 510-515; also: "The Martyrdom of Paul and Peter," *ibid.*, 377-384.

Both studies, which are written in a popular style, substantially reproduce in capsuleform all that has been previously stated by the scholars. They are intended to give the reader a 'general' idea of the subject.

597 FINK, J., "Archäologie des Petrusgrabes" — *Theologische Revue*, 50 (1954), 81-102.

An interesting and original study of the excavational results. The author's attempt to prove that grave theta (θ) was the actual grave of the Apostle is not accepted by the experts.

598 FISCHER, B., "Neues von den römischen Apostelgräbern" — BM, 25 (1949), 17-29.

> Basing himself on the long passage of Pius XII's radio discourse of May 13, 1942 (*Atti e Discorsi di Pio XII*, 4, 127-130) which is quoted here, the author compares the excavational findings of the scholars with the Pope's reference to Peter's grave beneath the basilica. There is included a reference to the tradition of the cult of the Apostle on the via Appia and the opinions of scholars. This is an excellent summary of the long-awaited information of the excavational findings under the Vatican basilica.

599 FORMIGE, J., "L'emplacement du cirque de Néron à Rome" — *Bulletin de la Société nationale des antiquaires de France*, 1954-1955, (Paris, 1957), 33-35.

> A new hypothesis regarding the position of the Neronian circus at Rome in the light of the excavations. Certainly the celebrated tomb was in the vicinity of the circus of Nero. An inscription confirms this. However, recent excavations have created a problem since it has been learned that it was situated in a different location than that supposed. The author continues his observations and suppositions.

600 FORSYTH, G. H. jr., "The Transept of Old St. Peter's at Rome" — *Late Classical and Mediaeval Studies in honor of Albert Mathias Friend, Jr.*, (Princeton, 1955), 56-70.

> This study is concerned with the origin of the transept wherein the author endeavors to explain the derivation of its form. One of the earliest examples of the through-transept appears in the fourth century in St. Peter's. The recent excavations under the floor of the present church have yielded much information relevant to the problem. It has been proven that the entire transept shown on Alfarano's plan of the Constantinian church formed part of the original construction. Therefore, the church

included from the beg'nning, a through-transept which extended across its full width and was terminated at each end by a pair of columns and a projecting wing. The excavations have also shown the original monument to St. Peter. The memorial which had existed on the spot even before the construction of the church was not submerged in a Confessio or beneath the Constantinian transept but was left free-standing in the great cross hall just as it had formerly stood in the open air. The author continues to give a description of the monument and its later arrangement. He concludes that St. Peter's basilica can best be understood as an original development intended to satisfy the two-fold purpose of a pilgrimage church and a triumphal monument. The transept was not only the practical culmination of old St. Peter's as a pilgrimage church, but it was equally the aesthetic expression of its thematic culmination as an imperial monument dedicated to Christ.

601 FREY, G., & POLLAK, O., "Ausgewählte Akten zur Geschichte der römischen Peterskirche 1535-1621" — *Jahrbuch der Preussischen Kunstmittheil*, 36-37 (1915-1916).

602 FREY, K., "Zur Baugeschichte des Hl. Petrus Mitteilungen aus der Reverendissima Fabbrica di S. Pietro" — *Jahrbuch der Königl. Preussischen Kunstsammlungen*. (Berlin, 1913), 17 ff.

603 FUHRMANN, H., "Archäologische Grabungen und Funde in Italien und Libyen" — *Archäologischer Anzeiger*, 56 (1941), 524-530.

> The author speaks of some of the excavational findings under St. Peter's, scil., the graves and their inscriptions. He also includes some of the findings under San Sebastiano on the via Appia, principally the Christian (New Testament) theme on a sarcophagus.

604 GALVIN, J., "Fob and fisherman; tombs of Popilius Heracla and St. Peter" — *The Catholic Digest*, 15 (March, 1950), 75-77.

> We have here an article written in popular style. The author speaks of the fateful accident that occurred in 1939 when provisions were being made in the Sacre Grotte

beneath the Vatican basilica for the burial of Pius XI. The excavations that followed revealed an entire Roman cemetery. One of the mausoleums, that of Popilius Heracla, was presumed to have been situated near the site of the Circus of Nero where Peter is supposed to have suffered martyrdom.

605 GERKE, F., "Ist der Sarkofag des Junius Bassus umzudatieren ?" — RAC, 10 (1933), 105-118.

This is a reply to Professor I. Roosval who holds the hypothesis that the sarcophagus of Junius Bassus discovered in the excavations of the Grotte Vaticane should be dated to the third century. As a consequence he endeavors to establish—beginning with this date—a system of chronology for the ancient sarcophagi of Rome.

606 GIANNELLI, G., & MAZZARINO, S., "Il problema della sepoltura dell' Apostolo Pietro e le recenti esplorazioni" — *Trattato di storia romana*, vol. 2 (Roma: Tumminelli, 1956), 575-578.

In dealing with the history of Rome the authors devote a brief chapter to the Vatican excavations and the tomb of Peter with its inevitable problems.

607 GIOVANNONI, G., "Tra la cupola di Bramante e quella di Michelangelo" — *Archittetura e Arte decorative*, 1 (1922), 418 ff.

608 GIOVANNONI, G., "Sui lavori ed i trovamenti nelle Grotte Vaticane" — *Atti della Pont. Accad. rom. di arch., 3 ser., Rendiconti*, 17 (1940-41), 24-25.

The author gives a resumé of the excavational findings of the first phase which revealed the manner in which the early basilica had been constructed. The second phase revealed the stratification of the sarcophagi and the Roman funerary monuments which constituted the substrata of the Constantinian construction. He also speaks of E. Josi's observations, the series of burials in the 'forma' type grave—similar to a system found 'ad catacumbas,' and he describes some of the Roman sepulchral chambers that came to light beneath the Vatican grottoes.

609 GIOVANNONI, G., "Trovamenti nelle Grotte di S. Pietro in Vaticano" — *Scienza e tecnica*, 5 (1941), 517-521.

> This is a study of the regions which determined the excavational research and its results: the discovery of an ancient cemetery and its relation with the tomb of Peter.

610 GNIRS, A., "La Basilica ed il reliquario d'avorio di Samagher presso Pola" — *Atti e Memorie della Società istriana di Archeologia e storia patria*, 20 (1908), 48 ff.

> This is a description of the ivory casket unearthed in 1906 at Samagher near Pola which dates from the beginning of the fifth century, and which was the basis for reconstructing the missing portions of the Constantinian apse and Memoria of the Apostle Peter.

611 GREGOIRE, H., "Billet de Rome: Le Tombeau de S. Pierre" — NC, 4 (1952), 325.

> An observation is made here on how the discovery of the inscription "Peter" with the chrismon (which had gone unnoticed by Josi, Ferrua and other collaborators) by M. Guarducci has once again raised a question of the excavational findings.

612 GREGOIRE, H., "Le tombeau de Valerius Herma (Hermas) et l'inscription relative à S. Pierre" — NC, 4 (1952), 398-401.

> Basing himself on the two crudely drawn heads and Professor Guarducci's inscription in the tomb of Valerius Herma (H) (well to the east of the Confessio), the author feels that the 'crux ansata' which accompanies the famous text obliges us to date it much later, i.e., the end of the fourth century (though many date it in the late third or early fourth century). He further suggests that the Christians of the late second century localized the grave of St. Peter in that mausoleum (despite its unequivocally pagan stucco ornamentation) and identifies Gaius' *trophy* with it. He also suggests that Hermas (the 'Shepherd'), of whom St. Paul speaks in his Epistle to the Romans, was the proprietor of the tomb. It is interesting to note the author's postscript which speaks of the false epigraphs

that appeared in Rome in 1952. In this connection he refers to Prandi's communication wherein he demonstrates the authenticity of the graffito PETER found in this tomb of Valerius Herma.

613 GREGOIRE, H., "Le problème de la tombe de S. Pierre" — NC, 5 (1953), 48-58.

In this study the author endeavors to take up the question of the provisional results of the Vatican excavations: the location of Peter's tomb which was sought for (but in vain) under the Confessio of the Vatican basilica. He points out, in particular, the graffito read by M. Guarducci which seems to be tangible evidence of a funerary cult to Peter before the building of the basilica. He also maintains, as demonstrated, the theory that for three-quarters of a century before the basilica was built on the Vatican, the faithful believed that Peter's body was buried "ad catacumbas" on the via Appia. There is no reason to believe that there was a transfer from the Vatican to the via Appia. Mohlberg's theory is discussed here; it claims that the Memoria of the two Apostles and the Basilica Apostolorum erected at a later time were cult-centers not for Catholics, but for the Novatianists.

614 GRENIER, A., "Travaux récents de l'archéologie antique" — L'Amour de l'art, 46-48 (1950), 29-31.

615 GRIFFITHS, J. G., "The Vatican Excavations and the Tomb of St. Peter" — HJ, 55 (1956-57), 140-149; 284-286.

Without being able to justify his claim, the author seems to doubt the Christian character of the mosaics found in the tomb of the Julii. He thinks that the *red wall* and the upper two niches of the aedicula are of the third century. The lack of any evidence of cremation does not necessarily indicate Christian occupancy. He is inclined to believe that the Memoria Apostolica was a sepulchral monument rather than a cenotaph. This study was followed by an exchange of letters between the author and J. Toynbee which is seen on pages 284-86.

616 GRIMALDI, G., "Instrumenta authentica translationum . . .

cum multis memoriis basil. (Vaticanae) demolitae" — *Cod. Barb. Lat.* 7233, 277-278 and *Vat. Lat.* 6438, 42-43 and 51.

In his account of the works in St. Peter's basilica under Pope Paul V (1605-1621) the author mentions the discovery of mauseoleum E in the atrium. He also describes many pagan inscriptions that were discovered, and he sees other tombs.

617 GRISAR, H., "Le tombe apostoliche di Roma" — *Studie Documenti di Storia e Diritto*, 13 (1892), 321-372.

The results of his research are published here. The author supplies us with a very full description of the tombs of Peter and Paul in Rome.

618 GRISAR, H., "Le tombe Apostoliche al Vaticano ed alla via Ostiense" — *Analecta Romana*, 13 (1899), 259-306.

This is concerned with the very early excavations under St. Peter's. The spot at which the search for Peter's tomb was decided by the Niche of the Pallia (under the present Papal altar). It was here that the author began his investigations, unfortunately, however, without adequate technical equipment.

619 GRISAR, H., "Il prospetto dell'antica basilica Vaticana" — *Analecta Romana*, 13 (1899), 463-506.

A continuation of the subject of the earliest excavations beneath the Vatican.

620 GRISAR, H., "Le teste dei SS. Apostoli Pietro e Paolo" — CC, 58, 3 (1907), 444-457.

At Rome, which is the treasure-house of sacred relics, few are honored with such veneration as the heads of the Apostles Peter and Paul. What facts do we have to authenticate these relics?

The author examines the historical details of the veneration at Rome; He then speaks of the present state of the relics. He finally takes up the question of their genuinity. As is known, because of the Saracen attacks the relics were transported into the chapel of the Lateran palace known as the "sancta sanctorum."

621 GUARDUCCI, M., "Un documento precostantiniano su san Pietro nelle Grotte Vaticane" — *L'Osservatore Romano*, Nov. 22, 1952, p. 3.

> We have here a summary of the author's discovery in the tomb of the Valerii: the inscription with two naive portraits (Christ & Peter). This confirms why Constantine found it necessary to construct a basilica *there*, because of Peter's cult. That there was such a cult in this place is incontestable.

622 GUARDUCCI, M., "San Pietro in un documento precostantiniano della necropoli vaticana" — *Atti della Pont. accad. rom. di. arch., 3 ser., Rendiconti*, 27 (1952-1954; ed. 1955), 152-153.

> This is a resumé of the author's communication in the conference of Roman archeologists with regard to her discovery in the tomb of the Valerii. (See above and below).

623 GUARDUCCI, M., *Cristo e san Pietro in un documento precostantiniano della necropoli Vaticana*, (Roma: "L'Erma" di Bretschneider, 1953), 105 pp., with 17 figs., 45 plates.

> This is the first result of the second series of excavations. The famous authority on ancient epigraphs examines in great detail the Christian evidence in the tomb of the Valerii. The most noteworthy is the series of inscriptions traced in red, done over in black in the niche of Apollo-Harpocrates. With these are two portraits, one above the other: the heads of Christ (above) and Peter. To the left of one head (Peter's) are the letters PETRV and to the right the rest of the epigraph distributed through five lines. The other head (Christ) bears on its forehead the word VIBVS and is accompanied by the symbol of a phoenix. From the author's reading and the topographical elements involved, she concludes that Peter was venerated in the Vatican even before Constantine built his basilica. The book contains some excellent plates of the inscriptions and other aspects of the mausoleum.

624 GUARDUCCI, M., "Documenti del I secolo nella necropoli vaticana" — *Atti della Pont. accad. rom. di arch., 3 ser.*,

Rendiconti, 29 (1956-1957; ed. 1958), 1-27; 110-137, with 17 figs.

The first-century remnants from the Vatican necropolis are first collected and thoroughly analyzed in this communication presented to the Roman Pontifical Academy of Archeology. Based in part on the use of new material found by Prandi, and in part on the discoveries made (at times even before 1940) on the outskirts of the Vatican basilica, the author in presenting her research emphasizes the epigraphical elements and figured pieces (from the church of S. Stefano degli Abissini) of the first century to prove that burials were being made in that area during this period.

625 GUARDUCCI, M., *I graffiti sotto la Confessione di san Pietro in Vaticano*, 3 vols., (Vatican City: Libreria editrice Vaticano, 1958), vol. I, pp. XII and 536, with 258 figs.; vol. II, pp. 480 and 39 figs.; vol. III, pp. 228 and 65 plates.

This is an evaluation of the reading and an interpretation of the numerous graffiti and inscriptions discovered on the occasion of the excavations executed beneath the Confessio of St. Peter at the Vatican. The authoress deals with a new theory regarding early Christian epigraphy which she well terms "mystic cryptography." It is an attempt to prove symbolic values (previously unknown) existed in early Christian epigraphy. And this, to such an extent, that a "second" language is to be gleaned from the inscriptions—more or less as found in Sacred Scriptures and in other books where allegorical meaning is given the text beyond the literal sense. These symbolic values consist mainly in abbreviations and suspensions which up to the present time have gone unnoticed. With this new vocabulary entire phrases are formed through the medium of a syntax, quite novel, to say the least. The volumes contain many such examples with some excellent plates.

626 GUARDUCCI, M., "Le indagini archeologiche ed epigrafiche sotto la basilica di San Pietro" — *Rendiconti dell'Accademia*

Nazionale dei Lincei. Classe di scienze morali, storiche e filolo-giche, 14 (1959), 173-178.

627 GUARDUCCI, M., "Nuove iscrizioni nella zona del circo di Nerone in Vaticano" — *Atti della Pont. accad. rom. di arch., 3 ser., Rendiconti*, 32 (1959-1960), 123-132.

The exact localization of the circus of Nero (as well as the obelisk) has been positively clarified—indeed, invaluable topographical evidence in conjunction with the Vatican excavations. The authoress takes up some of the epigraphic monuments which can be put into relation to the circus and its ambience. She analyzes the oldest inscription concerning the circus: an epigraph incised on the base of the obelisk and then considers some of the funerary inscriptions and graffiti. Her conclusions which are not without importance are: around the middle of the second century, and even before, Christian tombs were in the area of the circus, precisely near the obelisk. It is very probable that those Christian burials had some kind of link with the tradition which points out the place of Peter's martyrdom as being in the circus of Nero.

628 GUARDUCCI, M., "Scoperte epigrafiche sotto la Confessione di San Pietro" — *L'Osservatore Romano*, March 19, 1959, p. 3.

This is an interesting announcement of the epigraphic discoveries in the Vatican excavations. In a recapitulation the authoress mentions the various phases of the excavational campaigns: the first, 1939-1949 concluding in 1950; the second, 1952, which is still incompleted. Mention is made of the *official report* and its brief reference to the graffiti. She then takes up the subject of her own epigraphic research: the graffiti-wall and the "mystic cryptography" which she claims is based on the following three elements:
1) To the individual letters there is attributed a religious value (an amplification of the use is to be seen in the already known apocalyptic letters Alpha and Omega).
2) There is a joining of letters by signs of ligature to create new expressions of mystic character and sometimes entire new phrases.

3) There is what she terms an "alphabetic-transfiguration."

Her research in this respect is limited to the graffiti of the *red wall* and mausoleum R. From all this she arrives at the conclusion that when Gaius speaks of Peter's *trophy* he is actually referring to his tomb.

629 GUARDUCCI, M., "Un'iscrizione greca della necropoli Vaticana" — *Atti del III Congresso internazionale di epigrafia greca e latina*, (Roma, 1959), with 3 plates.

This is a study of the graffito Εμνήσθη found on the facade of mausoleum R.

630 GUARDUCCI, M., *La Tomba di Pietro. Notizie antiche e nuove scoperte*, (Roma: editrice Studium, 1959), 255 pp. and 13 plates, 48 figs. In English: *The Tomb of St. Peter, the new discoveries in the Sacred Grottoes of the Vatican*, trans. by J. McLellan, (New York: Hawthorn Books, 1960), 198 pp., 50 figures and 13 plates.

This was written for those who seek precise information on St. Peter's tomb and the excavations and who may not be professional scholars. It is an excellent summary of the excavational discoveries in which the following sections are contained:
1. The Vatican in ancient times.
2. The necropolis under the basilica.
3. The Memoria of the Apostle.
4. The testimony of the inscriptions.
5. The cult of the Apostles Peter and Paul on the via Appia.
The chapter on the readings of the graffiti was made also in her earlier writings. It is interesting to note that she rejects the theory of a translation of the Apostle's body to the via Appia.

631 GUARDUCCI, M., "La crittografia mistica e i graffiti Vaticani" — RAC, 13 (1961), 183-239.

Our distinguished epigraphist, after much research, analyses the graffiti-wall 'g' Noteworthy is her discovery of a cryptic play on letters. She believes she can demonstrate the frequent appearance (among many other symbolic letters and combinations of letters) of a logogram for Peter consisting in the association of the shortened PE with the familiar Christ monogram. Much of her earlier work in this respect is substantially reproduced here.

632 GUARDUCCI, M., "La crittografia mistica e i graffiti Vaticani (a proposito di una recensione del p. Antonio Ferrua)" — *Archeologia classica*, 13 (1961), 183-239.

This is the authoress' reply to A. Ferrua's review of her research with the Vatican graffiti and her mystic cryptographic readings and interpretations. She claims that he is not able to prove any of his allegations which attempt to belittle her conclusions.

633 HAARSEN, M., "Pope Gregory the Great as Guardian of the Apostolic Relics" — *Nederlands kunsthistorisch jaarboek*, 5 (1954), 305-307.

This is a brief study of a Dutch miniature of the fifteenth century depicting Gregory the Great holding a painting on which Peter and Paul are seen.

634 HEMMICK, W., "Under St. Peter's in Rome" — *The Catholic Digest*, 17 (May, 1953), 45-47.

This is a popular account describing the Vatican excavations which have revealed a city of the dead and the tomb of the first Pope.

635 HERMELINK, H., "Die Forschungen nach dem Petrusgrabe" — *Kirche in der Zeit*, 7 (1952), 77-78.

636 HOMANN-WEDEKING, E., "Fundbericht Italien. Vaticanum Grotten" — *Archäologischer Anzeiger*, 57 (1942), 329-333.

We have here a report of the excavations under the Grottoes of St. Peter's basilica which was previously recorded by H. Fuhrmann (*Arch. Anzeiger*, 56 (1941), 524 ff.) A particular reference is made to C. Cecchelli's study in *Capitolium*, 17 (1942), 173 ff., and A. Ferrua in *Civiltà Cattolica*, Oct. 7th and Nov. 21, 1942, who commented on the inscriptions, decorations of various sarcophagi, etc. The excavations, however, have still not revealed the location of the Neronian circus nor the via Cornelia.

637 HUDEC, L. E., "Recent excavations under St. Peter's basilica in Rome" — JBR, 20 (1952), 13-18.

No one ever expected that the beginnings of the Vatican excavations in 1940 would lead to the discovery of a Roman necropolis, which in turn would lead to the recovery of Peter's tomb. The author describes the outstanding results of the excavations: the mausoleums, paintings, inscription of C. Popilius Heraclea. It was also a great surprise that no trace could be found of the via Cornelia, which was supposed to run under the north walls of Nero's circus. Mention is also made of what had been seen in the very earliest excavations, and reference is made to the translation theory of Peter and Paul to the via Appia in A. D. 258. (Forty years later they were returned to their respective tombs). The author concludes that Peter was buried in Rome under the Papal altar. In his opinion, the question of identifying the remains can be regarded as of secondary importance in comparison with the archeological proofs of the existence of the tomb.

638 HÜLSEN, C., "Il Gaianum e la naumachia Vaticana" — Diss. della Pont. accad. rom. di arch. 2 ser., 8 (1903), 3-34.

In dealing with the subject of the Vatican region during classical times, our author examines the two locations of the Gaianum and the Vatican Naumachia. Their exact position is of extreme importance for a knowledge of the very ancient history regarding the Christian-Vatican. The study contains three sections:
1. The Gaianum.
2. The supposed circus of Adrian.
3. The Naumachia in the Middle Ages.
The author recognises the Naumachia in the ruins behind the Castle of Sant'Angelo.

639 HÜLSEN, C., "Il circo di Nerone al Vaticano" — Miscellanea Ceriani, (Milano, 1910), 255 ff.

This study examines the problem of the location of Nero's circus.

640 JONGKEES, J. H., "De stichting van de oude St. Pieter te Rome" — *Nederlandsch Archief voor Kerkgeschiedenis*, 43 (1949), 67-86.

> Kirschbaum's theory of a late completion of St. Peters basilica (middle of the fourth century at least), which was started after 324, is rejected by the author. The latter proposes earlier dates based on the cruciform plan of the edifice which must have been inspired after Constantine's vision of the Sign of the Cross in 312.

641 JONGKEES, J. H., "The Tomb of St. Peter" — Mnem. ser. 4, 13 (1960), 143-155.

> The author feels that this will be a modified view by the many subsequent studies on the subject. The main point of consideration is the "tomba scomparsa", which from about A.D. 160 at least, was firmly believed to contain the Apostles' remains. That this tomb existed has not only been argued by inference, but we may understand from the *official report* that it actually has been established by observation: the excavators found the shaft and the bottom of the shaft. However, there is no tile or other object that might date the tomb. Its date has to be established by circumstantial evidence. This, then, is what the author endeavors to do. His conclusions are: Since all the available chronological evidence has been exhausted, the "tomba scomparsa" must date from about 130-150 A.D. It is therefore beyond doubt that this grave is not Peter's original grave. However, it would be rash to infer from this that it could not be the Apostle's grave at all for there is always a possibility that in the first half of the second century his remains were reburied on this spot. On the other hand, there is no proof whatever that it is in fact Peter's grave—no more than we have proof to the contrary. But there is more possibility in favor of the former as circumstances indicate. The people who made the monument surely believed it was Peter's. This is obvious from the care and attention they gave it.

642 JOSI, E., "Ritrovamenti Archeologici" — *L'Osservatore Romano*, March 13, 1941, p. 4.

This is a supplement to G. Nicolosi's article appearing
on the same page which describes the work carried out
in the Sacre Grotte. In this account the author describes
the discoveries that were made, scil., the ancient necropolis and its tombs. Several pictures accompany the
article.

643 JOSI, E., "Le sacre Grotte Vaticana" — *L'Osservatore Romano*,
June 30, 1941, p. 2.

The author speaks of an ancient reference which gives
an indication of a crypt or grotto beneath the Constantinian basilica. A reference is also made to Gregory the
Great and Gregory of Tours in this same respect. He then
gives an explanation of what is to be understood by the
expression 'Sacred Grottoes of the Vatican.' This is followed by a historical reconstruction of the 'Grotte Nuovo'
and 'Grotte Vecchie' and those buried there.

644 JOSI, E., "Sulla scoperte archeologiche nelle Grotte Vaticana"
— *Atti della Pont. accad. rom. di arch. 3 ser. Rendiconti*, 17
(1940-41), 25.

This is a 'refresher' report on the results of the first
phase of the excavations. The author sees a similarity in
the types of burial here and 'ad catacumbas.' He then
describes the series of Roman sepulchral chambers discovered and their decorations. Peter was buried in a large
sepulchral area in the open. However, the excavations
have not uncovered the road that is supposed to have run
between Peter's grave and the circus of Gaius and Nero.

645 JOSI, E., "La regalità di Cristo negli antichi monumenti
cristiani" — *L'Osservatore Romano*, Oct. 26-27, 1942, p. 2.

A reference is made here to a Greek inscription from the
cemetery of Priscilla which speaks of the kingship of
Christ. Armellini reads in it: "the divine reign of Jesus
Christ." The author himself found a reference to the
'adoration of the Magi' in the catacombs. In this connection he speaks also of the discoveries in the Vatican
Grottoes: principally, a marble-lid of a sarcophagus which
contains scenes from the Old Testament on either side and

the Blessed Virgin and child in the center. Thus, we have here again the earliest manifestation of the Christian thought of the faithful regarding the kingship of Christ.

646 JOSI, E., "La tomba di s. Pietro e i recenti lavori nelle Grotte Vaticane" — BAC, 13 (1943), 29-43.

> This is substantially a repetition of the excavational findings beneath the Vatican Grottoes as appeared in the author's earlier writings.

647 JOSI, E., "Seconda relazione sugli scavi nelle Grotte Vaticane: nuova serie di mausolei" — *Atti della Pont. accad. rom. di arch., 3 ser., Rendiconti*, 19 (1942-1943), 7-8.

> This is a description—in a second report—of the new series of mausoleums that were discovered in the Grotte Vecchie. There were at least thirty that came to light. The author briefly describes their contents, pictorial decorations, the sarcophagi, epigraphical materials, etc. He also notes the double parallel row arrangement of the mausoleums. By way of conclusion he calls attention to the fact that the location of the circus still remains a problem.

648 JOSI, E., "Sul coperchio del sarcofago di Giunio Basso" — *Atti della Pont. accad. rom. di arch., 3 ser., Rendiconti*, 20 (1943-1944), 9.

> In this brief account the author gives a historical reconstruction of the lid of the sarcophagus of Junius Bassus, and in this connection, relates that among the excavational findings beneath the Vatican basilica were three fragments of an epigram which were recognized as belonging to the lid of the above mentioned sarcophagus.

649 JOSI, E., & NICOLOSI, G., "Gli scavi nelle sacre Grotte Vaticane" — *Il Vaticano nel 1944*, (1944), 188-200 with illus.

> This is one of the first reports on the beginnings of the excavational projects beneath the Vatican when the project was still shrouded in secrecy. The authors speak of the pre-Constantinian mausoleums; the pavement of the Constantinian basilica was discovered twenty centi-

meters below the floor of the Grotte Vecchie. The tombs
were placed beneath the pavement after Constantine. The
authors then speak in detail on the foundation of the
actual basilica and its present-day tombs.

650 JOSI, E., "Le Sacre Grotte" — *Vaticano*, (ed. G. Fallani &
M. Escobar, Florence: Sansoni, 1946), 23-53.

We have here documentation on the Vatican necropolis with a partial account of the tombs discovered beneath the Vatican basilica. Pages 1-22 is a study of the
classical topography by G. Lugli.

651 JOSI, E., "Roman Cemetery under St. Peter's" — *London
Times*, Feb. 27, 1947, pp. 5-6.

In this popularly written article the expert archeologist,
E. Josi, gives us a long account (with illustrations) regarding the discoveries made as a result of the fateful accident
in 1939 when alterations were being made in the Sacre
Grotte beneath the Vatican basilica to make room for the
sarcophagus of Pius XI. The excavations begun in 1940
revealed Roman graves. Under the initiative of Pius XII
the extensive project undertaken by the archeologists
uncovered a complete Roman cemetery with pagan and
Christian graves dating to the second and third centuries,
A.D. Obviously, the entire basilica had been erected over
a regular necropolis. However, one of the major surprises
was the failure to find any trace of the circus and via
Cornelia where it was assumed that Peter had suffered
martyrdom. The excavations brought to light two rows
of tombs that stretch in an east-west line. Some contain
the names of their owners. One, definitely Christian,
constitutes the earliest known example of the use of
mosaics in Christian funerary art.

652 JOSI, E., & NICOLOSI, G., "Vaticano. Scavi nelle grotte
vaticane" — *Enciclopedia Italiana* (Secondo Appendice), 2
(1949), 1091-1093.

At various times, before and during the work of constructing the actual basilica during the pontificates of
Nicholas V and Pius VI, both pagan and Christian

sepulchres had been discovered. However, it was only in Jan. 1941 that for the first time a systematic archeological exploration had taken place precisely in the area of the Vatican Grottoes which correspond to the central nave of the basilica. The authors then give a description of the archeological findings.

653 JOSI, E., "Una nuova iscrizione relativa al Phrygianum" — *Atti della Pont. accad. rom. di arch., 3 ser., Rendiconti,* 25-26 (1949-51), 4 ff.

This study deals with the new inscription relative to the "Phrygianum" that came to light in the excavations under the Piazza of St. Peter's. The author also speaks of the other epigraphs mentioned by Grimaldi and discovered in 1606. Such a discovery is valuable for dating the construction of the Vatican basilica.
See next.

654 JOSI, E., "Le Phrygianum; les témoignages de France à la Confession de Saint-Pierre" — *Comptes Rendus de l'Académie des Inscriptions et belles lettres,* 1950, 434 ff.

In this study the author presents a hypothesis with regard to the period of duration for the construction of Constantine's basilica based on observations derived from the altar of the "Phrygianum," presently in the Lateran Museum. Marucchi and others have shown that sacrifices were interrupted for twenty-eight years, and this interruption could be explained by the construction of the basilica. The dates of interruption can be fixed between 319 and 350. Hence it could be theorized that the work was commenced about that time and terminated about 350.

655 JOSI, E., "Il ritrovamento del sepolcro di S. Pietro in Vaticano" — *Alma Mater,* (1951), (Rome, Pontificio Collegio Urbano de Propaganda Fide, 1952), 3-16.

656 JOSI, E., *L'Osservatore Romano,* Dec. 22, 1951, p. 1.

The author gives an official report of his work on the Vatican excavations.

657 JOSI, E., "Pietro."

See no. 158.

658 JOSI, E., "Il contributo dell'archeologia cristiana alla storia della Chiesa antica" — *Studi sulla Chiese e sull'umanesimo, Analecta Gregoriana 70* (Roma, 1954), 3-7.

An examination of the numerous archeological discoveries will not only reveal the basic content of the Christian message, but also the depth to which the truths of the faith penetrated the early Christians. The significance of Christian archeology for the history of the ancient Church is invaluable.

659 JOSI, E., "Vaticano," III. — EC, 12 (1954), 1053-1097.

A detailed account of the archeological area of excavations beneath the basilica. The author first analyzes the Vatican region, the sepulchral monuments of the area, and the excavations, 1941-49. A detailed description of the findings follows. The Constantinian basilica and date of its completion is also considered. One can also find here general information about the Vatican and a description of the present basilica.

660 JOSI, E., "Pio XII e l'archeologia cristiana" — *Pio XII Pont. Max. Postridie kalendas Martias MDCCCLXXVI-MDCCCCLVI*, (Vatican City, 1956), 331-361.

The pages 339 ff. deal with the excavations.

661 JOURNET, C., "Les fouilles du Vatican (1939-1949)" — *Nova et vetera*, 28 (Geneva, 1953), 311-314.

A description of the archeological findings beneath the Vatican basilica during the first campaign.

662 KELLNER, W., "The Search for Peter's Tomb" — *The Catholic Digest*, 21 (1957), 106-110.

This brief essay written in popular style presents a historical reconstruction of Peter's death and burial and the beginnings of the Vatican excavations. The author asserts that repeated critical investigations have ruled out any doubt as to the identity of Peter's grave that was discovered. In reply to the question has the grave of St. Peter really been rediscovered? The voice of Pius XII (Dec. 23, 1950) replied—YES!

663 KIRSCHBAUM, E., "Die Reliquien der Apostelfürsten und ihre Teilung" — *Xenia Piana, Miscellanea Historiae Pontificiae*, 7 (Roma, 1943), 51-82.

    The feeling that was widespread in the early years of the twelfth century that half of each Apostle (Peter and Paul) reposed in St. Peter's basilica, and the remaining halves at St. Paul's basilica. This opinion was held for more than five hundred years. In endeavoring to get at its real origin, the author sees the earliest hint of the idea appearing in an inscription on the ancient sarcophagus of the Muses in which Petrus Leonis was buried at St. Paul's.

664 KIRSCHBAUM, E., "Intorno ad un mausoleo cristiano scavato sotto S. Pietro" — *Atti della Pont. accad. rom. di arch.,* *3 ser., Rendiconti*, 22 (1946-1947, ed. 1948), 7.

    This is a summary of a communication delivered on Feb. 27 regarding the discovery of a small Christian mausoleum (M) beneath the Vatican basilica.

665 KIRSCHBAUM, E., "Gli scavi sotto la Basilica di S. Pietro" — *Gregorianum*, 29 (1948), 544-557.

    On June 27, 1940 while the author was inspecting a project in the Grotte Vecchie beneath St. Peter's where workmen had dug an aperture in the south wall of the grotto to create more space for papal sarcophagi, something unique occurred. By this singular accident of fate some interesting findings came to light. The author speaks of the project of excavations under the Vatican basilica. He then gives a historical reconstruction of the necropolis, the Constantinian basilica, the circus of Nero, der and the via Cornelia.

666 KIRSCHBAUM, E., "Ein altchristliches Mausoleum unter der Peterskirche" — *Das Münster*, 2 (1949), 400-406.

    Here we have a detailed account of the discovery of a

small Christian mausoleum (M) beneath the Vatican
basilica. This is similar to an earlier account but more
descriptive.

667 KIRSCHBAUM, E., "Die Ausgrabungen unter der Peterskirche in Rom" — *Stimmen der Zeit*, 144 (1949), 292-303.

In this account the author speaks of the event which
initiated the Vatican excavations when arrangements
were being made in the the Vatican Grotto for the sarcophagus of Pius XI. He then gives a historical reconstruction of:
1. The Vatican necropolis.
2. The circus of Nero.
3. The via Cornelia.
4. Constantine's work.
5. Peter's grave.
All the elements fit harmoniously with the Pope's announcement of the excavational findings. Cf. AAS 34
(1942), 163-164.

668 KIRSCHBAUM, E., "Die Grabungen unter der Basilica von
St. Peter in Rom" — *Das Münster*, 2 (1949), 395-406 with
4 figs.

The first part of this study reproduces essentially that
which appeared in the *Gregorianum*, 29 (1948), 544-557.
In the second part the author speaks of the early Christian
mausoleum of Julius Tarpeiano (M) which Tiberio Alfa-
rano (in his description of St. Peter's) mentions as having
been discovered in 1574. It dates back to the end of the
second century after Christ. Of special significance here is
the mosaic decorations depicting Jonah, the Fisherman,
and Helios. The Fisherman is interpreted to be Peter and
Helios, Christ. These mosaics represent the earliest known
in Christian sepulchral art.

669 KIRSCHBAUM, E., "Das Petrusgrab" — *Stimmen der Zeit*,
150 (1952), 321-332; 401-410.

This is a detailed account of the recent excavations beneath the Vatican. In seeking for the one who might have

constructed the shrine beneath the Vatican (Anicetus, 154-165, or Anacletus, 88-97), the author suggests that the natural tendency to assign greater antiquity to events may have helped to confuse the two names in tradition. Thus, the name Anacletus would have been substituted for Anicetus. He also includes another interesting aspect: he gives an explanation for the total absence of the name of Peter on the wall of the graffiti.

670 KIRSCHBAUM, E., JUNYENT, E., VIVES, J., "La tumba de san Pedro y las catacumbas romanas" — (=*Biblioteca de autores cristianos*, 125), (Madrid: La Editorial catolica, 1954), 3-56; 596-599.

This study is concerned in general with the subject of Christian cemeteries in Rome, the sanctuaries of the martyrs, iconography and epigraphy. In the pages mentioned, scil., 3-56, the question of Peter's tomb is handled by E. Kirschbaum in his usual scholarly way. Fifteen figs. based on the *official report* are included. Pages 596 ff. are an appendix dealing with the *Depositio episcoporum* and *Depositio martyrum*, etc., whose testimony is valuable for a knowledge of the excavations.

671 KIRSCHBAUM, E., "Besprechung von Klauser, "die römische Petrustradition" — RQ, 51 (1956), 247-254.

This is an evaluation of T. Klauser's well-known work. The book consists of three major sections:
1. The Roman tradition about Peter.
2. The recent excavations beneath St. Peter's.
3. An evaluation of the Peter-Roman tradition in light of the results of the excavations.

Kirschbaum points out that Klauser's thesis is dependent on his opinions regarding the results of the excavations. According to Klauser, Gaius' topographical reference to the *trophy* is correct, and he admits that the *trophy* has been found *in situ*. On the negative side he states that it is certain that the *trophy* is not above Peter's tomb, nor has any real tomb been found in the excavations, nor are there any proofs which make the conclusion possible that it was in this place. The question is still unsolved as to when and how a tradition about localizing the Vatican hill as the place of his burial, originated. Klauser then attempts to prove that the rising force behind the idea of "Apostolic succession" (around 165 A.D.) gave the major impetus to this tradition. Prior to that period there was no interest in Peter's tomb and no continuous cult, because the day when Peter died was forgotten.

Kirschbaum points out that Klauser reached his conclusions by research on the tombs around the central area—based on A. von Gerkan's conclusions. It is a known fact that the reconstruction of the terrain and the erroneous chronology regarding the central group of tombs is bound to lead to such an untenable interpretation of the facts. It is no surprise then, that when Klauser bases himself on such false premises (thanks to von Gerkan), he should come to such false hypotheses.

On the question of "Apostolic succession," Klauser bases himself on Clement (100) and Irenaeus (185), and Gaius (around 200). Kirschbaum denies that Klauser's thesis of the idea of Apostolic succession originating around 165 can be proved. If someone attempts to prove the idea of Apostolic succession based on a "tomb," then such evidence is available only from a time around 200—the time when the *trophy* was already in existence. Klauser's main problem is attributed to the differences regarding the basic archeological assumptions which, naturally, have influenced all his subsequent conclusions.

672 KIRSCHBAUM, E., *The Tombs of St. Peter and St. Paul*, trans. by J. Murray, (New York: St. Martin's Press, 1959), 57 figs., 44 plates, 242 pp. Also in German: *Die Gräber der Apostelfürsten*, (Frankfort a.m.: Scheffler, 1957), 256 pp. with figs. and plates. Also in Spanish: *Las Tumbas de los Apostoles*, (Barcelona: Agros, 1959), 286 pp. with figs. and plates.

This scholarly work is directed against the studies of A. M. Schneider and A. von Gerkan. It is a detailed scientific-technical exposition of the excavations beneath the Confessio of St. Peter in the Vatican and of St. Paul on the via Ostia. It is also a critique of the critics and a history of the Apostolic remains.

The author defends the thesis of the excavations that Peter's tomb was really discovered, though he admits that the reports of the excavations are not entirely accurate. He himself was a member of the team commissioned by Pius XII to engage in the excavations and he is fully acquainted with the matter he discusses. He describes the necropolis (pagan and Christian burials) beneath St. Peter's that adjoined Nero's circus. From the mausoleums he demonstrates that Peter was probably buried at the spot in 67 A.D. From the levels of the ruins he reconstructs the fate of the body that was transferred from crypt to crypt in subsequent years. This is the first scholarly account in English.

673 KIRSCHBAUM, E., "Petrusgrab" — *Lexikon für Theologie und Kirche*, 8 (1963), 387-390.

In this brief study the author sums up the literary testimony that associates the cult-center of San Sebastiano on the via Appia with the grave of Peter (and Paul). It was on the basis of such testimony that some (Duchesne, Lietzmann, etc.) have put forth the theory that at the time of the Valerianic persecutions in 258, the bodies of Peter (and Paul) were transferred for safety to the via Appia. The tradition seemed confirmed by the excavations under San Sebastiano in 1915-1923 when the graffiti, triclia etc. came to light. In the second section the author takes up the Vatican excavations of 1940-49, 1953-57, wherein he briefly describes the findings of the experts. Critical investigations confirm the fact of Peter's burial beneath the *trophy* which Constantine had isolated as a monument, and which the architect was fully aware of when he constructed the basilica. This conclusion, however, is not acceptable to all. The author mentions the theory of Von Gerkan, Prandi, Dinkler, Klauser.

674 KLAUSER, T., *Die Römische Petrustradition im Lichte der neuen Ausgrabungen unter der Peterskirche*, (=*Arbeitsgemeinschaft für Forschung des Landes Nordrhein-Westfalen, Geistes-*

wissenschaft, 24) (Cologne-Opladen: Westdeutscher Verlag, 1956), 122 pp. with 16 ill., 19 plates.

This is a lecture delivered by the author in December, 1953 and brought up to date with copious footnotes.

The fundamental purpose of the work is to evaluate the extent to which the literary tradition of Peter's sojourn and death in Rome has been confirmed by the archeological excavations of 1939-1949. To this end the author gives an analysis of the oldest literary tradition, a critical summary of the excavational findings based largely on A. von Gerkan, and he reconstructs the historical development of the cult of Peter at Rome.

The author concludes that there never was any real tomb of St. Peter. However, about the year 165, the Roman Christians began for the first time to be interested in having a tomb of St. Peter. The real reason for the interest shown at that time is *Apostolic succession*. One group of Roman Christians claimed to have the tomb of St. Peter on the Vatican hill. Another group located the tomb of Peter at San Sebastiano. So the year 165 signifies the earliest beginning of a cult of the tomb of Peter. Before this time there was no such veneration. As a result, the translation-hypothesis must be totally discarded, also, the idea that an altar stood above the so-called Peter's tomb in the Constantinian basilica from the beginning. On the other hand, the author is convinced that the literary proof for the sojourn and martyrs' death of Peter and Paul has not been disproven by the excavations. He further is of the opinion that the *tropaion* mentioned by Gaius about the year 200, has been found. But this *tropaion*, contrary to Gaius' own opinion, was not located above the real tomb of St. Peter. As a conclusion, the author states that the excavations have not produced the real tomb, nor anything else which would enable us to believe that there ever was a real tomb of the Apostle.

675 KLAUSER, T., "Christlicher Märtyrerkult, heidnischer Heroen-kult und spätjüdische Heillgenverehrung" — (=*Arbeitsge-meinschaft für Forschung des Landes Nordrhein-Westfalen, Geisteswissenschaft*, 91) — (Cologne-Opladen, 1960), 27-38.

676 KIVEKÄS, E., "Das Problem vom Grabe des hl. Petrus" — *Teologinen Aikakauskirja*, 64 (1959), 34-48.

677 KOLLWITZ, J., "Die Grabungen unter Sankt Peter" — *Hochland*, 45 (1952), 15-25.

This is a good summary of the archeological results of the Vatican excavations to which the author adds some relevant remarks. However, because of the problems raised by the excavations, he questions whether or not we are able to demonstrate with certainty that we are dealing here with Peter's tomb.

678 KRAUTHEIMER, R., "Some drawings of early Christian basilicas in Rome: St. Peter's and S. Maria Maggiore" — *The Art Bulletin*, 31 (1949), 211-215.

We have here an interesting drawing by Martin Heemskerk (1532-1535) in which St. Peter's basilica is seen from the northeast corner of the Constantinian transept. The famous columns found in the basilica are also included.

679 KRONSTEINER, H., *Das Petrusgrab. Rom hat sein Herz entdekt.* (Graz-Wien-Altotting: Verlag Styria, 1952), 167 pp. pp. with 16 figs.

This is a brief and concise exposé—written in a popular style—of the excavational findings of the Vatican. It contains the following sections:

1. The world is listening.
2. We go as pilgrims to the grave.
3. The necropolis under the dome.
4. The series of mausoleums.
5. Hope from a grave.
6. Peter's grave and the Peter-question.
7. The sermon of the seven hills.
8. Peter and Paul.
9. Proof of the truth.
10 The builder and inhabitant is Christ Himself.
11 We are once again blessed.

680 KWIECINSKI, A., "Donioste odkrycie pod watykańska św. Piotra" — *Ateneum Kaplanskie*, 51 (1949), 489-495.

681 KWIECINSKI, A., "Tropaea" Piotra i Pawla Apostolów w Rzymie wedlug naidawnieszych dokumentow historyczno-archeologicznych" — *Collectanea Theologica*, 25 (Warsaw, 1954) 268-320.

682 LAST, H., "St. Peter, the Excavations under his Basilica in Rome and the Beginnings of Western Christendom" — *Proceedings of the Classical Association*, 51 (1954), 50-51.

> This is a summary of a paper read at King's College. The author distinguishes the questions that might be asked about Peter's association with Rome;
> 1. Whether he did or did not visit that city.
> 2. If he did and died there; whether his body was buried in the spot now covered over by the Papal altar.
> The author suggests that the main result of the recent excavations was to confirm the generally accepted view that Constantine built this church on this site for a compelling reason—probably some association of the site with Peter. He then describes the excavations and says it seems almost certain that the monument found behind and below the Niche of the Pallia was Gaius' *trophy*. The mass of graffiti on wall 'g' (which contained no reference to Peter), written probably in the latter part of the third century, did not suppose his relics to be nearby when they were written. These graffiti have to be considered in connection with those at San Sebastiano—which explains an association with the two Apostles—and could well be explained by the presence of their relics in that site for a time. The author concludes that several problems involved with the fate of Peter's body—if he died at Rome—demand a solution before it is possible to give an account commanding general assent of Peter's relation to the site of his basilica.

683 LAST, H., *Journal of Roman Studies*, 44 (1954), 112-116.

> This is an evaluation of Carcopino's "Études d'histoire chrétienne," etc., which consists of two studies. The first

is concerned with the letter-square SATOR which Carcopino believes is crypto-Christian. The second and larger part of the book is occupied with a treatment of the Vatican excavations. Carcopino's main conclusion is that Peter was buried at the time of his death on the spot marked by the *tropaeum*. He does not regard the bones found in the soil under Niche I of the *tropaeum* as having any serious claim to be the Apostle's. He also comments on the graffiti of wall 'g' which lack any invocation to St. Peter and which strongly suggest that the relics of the Saint were not thought by the writers of the graffiti to be nearby at the time they wrote. He believes that at that time, the body of Peter was at San Sebastiano. He also believes that the bulk of graffiti at San Sebastiano is not exactly explained without the assumption that the Apostles were there.

684 LEBUFFE, F. P., "Earthquakes in the Vatican: tremors reveal history" — *The Catholic Digest*, 16 (Jan. 1952), 97-102.

This article deals with the interesting account of the expedition sponsored by the 'American Weekly.' The experts made use of seismographs since it is the opinion of seismologists that artificial earthquakes will help shed light on the site of Nero's circus.

685 LECLERC, J., "Les fouilles faites récemment à Saint-Pierre de Rome et la tombe du Prince des Apôtres" — *Revue ecclésiastique du diocèse de Metz*, 35 (1953), 244-252.

This study contains an informative summary of the results of the excavations with some pertinent replies to the negative critics. Among his observations the author skillfully emphasizes the positive value of the conclusions drawn in the *official report*.

686 LECLERCQ, H., "Saint Pierre" — DACL, 14 (1939), 838-921.

One of the few scholarly studies that is informative in every aspect of the subject of "Peter." The author gives a wide range of his knowledge with regard to the theological, historical, literary and archeological problems about St. Peter. It contains the following sections:

1. Peter's coming to Rome.
2. His sojourn at Rome.
3. The duration of his sojourn.
4. His death and tomb.
5. The tradition of the hypothesis.
6. The martyrdom of Peter: history and legend.
7. The feast "ad catacumbas."
8. Damasus and "catacumbas."
9. Popes Gregory I, Leo III and Nicholas I.
10. The opportunity for a translation "ad catacumbas."
11. The inscription "hic habitasse."
12. The basilica of the Apostles.
13. The texts re: the Memoria Apostolorum.
14. Excavations at the Memoria Apostolorum.
15. The graffiti.
16. The translation of St. Paul.
17. The translation of St. Peter.
18. The 'domus Petri'.
19. Conclusions.
20. The tomb of Peter at the Vatican.
21. A reconstruction and modification.
22. During the time of Paul V and Clement VIII.
23. Aspects of the actual tomb.

687 LEMERLE, P., A propos de la basilique constantinienne de Saint-Pierre à Rome" — *Revue Archéologique*, 25 (1946), 79-81.

This is a summary of the studies by E. Josi: "Gli scavi nelle Sacre Grotte Vaticane," appearing in *Il Vaticano nel 1944*, pp. 188-200, and that by G. Nicolosi: "Questioni nuove intorno alla basilica costantiniana in Vaticano," *ibid.*, pp. 202-210 (see no. 729).

688 LEMERLE, P., "Les fouilles de Saint-Pierre de Rome" — NC, 1-2 (1950), 393-411.

One finds here a comparison between the knowledge obtained from literary tradition and the presumed results of the excavations beneath the Vatican. The author objects to some of the interpretations of the archeological findings of the experts. He claims that there is nothing to allow us to affirm that the authentic relics of Peter ever

existed, and nothing (up to the time of this writing) to
affirm that the Apostle's remains (authentic or not) were
venerated here either before Constantine or after him. It
seems improbable to speak of the Vatican as the tomb of
the Apostle and rather difficult to identify the small
monument in that place with the *trophy* of Gaius.

689 LEMERLE, P., "Les persécutions et le tombeau de Saint-
Pierre" — *Revue Archéologique*, 38 (1951), 147-151.

> An article of almost the same material as that found in
> Gregoire's study on the date of Polycarp's death and the
> persecutions of the Roman Empire. However, the ideas
> were subsequently modified.

690 LEMERLE, P., "La publication des fouilles de la Basilique
Vaticane et la question du tombeau de Saint-Pierre" — RH,
208 (1952), 205-227 with 6 figs.

> The author examines the *official report* (Esplorazioni)
> and expresses a great skepticism. The excavations have
> not yielded positive results regarding Nero's circus, the
> via Cornelia, the Apostle's tomb. The conclusions, there-
> fore, as to the interpretation of the archeological findings:
> the niches, the 'red wall' and associated details—are
> without foundation and open to dispute.

691 LEMERLE, P., "Saint-Demétrius de Thessalonique et les
problèmes du martyrium et du transept" — *Bulletin de corres-
pondance hellénique*, 77 (1953), 660-694.

692 LEMERLE, P., RHR, 151/2 (1957), 104 ff.

> This is an evaluation of T. Klauser's "Die Römische
> Petrustradition, etc."

693 LEITE, J., "A Sepultura de S. Pedro" — *Broteria*, 58 (1954),
385-511 with 17 figs.

> A long and rather ordinary treatment of the present
> St. Peter's in which the author traces its origin back to
> the Memoria of the Apostle. The plans herein can also be
> seen in P. Vogt's article in *Biblica*, 33 (1952), 165-168;
> 306-309.

694 LETAROUILLY, P., *Le Vatican et la basilique de St.-Pierre de Rome*, 2 vols. (Paris: A. Morel & Co., 1882), with 133 plates.

General information on the Vatican and the basilica.

695 LLORCA, B., "Las excavaciones de San Pedro y la authenticitad de su sepulcro" — *Salmanticensis*, 3 (1956), 474-484.

696 L'ORANGE, H. P., "The "Adventus" ceremony and the slaying of Pentheus as represented in two mosaics of about A.D. 300" — *Late Classical and Mediaeval Studies in Honor of Albert Mathias Friend, Jr.*, (Princeton, 1955), 7-14.

In this brief study the author gives an interpretation of two mosaics, one of which (pp. 10-14) is concerned with the mosaic on the facade of the mausoleum of the Marcii which was uncovered in the excavations under St. Peter's.

697 LUGLI, G., "Il Vaticano nell'antichità classica" — *Vaticano*, (ed. G. Fallani & M. Escobar, Florence, 1946), 3-22.

698 LUGLI, G., "Qui fu sepolto Pietro" — *Le vie d'Italia*, 64 (1958), 449-456, 11 plates.

The ever-puzzling Damasian inscription and the translation-theory at San Sebastiano, and Eusebius's quote of Gaius' trophy prompted this study. The author deals with the excavational results at the Vatican and concludes that the findings prove the truth of the tradition that Peter was buried here also (at the Vatican) immediately after his martyrdom and that Constantine built a basilica (began in 324) over the memoria of Peter.

699 MacKENDRICK, P., "Caesar and Christ" — *The Mute Stones Speak*, (New York: St. Martin's Press, 1960), 340-351.

We have here an account of the beginnings of the excavations beneath the Vatican at the direction of Pius XII. Basing himself upon the *official report*—which the author feels is quite objective (no conclusions are drawn which exceed the archeological evidence), he gives here a description of the findings; the mausoleums, decorations etc. But as interesting as the cemetery is, it is not the centrally important discovery under St. Peter's nor does it supply the motive for Constantine's location of his church here. The excavators found the motive in Campo P where there was a niche, in front of which existed an Aedicula. The conclusion is inevitable that Constantine in A.D. 322 planned his basilica to rise just here, because he believed the lower niche, under the Red Wall, contained the bones of St. Peter. The author then answers the question: how early can the burial be demonstrated to be? But this is not the only spot in Rome associated with St. Peter. He takes up a brief history of San Sebastiano on the via Appia where it was believed that Peter's body in whole or in part, was moved from the Vatican hill for safety during the Valerianic persecutions in A.D. 258.

700 MAGI, F., "Relazione preliminare sui ritrovamenti archeolo-gici nell'area dell'autoparco vaticano" — *Triplici omaggio a Sua Santità Pio XII*, vol. 2, (Vatican City, 1958), 187-201.

All of the archeological research up until 1956 centered around the ancient burial place beneath the Vatican basilica. Since the *official report* was published, the author made a wonderful discovery. It was in 1956 when exca-vations were undertaken to build a new garage in the Vatican, when another ancient burial place (which had been in use from the first to the fourth centuries A.D.) was discovered. Some fifteen mausoleums and seventy individual tombs had been excavated under the direction of the author. Among the mausoleums and inscriptions discovered, a good bit of archeological evidence was found dating from the first century. Thanks to this discovery, it was possible to continue research in a wider frame of reference, scil., the topography of the Vatican in ancient times.

701 MAHN, M., "Rome chrétienne. Des catacombes à Saint-Pierre de Rome" — *La Vie Spirituelle*, 82 (1950), 487-504.

702 MANN, H. K., *Tomb and Portraits of the Popes of the Middle Ages*, (London: Sheed & Ward, 1928), 1-4.

Any account of Papal tombs must begin with the story of the tomb of the first Pope, Peter. In these few pages the author gives a brief reconstruction of the tomb based on literary testimony.

703 MANTHEY, J., "Grob sw. Piotra" — *Duszpasters Polski za granica*, 3 (1952), 336-350, with 8 figs.

This little study was written to confute the doubts advanced by some Protestant scholars and at the same time to acquaint others with a cursory idea of the scientific results of the excavations. The author bases himself on the *official report*.

704 MARUCCHI, O., "Il cimitero del vaticano" — *Le Catacombe Romane*, (posthumous ed. by E. Josi, Rome: La Liberaria della Stato, 1932), 34-54.

In this outstanding work the author discusses the Vatican cemetery and the tomb of Peter according to the literary, archeological, and monumental testimony. Many of the aspects revealed in the most recent excavations are described herein.

705 MARROU, H. I., "L'épitaphe vaticane du consulaire de Vienne Eventius" — *Revue des études anciennes*, 54 (1952), 326-331.

The author treats of the inscription discovered in the archeological excavations under St. Peter's in 1941. His chief endeavor is to establish its date.

706 MARROU, H. I., "Vatican (fouilles du)" — DACL, 15 (1953), 3291-3346.

The material included here—based on scientific data only—furnishes us with ample proof that history can be corroborated or denied by archeology. The author deals with the excavations beneath the Vatican grottoes from 1940-49, including the research that took place up until Christmas, 1952. In this research the author shares credit with another eminent archeologist, M. J. Carcopino.

707 MATZ, F., "An evaluation of J. Toynbee-Ward Perkins: The Shrine of St. Peter" — *Gnomon*, 3 (1958), 500-503.

We have here an assessment of the famous work. The

author gives a break-down of its contents according to chapters. He concludes: "We could not ask for a better introduction to the Vatican cemetery."

708 MAURICE-DENIS, N., & BOULET, R., "A propos des fouilles de Saint-Pierre. Questions liturgiques et historiques" — RSR, 34 (1947), 403-406.

The author gives a historical reconstruction of the Constantinian basilica: its date and purpose. He endeavors to see a relation between the two dates of the chronography 25 dic. and June 29, and he imagines that the Vatican basilica was consecrated on 25 dic. 335 and 336. Further, basing himself on the literary evidence he studies the Confessio of Peter, the character and primitive plan of the basilica. Finally, he speaks of the Memoria ad catacumbas. His interpretation of the famous Damasian inscription allows him to conclude that Peter and Paul were buried on the via Appia for a period—though we do not know how long they were there.

709 MAURICE-DENIS, N., & BOULET, R., *Romée ou le pèlerin à Rome*, (Brussels-Paris: Desclée-De Brouwer, 1950), 3d. ed., 5-50.

This is a study of the excavational findings under the Vatican basilica.
See next.

710 MAURICE-DENIS, N. & BOULET, R., *Fouilles et découvertes faites dans la crypte de Saint Pierre en 1952* (sic).

The material contained herein—published in a separate fascicle—is almost the same as that above.

711 MAURY, J., & PERCHERON, R., *Itinéraires romains*, (Paris: Lethielleux, 1950), xxviii-664 pp.

This is one of the best guides on Rome wherein the monuments are arranged in their chronological order and in their historical setting. It also contains a brief historical-archeological introduction.

712 MAZZARINO, S., "Il problema della sepoltura dell'apostolo

Pietro e le recenti esplorazioni" — *L'impero romano*, (= G. Giannelli et S. Mazzarino, *Trattato di storia romana*, 2), (Roma: Tumminelli, 1956), 575-578.

713 MERLIN, A., "De Pythagore aux Apôtres" — *Journal des savants*, 1956, 145-165.

> This is a review of J. Carcopino's well-known work. (See no. 507).

714 MESLIN, M., "Fouilles archéologiques à Rome" — *Larousse Mensuel illustre*, vol. 13, n. 461, (Jan. 1953), 199-201, with 4 figs.

> The author describes the fateful accident in the Vatican Grottoes which prompted Pius XII to initiate the excavations under St. Peter's basilica. He describes the discovery of the cemetery, its mausoleums, and other artistic finds, and cites the Pontiff's message which announced to the world the results of the excavations.

715 MEYER, C. R., "Recent Excavations Under St. Peter's Basilica" — *Chicago Studies*, 1 (1962), 89-103.

> As indicated by the author himself, since the results of the excavational discoveries beneath the Vatican and the arguments connected with them are apt to be presented in too scholarly a fashion, he proposes to "simplify" the report for the 'ordinary' folk. The article is based on the *official report*.

716 MIGNANTI, F. M., *Istoria della Sacrosancta Patriarcale Basilica Vaticana*, vol. I, *Basilica antica*, (Roma-Torino, 1867), 339 pp.

> We have here valuable information for a knowledge of the ancient Vatican basilica.

717 MOHRMANN, C., "A propos de deux mots controversés de la latinité chrétienne, "tropaeum-nomen" — *Vigiliae Christiniae*, 8 (1954), 154-173.

> This is a valuable word-study of the term "tropaon" which is rich in material and acute in reasoning. The author's suggestion is that Gaius could not have used it

to indicate "the place of martyrdom" since such a usage is not found in any other document. It is preferable not to apply the word "trophy" to a funerary monument that marked the resting place of the relics. The passages read in Eusebius and in the light of contemporary usage (presumably also Gaius) had rather in mind the *actual relics* of the Apostles. In the second part of her study, the author takes up an analysis of the Christian evolution and usage of the term "nomen" with a reference here to the celebrated epigram about the Apostles Peter and Paul which Pope Damasus inscribed in the basilica ad catacumbas. Though others have concluded that the word refers to "relics," the author claims that all inscriptions wherein the word is found are of North-African origin. In its reference to relics, it is not proven for Italy. Frequently, Damasus himself uses the word but never in this sense. She concludes that it could be considered as a poetic paraphrase of *Petrum Paulumque*.

718 MONTENOVESI, O., "La tomba dell'apostolo san Pietro" — *Archivi*, 2nd ser., 20 (1953), 80-83.

719 MONTINI, R. U., "Il sepolcreto papale delle Grotte Vaticane" — *Capitolium*, 26 (1951), 269-284, 8 plates.

> The recent and wonderful systematization of the Vatican grottoes, which yielded the discovery of Peter's tomb, has given a new and noteworthy emphasis to the Pontifical necropolis which has existed for many centuries in the Vatican basilica. The author gives a detailed account of the Pontiffs buried here.

720 MULDER, H., *Het graf van Petrus* (=Reformatorische Stemmen, The Hague: Willem de Zwijgerstichting, 1953), 32 pp.

721 MULDER, H., "Het graf van Petrus" — *Christian Encyclopedia*, (Kampen), 2nd ed., 5 (1960), 439-440.

722 MÜNTZ, E. & FROTHINGHAM, A. L., "Il tesoro della basilica di S. Pietro in Vaticano dal sec. XIII al XV" — *Archivio della soc. rom. di st. patria*, 6 (1883), 1-137.

> The treasury of relics at the Vatican basilica is of great

importance for archeological studies. This deals with those relics from the time of Constantine, and gives a detailed list of the benefactors of the basilica.

723 MURPHY, F. J., "St. Peter's. The Excavations" — *Roman Echoes*, (An annual publication of the Undergraduate Students of the Pontifical North American College), (Roma: Arte grafiche italiane, 1956), 37-44; 245-252.

A cursory survey of the Vatican excavations based on the *official report*.

724 MURPHY, F. X., "Exploration Beneath St. Peter's" — *Thought*, 24 (1949), 581-586.

An editorial briefly summarizing the occasion for initiating the excavations in 1940, its full significance as expressed by Pius XII and the comforting first-hand evidence of the truths already expressed in history concerning the martyrdom and burial of the "Rock" that was Peter.

725 MURPHY, F. X., "Round the Tomb of St. Peter: The Vatican Excavations" — *The Tablet*, 193 (April 2, 1949), 215-216.

The author gives a brief survey explaining why modern non-Catholic historians during the last twenty years have been compelled to admit the probative evidence pointing to the fact that St. Peter was in Rome. The article mainly describes how this is now all possible because of the excavational findings under the Vatican.

726 MURPHY, F. X., "Exploration beneath St. Peter's" — *Catholic Mind*, 48 (1950), 257-261.

The article is the same as the one reproduced in *Thought*, 24 (1949), 581-586. (See no. 724).

727 MURPHY, F. X., "Saints Peter and Paul."

See no. 406.

728 NICOLOSI, G., "I lavori di ampliamento, risanamento e sistemazione delle Sacre Grotte Vaticane" — *L'Osservatore Romano*, March 13, 1941, p. 4.

A history of the excavations and their results are described here in great detail. The author speaks of the work of extension that was carried out in the Sacre Grotte in 1939 (the immediate occasion for the excavations) to prepare a tomb for Pius XI who had expressed the wish to be buried in the Grotte near the tomb of Pius X. The article tells how it was enlarged by lowering the floor of the crypt famous for its tombs of popes and princes. There is an accompanying floor-plan of the entire Vatican basilica pin-pointing the area where the project was undertaken.

729 NICOLOSI, G., "Questioni nuove intorno alla Basilica Constantiniana in Vaticano" — *Il Vaticano nel 1944*, (Roma, 1944), 200-210.

Much has been said and written about the famous circus of Nero and Gaius and especially with regard to the site occupied by the Vatican basilica. (Until 1940 it was generally believed that the southern foundation-walls of the fourth-century basilica rested on the northern walls of the circus of Gaius and Nero. Recent excavations have not been able to find traces of the circus). In this study the author examines the tradition with regard to the circus of Nero and its obelisk. He also makes some technical observations as regards the Constantinian basilica, the findings of the drainage-system of Pope Damasus, etc.

730 NICOLOSI, G., "Ritrovamenti e sistemazioni nelle sacre grotte Vaticane" — *Scienzae tecnica*, 8 (1947), 20-34, with illus., & plans.

The author gives here a more detailed account describing the work of extension in the Sacre Grotte, its systematic exploration, and the evidence that was brought to light.

731 NICOLOSI, G., "Un decennio di lavori nelle Grotte Vaticane" — *Ecclesia*, (Citta di Vaticana), 9 (1949), 310-317. 12 plates.

In anticipation of the anticipated official publication (the *official report*) regarding the excavations beneath the

Sacre Grotte Vaticane, the author (one of the collabora-
tors) takes up again the task of showing the many questions
that have resulted of a technical and statistical nature.

732 NICOLOSI, G., "Alcuni sarcofagi romani della necropoli
vaticana" — *Archeologia classica*, 7 (1955), 32-49.

In the course of the excavations commenced in 1939
(and continued) beneath the Vatican grottoes, a large
Roman necropolis came to light which is interesting for
its topography, architecture of the mausoleums, decorations in stucco and mosaics, paintings, and certain
sarcophagi. In this study the author deals with three of
the sarcophagi which contain elements of great use for the
study of the currents of Roman sculpture of the second
and third centuries. The sarcophagi are from:
1) The mausoleum of the Egyptians.
2) The mausoleum of the Marci.
3) The mausoleum of the Valerii.
The author gives a descriptive analysis and interpretation of these three sarcophagi.

733 NORTH, R., *Verbum Domini*, 32 (1954), 244-247.

This is a review of M. Guarducci's "Cristo e San Pietro
in un documento precostantiniano della necropoli vaticana." The book is concerned with the inscription found
in the tomb of the Valerii: the crude inscription traced in
red and done over in black. With the inscription two
portraits are seen one above the other. To the left of the
head are the letters PETRV, to the right, the rest of an
epigraph. The author analyzes Guarducci's methods of
establishing the authenticity of the text that she purports
to read. He seriously objects to her interpretation.

734 O'CALLAGHAN, R. T., "Recent Excavations underneath the
Vatican Crypts" — *The Biblical Archeologist*, 12 (1949), 2-23,
13 figs.

Basing himself on expert sources, the author gives a
scholarly summary of the remarkable excavational
findings. Included is a description of the rich and pre-
dominantly pagan cemetery which the findings revealed

(though it yielded less positive results regarding the circus of Nero and the via Cornelia). The earlier archeological work in conjunction with Peter's tomb is evaluated, and the solid literary traditions which fixed the site of his burial in Rome and the Vatican area is reviewed. This is one of the first reports to have appeared in English which is substantially that of the *official report*.

735 O'CALLAGHAN, R. T., "The Tomb of Peter" — *American National Catholic Weekly Review*, 89 (April 4, 1953), 9-11.

This is a brief resumé written in a popular style with regard to the archeological findings beneath the Vatican basilica, and based on the *official report*.

736 O'CALLAGHAN, R. T., "Vatican Excavations and the Tomb of Peter" — *The Biblical Archeologist*, 16 (1953), 70-87, with 12 figs.

This is the second study by the author which is intended to supply a complete report on the question of Peter's tomb based on the most recent archeological material made available at the time of this writing. Except for a few minor additions, it is essentially that which is contained in the *official report*. The twelve figures are also taken from the same source. The author considers the question of Peter's burial under these two aspects:

1. Have Peter's bones been found?
2. Has the place of burial been found?

737 O'DOGHERTY, E., "The Tomb of St. Peter" — *The American Ecclesiastical Review*, 128 (1953), 438-444.

The author is concerned with the period prior to Constantine, and gives only a very brief glimpse at the important evidence uncovered with regard to the building of the Constantinian basilica. The information contained herein is based on the *official report*.

738 L'OSSERVATORE ROMANO, (Editorial) Dec. 20, 1951.

This is concerned with the scientific documentation of the discovery of Peter's tomb.

739 L'OSSERVATORE ROMANO, Dec. 25, 1943, p. 1.

The Pope's (Pius XII) Christmas allocution wherein he mentions the archeological excavations under St. Peter's basilica.

740 L'OSSERVATORE ROMANO, Jan. 29, 1949, p. 1.

Pius XII announces the significance of the excavations beneath St. Peter's. "Here in the circus of Nero, concerning which fact we possess incontestable archeological evidence, (Peter) died as confessor of Christ. Under the central point of the gigantic cupola (of St. Peter's) was and is the place of his burial."

741 L'OSSERVATORE ROMANO, Nov. 22, 1952, p. 3.

An exciting discovery is announced by M. Guarducci. In the niche of the tomb of the Valerii about 81 feet east of the Confessio, were found portrayed two heads, one above the other, sketched in charcoal and red lead. An inscription accompanied the sketches which contains a prayer to Peter to intercede for all the Christians who are buried near his body.

742 L'OSSERVATORE ROMANO, March 19, 1959, p. 3.

There is an announcement here of M. Guarducci's research: "I graffiti sotto la Confessione di San Pietro" and her 'mystic cryptographical readings.'

743 PALANQUE, J. R., "A-t-on retrouvé le tombeau de Saint Pierre?" — *Cahiers universitaires catholiques*, (March-April, 1954), 318-325.

The author presents a clear synthesis of the chief archeological and historical results of the recent excavations. The Esplorazioni, Carcopino and Marrou, are the basis for this treatment, although the author does not . always agree with their conclusions.

744 PANVINIO, O., "De rebus antiquis basilicae S. Petri" — (=A. Mai, *Spicilegium Romanum* IX) Rome, 1843, 194-382.

Material on the Roman basilica with precious information on St. Peter's back in the sixteenth century when this Augustinian monk of Verona gathered his materials.

745 PARIBENI, R., "Le tombe degli Apostoli Pietro e Paulo in Roma e i recenti scavi" — *Vita e Pensiero*, 32 (1949), 150-154.

A rather brief but clear study about the actual state of the question with regard to the subsequent places where the bodies of the Apostles were buried and the basilicas erected in these historical places. The author also includes a brief critique of certain essential points found in a recent study by Belvederi.

746 PARIBENI, R., "Recenti scoperte sotto S. Pietro in Vaticano" — *Vita e Pensiero*, 35 (1952), 676-678.

This study examines the tomb of the Valerii (uncovered in the Vatican excavations) with its stucco reliefs and the portraits of two heads, one above the other, traced in red and done over in black, and the accompanying inscription.

747 PAUL VI (POPE) *L'Osservatore Romano*, June 26, 1963, p. 1.

In his allocution to the pilgrims from Philadelphia, Pa., his holiness makes the interesting observation: "All around you there are numerous monuments, reminders of the glories of the Church and her faithful . . . And here, at the tomb of Peter, we traverse centuries to return to the times of the Apostles, Peter and Paul."

748 PENNA, A., *San Pietro*,

See no. 208.

749 PERLER, O., "Die Mosaiken der Juliergruft im Vatikan" — *Rektoratsrede zur feirierlichen Eröffnung des Studienjahres am 15. November 1952*, (Fribourg, 1953); *Freiburger Universitäts Reden*, 74 pp., 12 plates.

This is an extensive and elaborate discussion of the Christian interpretation of the mosaic iconography (which decorated the mausoleum of the Julii) in relation to Scripture, Liturgy, the Fathers, Christian sculpture and painting of the third century, and to comparable motifs in contemporary pagan art.

750 PETERSON, E., & ORGELS, P., "A propos du tombeau de S. Pierre" — *Le Flambeau*, 25 (1952), 486-495.

This is a translation of the same study that appeared in *Schweizer Rundschau*, 52 (1952), 326-331, to which translator's notes have been added.

751 PETERSON, E., "Ueber das Petrusgrab" — *Schweizer Rundschau*, 52 (1952), 326-331.

The author interprets the shrine (which was revealed in the Vatican excavations) as a second century localization of a very early oral tradition that Peter was buried somewhere on this part of the Vatican hill. The word "trophies" used by the priest Gaius in his famous disputation with Proclus (when referring to the places where the bodies of the Apostles were laid) is to be understood as "tombs." This is clear from the context. Gaius' testimony, therefore, constitutes a valuable oral tradition. The small monument discovered beneath St. Peter's altar resembles those of Isola Sacra and Ostia. However, it was erected to Peter as an Apostle, not as a martyr.

752 PIGANIOL, A., "L'état actuel de la question constantinienne" — *Historia*, 1 (1950), 82-96.

This study examines the date of construction of the Constantinian basilica. There have been many opinions in this respect. According to the author the actual construction of the basilica was commenced in 326.

753 PIUS XII (Pope) "Discorso nell'Occasione dell'inaugurazione del monumentale sarcofago di Papa Pio XI" — (Feb. 9). *Discorsi e radiomessaggi di Sua Santita Pio XII, vol. 2*, (Milano, 1941), 391-393.

This is Pius XII's grateful response to the donation of those who made possible the new sarcophagus to contain the mortal remains of Pius XI. Herein he mentions the Grotto Vaticane and the new riches, which through divine Providence, are beginning to be revealed.

754 PIUS XII (POPE) "Recenti scavi nelle Grotte Vaticane; Importanti scoperte archeologiche" — AAS, 34 (1942), 162-164; also RAC, 19 (1942), 29-32.

> This is a radio address of the Supreme Pontiff wherein the full significance of the discoveries made beneath the Vatican basilica is announced to the world. The Pope announces that a "monument of simple form" through the indefatigable efforts of the excavators, has been discovered. This proves that even before Constantine's time this was a place of cult. These graffiti ... furnish certain historical evidence that we have here the remains of the trophy of which the priest Gaius spoke about A.D. 200. The contents in RAC which follow C. Respighi's article are quoted (not only in the AAS) but also in articles by J. Zeiller and E. Kirschbaum.

755 PIUS XII (POPE) "Discorso alle rappresentanze dei gruppi degli Istituti medi superiori di Roma ove fiorisce l'Opera gioventù studentesca" — (Jan. 30). *Discorsi e radiomessaggi di Sua Santità Pio XII, vol. 10* (Roma, 1949), 358.

> Of particular significance in this allocution are the following words of the Pontiff: "It was a disposition of Divine Providence that St. Peter selected Rome as his episcopal See. For here in the circus of Nero, concerning which fact we possess incontestable archeological evidence, he died as a confessor of Christ; under the central point of the gigantic dome (of St. Peter's) was and is the place of his burial."

756 PIUS XII (POPE) (Radio allocution of Christmas Eve, 1950) AAS, 42 (1950), 132.

> The Pontiff in inviting the world to come to Rome for the Holy Year refers to Rome (St. Peter's basilica) and categorically affirms that this is the place where the ancient *trophy* of the glorious tomb of the prince of the Apostles had been found.

757 PIUS XII (POPE) "Ritrovamento della tomba del Principe degli Apostoli" — AAS, 43 (1951), 51-52.

> In his radio address to the world during the Holy Year

the Pontiff makes a brief report on the excavations which
were completed at that time under the Vatican. In reply
to the question "was Peter's tomb really found?" His
answer is YES! In reply to a second question (subordinate
to the first) regarding the Saint's relics: "were they
found?" Human relics were discovered in the area of the
Apostle's tomb, though (at that time) it had not yet been
determined with absolute certitude that they were Peter's
bones.

758 PIUS XII (POPE) (Allocution to the 10th. International
Congress of Historical Sciences, Rome, Sept. 7, 1955) AAS,
47 (1955), 672-682. See 675.

In this allocution the Pontiff refers to the Vatican
excavations and reaffirms the fact that the site of St.
Peter's tomb has been established beyond all reasonable
doubt.

759 PIUS XII (POPE) (Discourse to the participants of the 3rd.
International Congress of Greek and Latin epigraphy) *L'Osservatore Romano*, Sept. 11, 1957, p. 1.

The Pontiff observes the great value that epigraphy
has for a knowledge of the ancient church as witnessed
in the recent Vatican excavations.

760 PLINY *Nat. Hist.*, *36*, *11* (ed. Teubner, Leipzig, 1897).

An interesting reference here to the famous obelisk
which eventually Sixtus V arranged in the center of the
piazza before the new basilica. Speaking of the obelisk and
its location Pliny says: "Tertius (obeliscus) est Romae in
Vaticano Gai et Neronis principum circo . . ."

761 PRANDI, A., "Billet de Rome" — NC, 4 (1952), 395-397.

The author examines M. Guarducci's reading of the
inscription found in the tomb of the Valerii beneath the
Vatican basilica.

762 PRANDI, A., *La zona archeologica della Confessio Vaticana.
I monumenti del II secolo*, (Vatican City: Tipografia Poliglotta
Vaticana, 1957), 95 pp. with 124 illus. and plans.

This is a report on the results of the findings of the excavations after those of the *official report*. This study is the result of archeological research conducted under the Papal altar. The excavations carried on personally by the author reaffirm the main points in the *Esplorazioni*. It stresses the fact that all the archeological documents which were found dated from the second century. It contains some excellent plates and offers new elements for consideration with regard to the dating of the monuments. Besides the tombs found by the first Commission, there is the discovery of many other tombs with further interesting observations about the mausoleums along the *clivus*.

763 RADKE, G., "Vaticanus, I" — *Realencyclopädie der classischen Altertumswissenschaft*, (1955), 490-493.

764 RALEGH RADFORD, C. A., (a Review of T. Klauser's "Die Romische Petrustradition, etc.") *Journal of Roman Studies*, 48 (1958), 229.

This deals with T. Klauser's: *The Peter-Question*. The book (according to Ralegh Radford) which contains an analysis of the oldest literary tradition, a critical survey of the excavational report, and a reconstruction of the historical development of the cult, is unduly weighted on the side of skepticism. The historical reconstruction is an interesting essay but open to criticism.

765 RESPIGHI, C., "La tomba apostolica del Vaticano" — RAC, 19 (1942), 5-27.

The author, secretary of the Pontifical Commission of Sacred Archeology, speaks especially of the works executed under St. Peter's in 1594 when the new Pontifical altar was erected by Clement VIII, and in 1626, when the Bernini baldachin was erected by Urban VIII. He seems to feel that the relics of Peter and Paul might not be found in the basilicas at Rome which bear their names, and it could be that the sarcophagus of Peter might not be under the altar of the basilica.

766 RESPIGHI, C., "Esplorazioni recenti nella confessione Beati Petri" — RAC, 19(1942), 19-26.

At the time when the whole project of the Vatican excavations was initiated, it was shrouded in the strictest secrecy. This is one of the very first few reports that was released. In these few pages there is a wealth of material. The author gives an account of the history of the work: the beginning of the first excavations beneath the Confessio which endeavored to search for the Apostle's tomb, or at least his relics, inside the existing Niche of the Pallia and the altars associated with it.

767 REY, E., "Yace Pedro en el Vaticano?" — Razón y fe, 155 (1957), 277-287.

768 ROMANELLI, P., "La documentazione scientifica del ritrovamento della tomba di S. Pietro al Vaticano" — L'Osservatore Romano, Dec. 20, 1951, p. 1.

The article speaks of the momentous occasion, Dec. 19, 1951, when Pius XII received in audience those responsible for the excavations beneath the Vatican. They in turn presented the Holy Father with the first *official report* consisting of two volumes, the first: the written text; the second: illustrations. Romanelli, a member of the Pontifical Commission for Sacred Archeology, though not engaged in the official work itself, had been given access to it. In the article he continues his account by reaffirming the fact that the site of Peter's tomb has been established beyond all reasonable doubt. A photograph of the event (the presentation of the *official report* to the Pontiff) is included in this front-page news.

769 ROSENBAUM, E., "The Vine columns of Old St. Peter's in Carolingian Canon Tables" — *Journal of the Warburg & Courtauld Institutes*, 18 (1955), 1-15.

Among the classic works of art and a source of inspiration to artists are the vine columns from the shrine of St. Peter in Rome. This paper is an endeavor to use their imagery (testifying to the impression which the ancient sanctuary had made on the imagination of early Christian artists) as an aid in throwing some new light on the history of the Canon Tables with the Evangelist's symbols

— the so-called Beast Canon Tables. This is a very scholarly work and of interest in the general scope of the basilica and the excavations.

770 RUYSSCHAERT, J., "Het graf van de H. Petrus en de opgravingen onder de Vaticaanse basiliek" — *Nova et vetera*, 29 (1951-52), 217-228, 2 figs.

This is a critique of the critics in the light of the *official report* on the excavations and the diverse reaction it provoked.

771 RUYSSCHAERT, J., "La tombe de S. Pierre et les fouilles sous la basilique Vaticane" — *Revue diocésaine de Tournai*, 7 (1952), 171-180, 3 figs.

The material here is substantially the same as that reproduced above: *Nova et vetera*, 29 (1952), 217-228.

772 RUYSSCHAERT, J., "Les fouilles de la basilique Vaticane et la memoria apostolique pré-constantinienne" — *L'Antiquité classique*, 21 (1952), 384-403, 7 figs.

This is a thorough summary of the results of the excavations centered on the *locus petri*, and containing sketches found in the *Esplorazioni* but presented more intelligibly here. A very good bibliography is also to be found.

773 RUYSSCHAERT, J., "La biografia del Papa Anacleto e la tomba apostolica vaticana" — RAC, 29 (1953), 97-98.

In the light of a new reading in the biography of Pope Anacletus (Liber Pontificalis) (after Kirschbaum and Carcopino had presented their hypotheses) the author proposes a more detailed examination of graveyard P which surrounded the Apostolic tomb.

774 RUYSSCHAERT, J., "Réflexions sur les fouilles vaticanes. Le rapport officiel et la critique: données archéologiques, données épigrafiques et littéraires" — RHE, 48 (1953), 573-631; 49 (1954), 5-58.

In both studies we have a careful evaluation of the archeological arguments and counter-arguments based on the official findings of the excavations. The author divides his subject-matter into two articles. In the first he deals with the archeological evidence, scil., the Apostolic tomb and its pre-Constantinian arrangement. In the second article he takes up the epigraphical and literary evidence connected with the tomb of St. Peter, ending with the account of St. Sylvester's activities, i.e., the building of the basilica, etc. This is indeed an admirable and exhaustive study which makes a positive contribution to the problem. Though in no way does the author want his own subsequent considerations either to counter the findings of the Commission or to be thought more important than their primary conclusions.

775 RUYSSCHAERT, J., "La tradition romaine des tombes apostoliques et Eusèbe de Césarée" — *L'Osservatore Romano*, April 1-2, 1957, p. 5.

This is a resumé of a communication presented on March 28, 1957, to the Pontifical Roman Academy of Archeology. The matter deals with the Roman tradition of the Apostolic tombs and the text of Eusebius of Caesarea, in the light of recent studies by Josi, Kirschbaum, Künzle, Carcopino, Klauser, and their analyses.

The literary evidence testifies to the historical fact that Peter's tomb was known to be beneath the Vatican basilica for a period of time prior to the end of the second century. It is interesting to observe Eusebius' silence with regard to the via Appia. This must be interpreted as a denial of every hypothesis of a total translation of the bodies of the Apostles (Peter and Paul) from their respective tombs to the via Appia. This is confirmed by the two texts (*Eusebius IV, 7*) and the *Depositio Martyrum*. Thanks to both, we have proof that in 333-354 Peter's tomb was at the Vatican while a liturgical commemoration is recorded on the via Appia. Josi recently proposed that there can be a reconciliation with Eusebius' text and a partial translation. He noted that the Damasian inscription should read 'hic habitare' (not habitasse). The via Appia tradition is explained by the development of a cultus to the Apostles in Rome during the third century, perhaps, linked with the presence of their relics here during Damasus time. But the real funerary cult (as was the case for martyrs at this time) was at the Vatican and via Ostia where their bodies were. This explanation seems best to reconcile all the literary data.

776 RUYSSCHAERT, J., "Recherches et études autour de la Confession de la Basilique Vaticane (1940-1958): État de la question et bibliographie" — *Triplice ommagio a Sua Santità Pio XII, vol. II,* (Vatican City, 1958), 3-47, 13 figs., 4 plates.

In the pages mentioned in this voluminous work the author studies the reports of both excavational campaigns under the Vatican and the important publications that resulted. The Roman-tradition of Peter's tomb is reconfirmed by the excavations. A vast bibliography is also included here.

777 RUYSSCHAERT, J., "Vaticano: III. Autenticità della tomba di S. Pietro" — *Dizionario ecclesiastico,* 3 (Turino, 1958), 1274-1276.

This is an analysis of the literary texts that refer to Peter's tomb at the Vatican. Once again the theories pertaining to a translation of the relics of the Apostles (Peter and Paul) to the via Appia is discussed. The Depositio Martyrum refers merely to a cultus, by no means to a translation.

778 RUYSSCHAERT, J., "Témoignages archéologiques concernant la tombe de S. Pierre" — *Revue générale belge* 95, 12 (1959), 67-77.

We have here a review of the excavations undertaken from 1940-58 which the author bases on the findings of the experts: B. M. Apollonj Ghetti, E. Josi, M. Guarducci, M. Prandi, M. F. Magi, A. Ferrua, E. Kirschbaum. He clearly distinguishes between the discovery of the actual tomb and the place of the tomb. The absence of the actual tomb is a proof of its historicity.

779 RUYSSCHAERT, J., "The Tomb of St. Peter: the Archeological Evidence" — *Thought,* 34 (1959), 5-15.

This is a masterful assessment of the archeological

facts resulting from the subsidiary discoveries made by
F. Magi in 1956 when the new Vatican garage was being
constructed. The author limits himself to the findings
within this area. The research made by Magi and Guarducci is his prime consideration, though he omits any of
the technical details.

780 RUYSSCHAERT, J., "Trois Campagnes de fouilles au Vatican
et la tombe de Pierre" — *Sacra Pagina, Miscellanea biblica,*
2 (1959), 86-97.

Much of the material here has already been reproduced
in the author's earlier writings.

781 RUYSSCHAERT, J., "La tombe de Pierre au Vatican" — *Bible et Terre Sainte,* 30 (1960), 4-12, with figs. and plans.

782 SARTORIO, G. A., "La colonne vitinee e le colonne tortili
della chiese romana" — *Capitolium,* 3 (1927-28), 595-607.

We have an interesting account here dealing with the
history of the spiral columns (with 16 figs.) in the Vatican
basilica and other churches of Rome.

783 SCHÄFER, E., "Das Petrusgrab und die neuen Grabungen
unter St. Peter in Rom" — *Evangelische Theologie,* 10 (1951),
459-479.

In his analysis of the results of the excavations in the
Vatican, the author speaks definitely against a transfer of
the remains of the two Apostles. He argues chiefly that
no reason existed for a transfer, since Valerian's prohibi-
tion against entering Christian cemeteries dates not from
the year 258, but from 257. Moreover, the grave of Peter
was located not in a Christian cemetery but in a pagan
one. Fear that the grave would have been violated would
have been groundless since, indeed, nothing is known of
violations of Christian graves in times of persecution.

784 SHADE, H., "Die Gräber der Apostelfürsten" — *Stimmen der
Zeit,* 162 (1957-58), 223-226.

This is a review of E. Kirschbaum's well-known work
(see no. 672). In agreement with Kirschbaum, the reviewer

holds the opinion that the discovery of the small monument of the second century has a decisive value for the solution of Peter's grave at the Vatican.

785 SCHÄFER, E., "Das Apostelgrab unter St. Peter in Rom" — *Evangelische Theologie*, 12 (1953), 304-319.

The *Aedicula* discovered by the excavators and the *tropaion* mentioned by Gaius and Eusebius are not to be identified. The *Aedicula* is of a later date.

786 SHEEN, F. J., "The Rome of the Pilgrims" — *This Is Rome*, (New York: Hawthorne, 1960) Image ed., 70-76.

An extremely interesting account—written in popular style—that reconstructs the history of the Vatican hill, the tomb of Peter, and Constantine's church.

787 SCHMIDT, H., "Het graf van Sint Petrus" — *Katholiek Archief*, 7 (1952), 101-110.

788 SCHMITZ, J., "Fouilles et découvertes sous la basilique de Saint-Pierre de Rome" — *Revue diocésaine de Namur*, n.s., 2 (1947), 48-63.

789 SCHNEIDER, A. M., "Das Petrusgrab im Vatikan" — TLZ, 77 (1952), 321-326, 2 figs.

This is a negative approach to the results of the archeological investigations beneath the Vatican. The author, basing himself on the *official report*, singles out particular findings to deny their positive value; e.g., he views the *trophy* of Gaius as a memorial-shrine unaccompanied by any burial. He is convinced that the pre-Constantinian shrine in Campo P cannot be a tomb-shrine marking a burial below, but represents only a memorial-shrine, a cenotaph, in which the Apostle, martyred in the nearby circus, was commemorated.

790 SEPPELT, F. X., "Das Petrusgrab."

See no. 228.

791 SESTON, W., "Les récentes fouilles de Saint-Pierre de Rome et la date de la basilique constantinienne" — RHR, 130 (1945), 186-188.

In endeavoring to date the Constantinian basilica, the author calls attention to the fact that the excavations initiated by Pius XII have brought to light the gigantic task undertaken by the Constantinian architects in constructing the five-naved basilica. The complexity of labor involved demanded a certain period of time for its completion. It is impossible to hold any theory that it was consecrated in 335 or 336. See next.

792 SESTON, W., "La date de la basilique constantinienne de Saint-Pierre de Rome" — *Bulletin de la Société des antiquaires de France*, 1945-46-47, 141-142.

This is a resumé of a communication of March 20, 1946. See the following.

793 SESTON W., "Hypothèse sur la date de la basilique constantinienne de Saint-Pierre de Rome" — *Cahiers archéologiques*, 2 (1947), 153-159.

We have here an hypothesis attempting to establish more precisely the date when the Constantinian basilica was begun. The author notes that in 349 the Emperor Constans passed a law severely punishing *violatio sepulcri*, which was made retrospective to cover the past sixteen years. The reason for this is that 333 was the year that Constantine had given orders to cover the necessary work of destruction in the Vatican necropolis—and that his subjects had taken advantage of the opportunity to plunder the tombs for building materials, and that now steps had to be taken to correct the abuse. The text of this law is in *Cod. Theod. IX. 17.2*. The foundation for the basilica was begun in 333 (not 324).

794 SESTON, W., "Die Constantinische Frage. B. Faits politiques, armees, finances" — *Relazioni del X Congresso internazionale di scienze storiche, Sept. 4-11, Rome, 1955*, Vol. VI. (Florence, 1955).

795 SEVERANO, G., *Memorie sacre della Sette chiese di Roma*, (Roma, 1630), 1-292, spec. 20.

An interesting reference is made here to the excavations

under St. Peter's in 1626 (Under Urban VIII) when Bernini placed his bronze baldachin over the confession-altar, and how, when the foundation was being laid, some graves were discovered.

796 SILVAGNI, A., *Inscriptiones cristianae urbis Romae septimo saec. antiquiores*, II, (Roma, 1935), n. 4093.

We find here the text of Constantine's and Helen's inscription that had been incised on the golden cross which was placed on Peter's tomb. Of added interest is n. 4092, which reproduces the mosaic inscription over the triumphal arch representing the Emperor Constantine offering the basilica to Christ.

797 SJÖQVIST, E., "The Shrine of St. Peter: A Review" — *Antiquity*, 31 (1957), 15-18.

This is a review of the *official report* in view of the many publications that attempt to interpret it. The author gives a concise account of the Vatican area in antiquity, its topography and history in which the discoveries under St. Peter's play so great a part. The location of the circus remains uncertain. He then speaks of Constantine's project and the necropolis. All agree here. The divergence of opinion arises when one comes to the absolute dating of the *Aedicula* and the assessment of the age of the Petrine tradition in Rome. Before this discussion the author gives a lay-out and chronology of the tombs, and the religious beliefs of the occupants. How old is all this and the consequent conclusions? The date assigned to the *Aedicula* is the decade between A.D. 160-170, i.e. about a century after Peter's death. What the shrine looked like and alterations it underwent is clearly put forward. All is original research and profound scholarship.

798 SMIT, J. O., "De voorgeschiedenis van de Sint Pieterskerk" — *Mededeelingen van het Nederlandsch historisch Instituut te Rome*, 5 (1947), 64-66.

799 SMOTHERS, E. R., "The Excavations under St. Peter's" — *Theological Studies*, 17 (1956), 293-321.

In this study the author answers the question as to the

historical significance of the discoveries (pagan and Christian) at the site of the reputed burial of Peter beneath the Vatican. The contents of the article is a summary of the famous work by J. Toynbee & J. W. Perkins: "The Shrine of St. Peter and the Vatican Excavations."

800 SPEIER, H., "Die Vatikanische Necropole unter den "Grotten" des Petersdomes" — *Wort und Wahrheit*, 4² (1949), 481-489.

This is a summary of the results obtained in the Vatican excavational project during the years 1940 to 1946 when information was limited. The author describes the Roman necropolis that came to light, and its existing mausoleums.

801 SPEIER, H., "Die neuen Ausgrabungen unter der Peterskirche in Rom" — *Vermächtnis der antiken Kunst*, (ed. Reinhard Herbig, Heidelberg: Kerle, 1950), 197-218.

A partial and popular account of the more recent (at that time) excavational discoveries beneath the Vatican basilica.

802 SPEIER, H., "Memoria Sancti Petri, die Auffindung des Petrusgrabes" — *Wort und Wahrheit*, 7¹ (1952), 262-272.

In this study the author deals with the interpretation and reconstruction of the "Memoria" of the Apostle based on the scene portrayed on the ivory casket of Pola. It is a clear and competent study with some excellent plates.

803 STEINHART, K., "Die Neuordnung der Vaticanischen Grotten" — *Münchener Theologische Zeitschrift*, 2 (1951), 109-114.

804 STUIBER, A., "Das Grab des Apostels Petrus" — *Der christliche Sonntag*, 4 (1952), 165-166; 173-174.

805 SULLIVAN, K., "Excavations under Saint Peter's" — *Liturgical Arts*, 26 (1958), 42-43.

This very brief article, written in a popular style, narrates the occasion (the fateful accident in the Grotte Vecchie) which inaugurated the excavational project beneath the Vatican. The author limits herself to the following questions:

1. What light do the explorations throw on the traditional claim that St. Peter's tomb is directly under the present high altar?
2. What is the nature of the long-hidden pre-Christian cemetery?

806 TAILLIEZ, F., "Notes conjointes sur un texte fameux d'Eusèbe I. La tombe de Saint Pierre. Correction au texte de H.E. II, 25" — OCP, 9 (1943), 431-449.

This scholarly study examines Eusebius' citation of Gaius' testimony regarding the tombs of the two Apostles at the gates of Rome. The author deals with the subject under these two main headings:

1. The tomb of St. Peter. A correction of the text of Eusebius H.E. II, 25.
2. Γάϊος or Gaius? The first "Father" of Latin Patrology?

807 TAILLEZ, F., "Βασιλικὴ ὁδός Les valeurs d'un terme mystique et le prix de son histoire littérale. Miscellenea Guillaume de Jerphanion" — OCP, 13 (1947), 299-354.

This study constitutes a developed answer to a question raised by the first of these two notes: the tomb of Peter: correction to the text of Eusebius (II, 25, see article above), where account is taken of the old mistakes according to which Βασικανόν was made to mean *Vaticanum* by reconstructing a corrupted text of the *Hist. Eccles.* Επι (τὴν) Βασι (ι)ικὴν οδόν, etc. The author gives a word-study of the expression Βασιλικὴ 'οδός: *Via Publica* which was found (thanks to Rufinus) in the text H.E. (II, 25).

808 TARDINI, G., "Il Vaticano e i Borghi attraverso i secoli. L'antica facciata e il "Paradiso;" gli edifici vaticani verso il "Forum S. Petri" — *L'illustrazione Vaticana*, 7 (1936), 801-806.

This is an interesting study describing the ancient facade of St. Peter's according to Medieval and later plans. There is also a description of the facade of the atrium, the

Forum Petri, Michaelangelo's ideas and successive transformation, the Bernini columns.

809 TARDINI, G., *Basilica Vaticana e Borghi*, (Rome: Instituto
grafico Tiberino, 1937), 114 pp., 59 figs.

This is a historical study on the topography and the
surroundings. of the city of Rome in reference to the
important Vatican basilica and the various questions in
regard and the transformations it underwent. An excellent
bibliography is also to be found here.

810 TERMES ROS, P., "El sepulcro de san Pedro" — *Cristiandad*,
10 (Barcelona, 1953), 253-259., 13 plans.

Basing himself on the *official report* the author takes up
the study of the following points:
1. The primitive tomb of Peter.
2. The 'trophy' of Gaius.
3. The Constantinian basilica.
4. Gregory the Great's reconstruction.
5. The new basilica.

811 TESTINI, P., "Cenni sui principali cimiteri cristiani di Roma"
— *Archeologia Cristiana*, (Roma; Desclée, 1958), 163-185.

The author takes up the matter of the Vatican excavations drawn principally from the *official report*.

812 TORP, H., "The Vatican Excavations and the cult of St.
Peter" — *Acta Archeologica*, 24 (1953), 27-66.

The author uses the *official report* as the basis for an
independent study of the questions of both dating and
interpretation. (According to the Esplorazioni, the vestiges
of the Memoria which were found can be dated to about
A.D. 175, and identified with Gaius' trophy. Further, some
graves at different levels under the monument are dated
back to the first century, A.D.; partly by relating these
graves to a primitive tomb of the Apostle, partly by
connecting this tomb with the Memoria, the excavators
then proceed to bridge the century which separates the
Memoria and the time of death of the Apostle. Thus, proof
is furnished of a continuous cult of Peter having taken
place on that spot from the time of his burial to the

erection of the monument.) Torp, however, attempts to prove that the excavations have been fundamentally misinterpreted mainly because of the fact that the entire Vatican cemetery was dated at least a half century too early. The ideas that he proposes in this descriptive account are hardly acceptable to the experts and in need of a reassessment. The author makes an addition of a few notes regarding the cult ad Catacumbas and the first church in Vaticano, the martyrium erected over the Memoria by Constantine.

813 TOWNSEND, G., "The Circus of Nero and the Vatican Excavations" — *American Journal of Archeology*, 62 (1958), 216-218.

In this study the author analyzes one of the problems raised by the *official Vatican report* in 1951 regarding the orientation of the circus. He employs the literary testimony that reveals a history of the circus rather different than has generally been supposed. He concludes: Thus, it appears possible by inferring from both the literary and archeological evidence for the circus—no more is given to explain the history of the site in such a way as to accept the traditional account, and to remove all the difficulties raised by the position of the obelisk as it was until the sixteenth century. This view will be confirmed if excavations round the former site of the obelisk reveal traces of a *spina*, but hardly refutes it, if not. The restoration of the circus to its traditional position (at the expense of its architecture) may facilitate explanations of the Aedicula beneath St. Peter's.

814 TOYNBEE, J. M. C., "The Shrine of St. Peter and its twelve Spiral Columns" — JRS, 42 (1952), 21-33.

The author presents a full and delightful discussion of the vine-scroll columns which were a gift of Constantine to surround the Memoria of the Apostle, and he comments on their subsequent history.

815 TOYNBEE, J. M. C., "The Shrine of St. Peter and its Setting" — JRS, 43 (1953), 1-26, 13 figs., 4 plates.

Among the very few scientific studies that have been published in English relative to the results of the excavations, this merits special attention. It is outstanding both for its clear presentation and objectivity. The questions raised pro and con are dealt with individually, and an endeavor is made to establish some degree of certainty. Solutions are proposed. This summary survey falls into three main headings:

1. The Vatican report. The Petrine tradition, the Scope of the Vatican excavations as a whole.
2. The topography and history of the Vatican zone in ancient times.
3. An account of the pre-Constantinian shrine of St. Peter beneath the high altar at the Vatican basilica.

In this excellent little study the author accepts as a historical fact the tradition linking Peter with Rome. It is perfectly consistent, has had no competitors worth considering and has never been contradicted by any positive evidence, written or material. There is also a study of Constantine's engineering operations and the problems involved, and the question of a translation ad Catacumbas with which the *official report* does not profess to deal. The author concludes that the results of the excavations have produced evidence for the pre-Constantinian cult of Peter under the basilica, a cult which we can at present trace back as far as the second half of the second century and may perhaps be able to trace back still further. However, we cannot be absolutely certain that the lowest level in the central space was St. Peter's actual tomb. It is unscientific to apply the word "tomb" categorically to what the excavations have revealed.

816 TOYNBEE, J. M. C., *Hibbert Journal*, 55 (1956-57), 284-286.

This is an exchange of letters between Dr. Griffiths and J. Toynbee on the matter of the excavational results. Toynbee repeats Griffiths' objections and refutes them as was originally done in her work with Perkins. The objections raised are as follows:

1. The "red wall" into which the primitive shrine of Peter (Aedicula) was built as that wall was being

erected; the clivus immediately to the west of the wall, and the drain—they are not contemporary.

2. The Aedicula dates from the third century.

3. Doubt is cast on the Christian character of the vault-and-wall-mosaics of the mausoleum of the Julii (M).

4. Isis and Hypnos are rendered in stucco in the tomb of the Valerii.

5. The suggestion that the first owners of tomb Z were members of an Egyptian family is rejected.

In replying, Dr. Griffiths attempts to justify his claims. However, he does conclude by saying: "in spite of these disagreements I support the book's (Toynbee-Perkins) main thesis that St. Peter's burial-place is now revealed."

817 TOYNBEE, J. M. C., "Under the Vatican Basilica" — *The Tablet*, 195 (June 10-24, 1950), 460-462; 480-482; 500-502, with illustrations.

In the series of three articles that follow Miss Toynbee offers a detailed account of the excavations as a whole by discussing the topographical and historical problems which they raise, by describing some of the treasures of art, pagan and Christian, which they contain, and by considering their bearing on the well-known "Memoria Apostolorum" on the via Appia, a few miles south of Rome, and on the history of the Apostle's remains from their martyrdom to the peace of the Church.

In the first article (pp. 460-462) the author describes the Roman necropolis and topography; In pages 480-482: the occupants of the Roman necropolis, architecture and art; In pages 500-502: the Apostolic tombs from Nero to Constantine.

818 TOYNBEE, J. M. C., (Discussion) *The Tablet*, 196 (July 15-22, Aug. 5-12, 1950), 56, 74, 114, 134.

Here one will find letters to the editor resulting from the above articles by Miss Toynbee. They reveal an awareness of the importance of the excavational findings beneath the Vatican as well as a keen interest.

819 TOYNBEE, J. M. C., "Tomb of St. Peter"—reply.—*The Tablet*, 200 (Aug. 30, 1952), 175.

Under 'letters to the editor' is found this reply by the author. It is a note commending the article referring to the Vatican excavations that appeared in the Aug. 23rd issue (1952) which summarized the main conclusions reached by the project. However, the author feels that a number of points were omitted in said account and, therefore, takes this opportunity to draw these to the attention of the readers.

820 TOYNBEE, J. M. C., "Tomb of St. Peter: the extent and limitations of the discoveries" — *The Tablet*, 202 (Sept. 26, 1953), 297-298.

821 TOYNBEE, J. M. C., & PERKINS, J. B., *The Shrine of St. Peter and the Vatican Excavations*, (New York: Pantheon Books, 1957), xxii-293 pp., 25 figs., 32 plates.

With a clear grasp of the technical problems involved, the authors have simplified this account of the recent excavations under the Vatican basilica. It is based on the *official report* of the excavations but, at the same time, presents the results in the light of a critical and independent reading of the evidence. The first half of the book is concerned with the cemetery which was either demolished or buried in the early fourth century, when Constantine built the basilica. There is a general account with a detailed description of three of the tombs. The art and architecture are the subject of one chapter: the owners, their status and belief, the subject of the others. This is an excellent source of information on Roman cemeteries. The second part of the book deals with the shrine of St. Peter. The archeological data are recorded with accuracy, the architectural problems are discussed, and solutions are given. This section is divided under these main headings:

a) The Petrine tradition.
b) The pre-Constantinian shrine which also includes the cult-center of Peter and Paul at San Sebastiano.
c) Constantine's Church; the original building and later reconstruction.

The authors have indeed given a full and fair summary

of the evidence and have endeavored to interpret the data revealed by the excavations. While some do not agree with their solutions on some points, all will admit that this is a positive contribution of great value, and that it is extremely important for an understanding of the Roman world of St. Peter and his shrine.

822 TOYNBEE, J. M. C., (An appraisal of T. Klauser's "Die Römische Petrustradition, etc.") — AJA, 62 (1958), 126-129.

According to Toynbee, the object of Klauser's work is to assess the extent to which the Roman literary tradition of St. Peter's residence and death in Rome has been confirmed by the excavations made between 1939-1949. In his preface he says that were this tradition proved to lack historical foundation, the belief in the bishop of Rome's Primacy and the whole Roman and western cult of the prince of the Apostles would be shown to rest on fiction. Klauser's conclusions are: The vatican excavations have confirmed the literary tradition of St. Peter's residence and death in Rome and the reliability of the topographical indications of Gaius, whose trophy has in fact been brought to light. The excavations have not revealed a grave below the trophy. But the possibility that this trophy was erected to mark the site of a burial (that the mid-second-century Roman Christians believed to be that of the Apostle), would (according to Toynbee) seem to be considerably stronger than the author is ready to admit.

823 TOYNBEE, J. M. C., "Graffiti beneath St. Peter's. Prof. Guarducci's Interpretations" — *The Dublin Review*, 233 (Autumn, 1959), 234-244.

This is an analysis of Guarducci's readings of the graffiti. That veneration of our Lady and St. Peter was flourishing in Rome in the late-second, third, and early-fourth centuries (the period covered by the bulk of Guarducci's material) is not in doubt. It is well attested both by literature and by some works of early Christian art. It would, none the less, have been a matter of the deepest interest to every Christian if there could be added to that testimony clear monumental evidence from early

Christian epitaphs and from the wall "g" graffiti beneath
the Confessio of St. Peter's. Guarducci claims to have laid
such evidence before us; and her work assuredly deserves
a prolonged and most careful examination. But while
sharing the full beliefs and values that inspired her to
undertake this arduous task, Toynbee must (at the end
of her lengthy journey through her pages and plates)
regretfully record "non-proven" as her verdict on Guarducci's case.

824 TURCIO, G., *La Basilica di S. Pietro*, (Firenze: Sansone
editore, 1946), 259 pp., 67 plates.

This is a historical-artistic survey of the Vatican basilica.
As is known, the basilica and the tomb of Peter are intimately related with the history of religion, the papacy,
and artistic thought. The purpose of this book (written in
a popular style) is to help one gain a better insight not
only into the artistic aspects of the basilica, but also to
inculcate a more vivid devotion to the prince of the
Apostle and his successors.

825 VACCHINI, F., "La Sua Tomba è stata trovata" — *Ecclesia*,
11 (Vatican City, 1952), 12-13.

A popularly written account of the Pope's radio-message
of Christmas 1950 announcing the discovery of Peter's
tomb, and a cursory reconstruction of the *official report's*
findings, scil., the necropolis and mausoleums, with some
excellent photographs. One of the few written articles
which also includes the photos of the expert archeologists
who were entrusted with the excavations.

826 VALENTINI, R., & ZUCCHETTI, G., *Codice topografico
della città di Roma, vol. II*, (=*Fonti per la storia d'Italia*,
58) Rome, 1942, 12-28.

While in general we find here a valuable topographical
document from the most ancient times, the pages mentioned above contain the texts of the Depositio Episcoporum
and Depositio Martyrum—the chief sources of the ancient
history of the Church.

827 VAN AKEN, A. R. A., "De opgravingen onder Sint Pieter" — *Streven*, n.s. 3. 2 (1950), 281-289.

828 VAN BUREN, A. W., "News letter from Rome" — AJA, 57 (1953), 211.

A reference is made here to the fact after the sumptuous publication devoted to the finds beneath St. Peter's appeared (the Esplorazioni), there followed M. Guarducci's deciphering of the painted inscription in a neighboring tomb, giving the name of St. Peter in an informative context.

829 VAN DODEWAARD, J. A. E., *Bijbels woordenboek*[2], (1957), 1370.

Speaking of the archeological excavations under St. Peter's at Rome, the author asserts that the results of these excavations have strengthened the tradition about Peter's grave.

830 VAN STEMPVOORT, P. A., *Petrus en zijn graf te Rome*.

See no. 240.
Chapter III (pp. 65-148) deals with the significance of the Vatican excavations with supplementary literary and historical testimony. The author holds that the discovery of the aedicula dating from the middle of the second century has decisive value for the solution of Peter's Roman sojourn, martyrdom, and burial on the Vatican hill.

831 VAWTER, B., "Tomb of St. Peter" — *Columbia*, 30 (April, 1951), 7, 21, 22, 23, with illus.

For the sake of the 'simple folk' we find here a brief article that speaks of the Pope's announcement (Dec. 24, 1950) that the first period of excavations was completed, and their findings confirmed a tradition here beyond doubt, viz., that before the St. Peter's (basilica) of the Renaissance, before the Middle Ages, before the barbarians, before Constantine and the Christians of the persecutions, the remains of Peter were buried. The grave has been found once more.

832 VAWTER, B., "St. Peter's Triumph" — *Columbia*, 31 (March, 1952), 6, 19, 20, with illus.

> The author reprints the official announcement of the *report* and its findings. The Christian tradition concerning the Vatican hill and St. Peter's martyrdom and burial is confirmed by the excavational findings.

833 VERSTRAETEN, M., "Het graf van de H. Petrus" — *Streven*, 6 (1953), 305-315, 3 figs.

> Another summary of the results of the excavations beneath the Vatican based on the *official report* and other studies. The work lacks the usual technical details.

834 VESA, I., "Mormantul Sf. Petru. Increstari in legatura cu sapaturille din Grotele Vaticane" — *Cultura crestiana*, 22 (1942), 278-284.

835 VILLETTE, J., "Les fouilles récentes de Saint-Pierre de Rome" — *La Vie intellectuelle*, 15 (1947), 42-51.

> An excellent summary of that part of the excavations —available at that time—under St. Peter's.

836 VILLIGER, J. B., "Die Ausgrabungen unter der Peterskirche in Rom" — *Theologie und Glaube*, 42 (1952), 321-328.

> Based on the *Esplorazioni*, the author presents a clear survey of the results of the Vatican excavations. He brings into relief new aspects of Christian burial practices and the value of tradition.

837 VLAD, L. B., "Sul carattere di autenticità di alcuni graffiti" — *Bollettino del Instituto centrale del restauro*, 13 (1953), 45-59.

838 VOELKL, L., "Vaticano" — RQ, 48 (1953), 244-245.

> The author speaks of the discovery of the inscription accompanying the figure of the heads of Christ and Peter in the tomb of the Valerii during the Vatican excavations and M. Guarducci's reading of the text.

839 VOGELSANGER, P., "Petrusgrab und Papsttum" — *Reformatio*, I, 6 (1952), 308-317.

> Without substantiating his arguments, the author

criticizes as unscientific E. Kirschbaum's conferences in Switzerland.

840 VOGT, E., "Sepulchrum S. Petri" — *Biblica*, 33 (1952), 165-168; 306-309.

> This is a summary of the important results of the archeological excavations beneath the Vatican. It is presented in a clear and systematic fashion. One of it's chief merits is the list of plans indispensable for this study. It is based on the *official report*.

841 VOGT, E., "Inscriptio de S. Petro sub Basilica Vaticana" — *Biblica*, 34 (1953), 124-125.

> The author deals briefly with the figure of Peter's head and the inscription accompanying it that was discovered in the tomb of the Valerii. He repeats M. Guarducci's reading and conclusion, viz., that Peter's body must have been buried in this locality.

842 VOLBACH, W. F., "Die Ikone der Apostelfürsten in St. Peter zu Rom" — OCP, 7 (1941), 480-497.

> This is a historical reconstruction of the famous picture of Peter and Paul "quam beatus Silvester papa ostenderat Constantino ad repraesentandam formam eorum, quas ante baptisma in visione viderat."

843 VON GERKAN, A., "Die Forschung nach dem Grab Petri" — *Evangelisch-Lutherische Kirchenzeitung*, 6 (Nov. 15, 1952), 379-382, 2 figs.

> The conclusions as presented by the excavators (and the facts on which they base them) with regard to the pre-Constantinian shrine, scil., Niches, "red wall," etc., are disputed by the author. Thus, he views the "trophy" as a memorial-shrine unaccompanied by any burial. He is convinced (like A. M. Schneider) that the pre-Constantinian shrine in Campo P cannot be a tomb-shrine marking a burial below, it was merely a cenotaph.

844 VON GERKAN, A., "Die Forschung nach dem Grab Petri" — ZNW, 44 (1952/53), 196-205.

The matter here is the same as originally appeared in the periodical: *Evangelisch-Lutherische Kirchenzeitung.* See above.

845 VON GERKAN, A., "Kritische Studien zu den Ausgrabungen unter der Peterskirche in Rom" — *Zeitschrift f. Geschichte u. Kunst des Trierer Landes*, 22 (1954), 26-55.

This is a critique on some of the conclusions drawn in the *official report*. The author's negative interpretation of some of the findings is rejected by many of the experts.

846 VON GERKAN, A., "Zu den Problemen des Petrusgrabes" — JAC, 1 (1958), 79-93, 3 figs.

The conclusions drawn previously by the author were not acceptable to E. Kirschbaum. This is a reply wherein the author reiterates his assertion that the Apostolica Memoria was neither a true grave nor a cenotaph, but a "token of remembrance," a monument in the sense of a "souvenir." A real depository beneath the Memoria is pure legend.

847 VON GERKAN, A., "Basso et Tusco consulibus" — *Bonner Jahrbücher*, 158 (1958), 89-105.

The author's conclusions in this study are as follows: There is still no evidence of St. Peter's tomb beneath the Aedicula in graveyard P. However, a veneration of martyrs had already existed in Rome prior to 258; otherwise, the following passage of an edict by Emperor Valerian (257), quoted in the *Acta Cypriani* (ch. 7) would not make sense, namely: "ne in aliquibus locis conciliabula fiant, nec coemeteria ingrediatur." Moreover, it may be rightly assumed that the damage in the "red wall" below the Aedicula was done when the Christians were searching for the relics which they afterwards illegally brought to the via Appia. (This is the direct opposite to the theory proposed by Von Gerkan in his previous studies). Furthermore, the triclia ad catacumbas was only for the usual Compagna-Osteria. It was about 258 that it came into the possession of a Christian and was then used for the "refrigeria." The relics of the Apostles were placed in the floor which is at the end of a stairway leading down ten yards. The entrance to the stairway was close to the triclia. A stone wall was constructed in front of the relics of the Apostles so that the Christians could not see them. However, they did scratch their graffiti on the walls as can still be seen today. The separating wall was torn down when the relics were retranslated during Constantine's time. Unfortunately, we do not know exactly where the relics were deposited at that time.

848 VON HEINTZE, H., "Nachtrag zum Petrus-Grab" — *Wort und Wahrheit*, 82 (1953), 637-638.

This is a brief commentary on the results of the excavational findings according to the Esplorazioni, Ferrua (*Messagero*, Jan. 16, 1952) & Guarducci's discovery of the inscription and accompanying sketch that came to light in the tomb of the Valerii.

849 WAND, A. C., "The Location of Constantine's Gold Cross" — *Theological Studies*, 2 (1941), 84-88.

Since the *Liber Pontificalis* gives a detailed, but not always clear account of the work done under the direction of Constantine and Pope Sylvester at the tomb of St. Peter, the author examines the text of the Liber in order to reconstruct the tomb and its other appurtenances, especially the famous cross that tradition claims was placed over the bronze casket by Constantine and Helena. The text in question reads: "At the request of Sylvester, Constantine Augustus made a basilica to blessed Peter the Apostle, near the temple of Apollo, the tomb with the body of St. Peter being thus covered over. The tomb itself he shut in on every side with cyprian bronze, so that it was built up with masonry: at the head five feet . . . thus he enclosed the body of blessed Peter the Apostle and covered it over. And he adorned the altar above with porphyry columns . . . and above the body of Peter, above the bronze that enclosed it, he made a cross of purest gold weighing one hundred and fifty pounds . . ."

850 WARD PERKINS, J. B., "The Shrine of St. Peter" — *The Listener*, 48 (Sept. 25, 1952), 509-511, 2 figs.

One of the very few articles written in the English
language for the general public which never loses sight of
the scientific scholarliness demanded by the nature of the
subject. It is a cursory survey of the results of the excavations with emphasis on the positive value of the findings
in confirming the Roman tradition of Peter's tomb.

851 WARD PERKINS, J. B., "The Shrine of St. Peter and its
twelve Spiral columns" — JRS, 42 (1952), 21-33, 2 figs., 7
plates.

The layout and early history of the Constantinian
sanctuary is excellently sumarized here. In its connection
the author speaks of a subject seldom dealt with: the
twelve spiral columns which surrounded Peter's tomb.
Six of these were Constantine's gift; the other six were
those of the Byzantine exarch of Ravenna. They are
examined historically in a very delightful way. The very
many imitations are accurately noted here.

852 WARD PERKINS, J. B., "Intorno alle colonne tortili di
S. Pietro" — *Atti della Pont. accad. rom. di arch.*, 3¦ ser.,
Rendiconti, 27 (1952-1954, ed. 1955), 153-154.

This is a communication (Dec. 18, 1952) regarding the
nine columns in St. Peter's. Presently there are eleven
there. Originally there were twelve and in this regard a
reference is made to the Liber Pontificalis which says
that they were placed here in two distinct periods: six
by Constantine, which came from Greece; and six as a
gift of the exarch of Ravenna, Gregory III in the eighth
century. Recent excavations have shown that the first 6
were arranged to ornament the Apostolic tomb, while the
other 6 were added in a second reconstruction of the tomb.

853 WARD PERKINS, J. B., "Constantine and the Origin of the
Christian Basilica" — *Papers of the British School at Rome*,
22 (1954), 69-90.

Apart from the various influences that may have entered
into the Christian tradition of monumental architecture,
there can be little doubt that the policy adopted by
Constantine with regard to his own ecclesiastical founda-

tions must have determined the pattern for the future development. It is against this background that the Constantinian Church of St. Peter must be viewed.

854 WARD PERKINS, J. B., "Letter to the Editor" — *Antiquity*, 29 (1955), 239.

> This is written in defense of the *official report* and concerned with *Antiquity's* characterization in a note (June 1955, p. 76) of H. Torp's article in *Acta Archaeologica* as being "a scholarly analysis of a bad excavation." The author endeavors to vindicate the position of the archeologists charged with the task of the Vatican excavations. While one may criticize some of the interpretations, the important thing is that the essential facts are noted and presented clearly and honestly: the evidence for agreement and disagreement is all there. It is a good and scrupulous account of a difficult piece of work well done!

855 WARD PERKINS, J. B., "A Roman Cemetery newly discovered in the Vatican, etc." — *The Illustrated London News*, Dec. 12, 1959, 849-850.

> This brief survey is about the burial place discovered when excavations were being made for a parking area in the Vatican. It was located some four hundred yards to the north of St. Peter's. This necropolis was evidently already in use in the year 67 A.D. which leads to the conclusion that the necropolis beneath St. Peter's also originated at the same time since it probably belonged to the same sepulchral area.

856 WELLES, C. B., (Archeological News. Classical Lands) AJA, 51 (1947), 284-285.

> We have here a description of the two mausoleums discovered in the Vatican excavations—one of which was pagan. The second one (Julius Tarpeianus) had been seen by Alfarano in 1574 but was lost again. The wall mosaics reveal its Christian character.

857 WENZEL, R., *Die Ausgrabungen unter der Peterskirche in Rom*, (= *Heilige Stätten*, 1), Leipzig, 1953, 34 pp., 8 figs.

This is an attractive little work describing the excavations under the Vatican. It is to be recommended for its comprehensiveness and originality in presentation.

858 WILPERT, J., *La Fede nella Chiese nascente*, (Roma: Pont. Ist. di Archeol. Crist., 1938), 205 & ff.

We find here the interesting theory that Peter's body was placed in an ordinary sarcophagus and covered over in bronze, according to the Liber Pontificalis.

859 WILPERT, J., "La tomba di S. Pietro" — RAC, 13 (1936), 27-41.

This study is concerned with the deposition of the tomb (and a description of its details) in which Peter was supposed to have been buried with an endeavor to reconstruct its bronze casing. Basing himself on the literary evidence the author examines the actual tomb in pre-Constantinian times. He then considers it during Constantine's time showing four figures of its appearance and the inscribed cross of dedication. He concludes with the remnants of the tomb after Constantine. According to the experts there is an unfortunate lapse in the author's critical judgement.

860 WILPERT, J., *Das Grab des hl. Petrus im Lichte der geschichtlichen Nachrichten.* (no date).

This small brochure which was written prior to the Vatican excavations of 1939 gives a historical reconstruction of the Apostle Peter's tomb according to the *Liber Pontificalis.*

861 WORONOSWKI, F., "Grob Sw. Piotra (na podstawie wykopalisk)" — *Ruch Biblijny i Liturgiczny*, 9 (Cracovia, 1956), 159-165.

862 WOTSCHITZKY, A., "Topographie von Rom" — *Anzeiger für die Altertums-Wissenschaft*, 10 (1957), 17-24.

A study of the Vatican topography as known in ancient times.

863 X., "O Sepulcro de Sao Pedro" — *O Pio Brasileiro*, 2 (1952), 34-41, 3 figs.

Taking them in their proper sequence the author (who signs himself "X") describes what has been revealed by the Apostle's tomb, Gaius' trophy, Constantine's basilica, and the new presbyterium.

864 X., "Het graf van Sint Petrus" — *Katholiek Archief*, 7 (1952), 101-110, 3 figs.

Based on Ferrua's article that appeared in CC, 103, 1 (1952), 15-29, the author gives an accurate description of the results of the Vatican excavations. He limits his discussion mainly to the Apostle's tomb and the Aedicula.

865 ZEILLER, J., "Les récentes fouilles des cryptes de Saint-Pierre de Rome" — *Revue Archéologique*, 24 (1945), 156-157.

This is a resumé of Pope Pius XII's radio message to the world in 1942 wherein he announced the significance of the discoveries made beneath the Vatican basilica.

866 ZEILLER, J., "Signification des ossements trouvés dans les fouilles du Vatican" — *Bulletin de la Société Nationale des Antiquaires de France*, (1957), 97-98.

This is a communication from M. Bernardi on the signification of the findings discovered in the Vatican excavations. Basing himself on C. Carcopino, he concludes that there is no doubt that the body of Peter was first buried here where there actually was a Memoria. On Feb. 22, 258, the Christians translated the body (of Paul, as well) ad Catacumbas to hide during the persecutions. The author also speaks of the work of Gregory the Great to enclose the relics (at the Vatican) in order to protect them.

867 ZIHLER, J., "Zur Diskussion um das Petrusgrab. — Orientierung" — *Katholische Blätter für weltanschauliche Information*, 17 (1953), 65-68.

The author gives a description of the "red wall" and the columns of the three niches discovered in the recent excavations. He also takes to task the superficiality of some publications on the subject. He further maintains that there was a translation of the Apostle's relics ad

Catacumbas in 258, and a re-translation in 556 (St. Peter to the Vatican, Paul to the via Ostia).

868 ZIHLER, J., "Het graf van Sint Petrus" — *Katholiek Archief*, 7 (1952), 101-110.

869 ZUNZUNEGUI, J., "Las excavaciones bajo el altar la Confession de San Pedro" — *Lumen*, 3 (1954), 193-214.

870 ZUCCHETTI, G., "l'Obelisco Vaticano" — *Ecclesia*, 9 (1950), 523-526.

Many legends and hypotheses have been associated with the famous obelisk before the Vatican basilica. It is a monument that has traversed three civilizations: the oriental, the Roman, and Christian-Catholic.

In this study the author reconstructs its history which is related to the work of the Vatican excavations.

INDEX OF AUTHORS

(References are to the numbered paragraphs)

DATE DUE
